ADMINISTRATIVE PROCEDURE

ADMINISTRATIVE PROCEDURE

A Practical Handbook for
the Administrative Analyst

COMSTOCK GLASER

Introduction
PROF. ARTHUR N. HOLCOMBE

American Council On Public Affairs

WASHINGTON, D. C.

American Council on Public Affairs

Dedicated to the belief that the extensive diffusion of information is a profound responsibility of American democracy, the American Council on Public Affairs is designed to promote the spread of authoritative facts and significant opinions concerning social and economic problems. The Council believes that the facts presented and opinions expressed under its sponsorship deserve careful attention and consideration. It is not, however, committed to these facts and opinions in any other way. Those associated with the organization necessarily represent different viewpoints on public questions.

In view of the increasing urgency for the diffusion of information on current affairs, the Council's publication program endeavors to implement a broader usefulness of research by encouraging properly qualified scholars to give greater attention to the background, analysis, and solution of contemporary problems. The objectives of the program are furthered through the assistance of experts in the following fields:

POLITICAL SCIENCE: Ernest Griffith, Kenneth Colegrove, William Yandell Elliott, Lowell Mellett, Frederic Ogg, C. J. Friedrich, William E. Mosher, Ernest K. Lindley, W. C. Johnstone, Robert J. Harris.

ECONOMICS: Sumner Slichter, Paul H. Douglas, Edwin E. Witte, Paul Homan, Leon C. Marshall, G. T. Schwenning, David Cushman Coyle, Arthur E. Burns, E. J. Coil, Jacob Viner, Eveline Burns, Herman Somers, George Soule.

SOCIOLOGY: William Ogburn, R. M. MacIver, Read Bain, Bruce Melvin, Mark May, Willard Waller, Harold A. Phelps, Edward Allsworth Ross, E. S. Bogardus.

SOCIAL WELFARE: Paul Kellogg, Abraham Epstein, Walter West, Frank P. Graham, E. C. Lindeman, Clarence Pickett.

LABOR: John B. Andrews, Leo Wolman, W. Jett Lauck, Hilda Smith, Elizabeth Christman, Willard Uphaus, Marion H. Hedges, Paul Brissenden, Frank Palmer.

FOREIGN AFFAIRS: Stephen Duggan, Esther Brunauer, Clark Eichelberger, Clyde Eagleton, Max Ascoli, Walter H. Lockwood, Brooks Emeny, Ralph H. Lutz, Edgar Mowrer.

LATIN AMERICA: Ernest Galarza, George Howland Cox, Rollin Atwood, J. D. M. Ford, John I. B. McCulloch, Samuel Guy Inman.

HISTORY: Guy Stanton Ford, Harry Elmer Barnes, Sidney B. Fay, Richard Heindel, Bernadotte Schmitt.

PUBLIC OPINION: Harold Lasswell, Peter Odegard, Delbert Clark, Harold Gosnell, Harwood Childs, Cedric Larson.

EDUCATION: George Zook, Clyde Miller, Frederick Redefer, Floyd Reeves, Chester Williams, William G. Carr, Carl Milam.

RELIGION: Henry Smith Leiper, Guy Shipler, Frank Kingdon, L. M. Birkhead, James Waterman Wise.

The Council's staff is composed of M. B. Schnapper, Executive Secretary and Editor; Victoria Doggett, Administrative Secretary; and William West 2nd, Business Secretary.

COPYRIGHT, 1941, BY THE AUTHOR
PRINTED IN THE UNITED STATES
AMERICAN COUNCIL ON PUBLIC AFFAIRS
2153 FLORIDA AVENUE, WASHINGTON, D. C.

To My Father
OTTO CHARLES GLASER

INTRODUCTION

The rapid expansion of the business of government in recent years—above all, the rapid expansion of the business of the Government of the United States—has created an unprecedented demand for better information about the methods of doing public business. Those for whose benefit the expanded services of government are administered and who have to pay for them directly or indirectly, wish to be assured that they are getting their money's worth. Those who have occasion to do business with the Government wish to understand more clearly how such business should be done. Those particularly who wish to work for the Government need to know better what will be expected of them by their employer and how best they can justify these expectations. It is not surprising that there should be a growing production of books on public administration.

Dr. Glaser's book on public administration is different from other books on the subject. He is not concerned with the law of public administration, and gives none of his space to such topics as the separation of powers or judicial control of administrative acts. He is not concerned with the policies which administrative officers have been authorized by the Congress to carry into effect, and has nothing to say about the development of the functions of government at Washington and the distribution of activities among the executive departments and independent establishments. He is not even concerned with administrative politics in the stricter sense of the term, and ignores the problems of patronage and propaganda which occupy so much of the time and thought of high executive officers. This book is devoted to the technical aspects of public business administration, which must be mastered by public business administrators, if they are to command the confidence of their real employer, the public.

Dr. Glaser is one of those modern students of public administration who believe that the province of scientific management should

ADMINISTRATIVE PROCEDURE

be broad enough to include the management of public business. Frederick W. Taylor demonstrated some of the possibilities of scientific management in the field of factory management and works construction. Others have explored the possibilities of scientific management for white-collar workers in private business offices. Latest and most difficult development in the science of management is the application of scientific methods to public business offices. Dr. Glaser has undertaken to show what scientific management has accomplished in this field and, more important, that much more might be accomplished in this field by the further application of scientific methods.

At the outset the author encounters the obstacle of an unstandardized vocabulary. The writer of a book on public administration would like to make his book intelligible and interesting to the public, but this aim presupposes that the language of the average man is adequate for the scientific discussion of administrative problems in the public service. Consider, for example, the familiar words, function, planning, staff, control, and administration itself. Is an administrative function a purpose (object) of administration, or is it a process (method) of administration? Does a functional type of administrative organization mean organization according to the nature of the services rendered or according to the kinds of activity employed in rendering a particular service? Both uses of the term seem to be logical, if the appropriate premises are adopted for purposes of classification, but sometimes one use is more convenient and at other times the other use is more convenient. A writer may use the term in both senses, according to the dictates of convenience, being careful to indicate in each case how he is using the term. This practice possesses the advantage of clarity, but it does not help much the process of standardization. A basic term remains ambiguous and intractable.

The exact definition of terms which a writer wishes to use for the purpose of scientific discussion offers two advantages. One is consistency in their use. This is generally, though not necessarily always, convenient and helpful to the reader. The other advantage is more substantial. By making his terms more intelligible, the author actually contributes to the development of his subject. Planning, for example, means many different things, and by being careful never to speak of planning, pure and simple, but always of some particular kind of planning, the author makes a solid contribution to that

INTRODUCTION

sense of fine discrimination which is the indispensable foundation for any instructive discussion of the subject. Dr. Glaser's use of terms may not greatly accelerate the process of standardization, but he certainly has made a solid contribution to the analysis of fundamental concepts in the science of public administration.

A student of public administration who is preoccupied with the problems of civilian agencies may neglect some useful ideas which have flourished particularly in the field of military administration. The familiar distinction, for example, between line and staff services calls for a thorough analysis of the concept of a staff. Here the military administrators have developed an important difference between special staff services and those of a general staff. Dr. Glaser's discussion of the comparative advantages and appropriate uses of staff and line agencies, respectively, relates particularly to what the military administrators would call the special staff agencies. His admirable discussion of program planning and management planning clearly shows that there is room for civilian as well as military general staffs. The extension of the general-staff type of agency from military into civilian administration is certainly one of the most promising developments of the near future.

Control is a subject hitherto more freely discussed by lawyers and accountants than by administrative analysts. Dr. Glaser shows convincingly that much can well be said on this subject without reference either to administrative law or fiscal accountability. The great subjects of centralization and devolution call for careful consideration from the stand-point of scientific management. It is evident that much research needs to be done in this field by competent administrative analysts. Meanwhile Dr. Glaser makes some significant observations which should be helpful to practical public administrators. His views obviously reflect the lessons of his own experience in the management of public business at Washington. For this reason, though more limited in application, they are also more persuasive than the broader but less explicit generalizations that might be sponsored by abstract theoreticians in the field of public administration.

The biggest and most fundamental question of terminology in the science of public administration is, what shall be the meaning of the word administration itself. Many writers give this basic term the broadest possible meaning. Dr. Glaser prefers to use it in the narrower sense of what he sometimes calls "direct administration,"

ADMINISTRATIVE PROCEDURE

and distinguishes carefully between this kind of administration and administrative management, as defined by the President's Committee on that subject. This distinction aids him in the analysis of the whole administrative process, whatever may be thought of his choice of terms. The general acceptance of these distinctions by administrative analysts should facilitate the eventual standardization of terms. To understand the need for a scientific terminology is the beginning of wisdom in the study of public administration. The better perception of necessary distinctions will bring, as Dr. Glaser shows very persuasively, solid gains to administrative managers.

Larger questions of political control over what hostile critics of modern administrative expansion call bureaucracy do not escape Dr. Glaser's attention. He makes an interesting proposal for the establishment of a Permanent Joint Congressional Committee on Administrative Management. It recalls the similar proposal of the President's Committee on Administrative Management four years ago for a Joint Congressional Committee on Fiscal Control. There are reasons for believing that a more promising line of development would be the strengthening of the staff of the existing House Committee on Appropriations. But this is not the place for a searching inquiry into the relative merits of such proposals. It is clear that there is need for a better kind of Congressional supervision over administration in general and administrative management in particular. Dr. Glaser's book should interest politicians as well as the administrative managers and analysts for whom it was specifically written.

ARTHUR N. HOLCOMBE

Professor of Government
Harvard University

PREFACE

This is a book about administration in general. It is not, however, a general book on administration. It is essentially an inquiry into the processes of administration and the anatomy of administrative organizations. It does not concern itself, except incidentally, with the content of the programs or activities which are being administered. Nor does it attempt to generalize or particularize on the social, technical, or ethical problems which are encountered by administrators. It is concerned only with strictly administrative problems—those which arise from the nature of administration itself and not from the particular activities concerned.

There has long been a need for standard methods and criteria for analyzing the day-to-day operations of administrative establishments. These must be realistic in terms of the phenomena observed and the administrative processes they represent. They must be based on a sound understanding of what administration is, and they must indicate that which can be improved and how to do so. An effort has been made herein to provide some basic tools for administrative analysis and to apply them to the common problems which arise from time to time in most organizations.

Any work about administration as such must contain a good deal of theory. But the author has tried constantly to keep in mind the needs of the operating official faced with the task of applying theories to practical problems. Most of the case material and many of the ideas contained in this book were gathered by direct investigation, including many interviews with officials of various agencies. Certain other problems have been selected from among the author's own experiences. For this reason, it has often been impossible to quote sources, and occasionally it has been necessary to disguise the agencies in which some of the situations occurred. All of the original material dealing with Government agencies mentioned by name has been cleared with officials of those agencies.

ADMINISTRATIVE PROCEDURE

Many of the problems which occur in Government agencies are found in similar form in private business concerns. It is hoped that the business man, as well as the Government official, will find something of interest in the chapters which follow.

The author has, of course, drawn upon his experience as Assistant Procedure Analyst in the Office of Budget and Finance of the U. S. Department of Agriculture and, more recently, as Procedure Investigator in the Coordinating and Procedure Division of the Social Security Board, but he wishes to state that the opinions and interpretations of fact presented herein are personal and not official.

Moreover, he wishes to thank the many people who have contributed ideas, suggestions, and criticisms, particularly the following: Dr. Frederick F. Blachly of the Brookings Institution; Mr. Oliver G. Brain, Chief Consultant, Farm Security Administration; Mr. Henry H. Farquhar, General Inspector, Forest Service; Mr. C. C. Hathaway, Chief, Information and Recruiting Division, United States Civil Service Commission; Professor Morris B. Lambie of Harvard University; Mr. Earl W. Loveridge, Assistant Chief, Forest Service; Mr. Ben D. Mills, formerly Chief of the Production Control Unit, Rural Electrification Administration; Mr. H. A. Nelson, Assistant Director of Finance, Department of Agriculture; Dr. Harlow S. Person, Consulting Economist, Rural Electrification Administration; Miss Florence W. Riddle of Washington, D. C.; and Mr. Joseph B. Riddle of McLean, Virginia.

COMSTOCK GLASER

Washington, D. C.

CONTENTS

Introduction—*Arthur N. Holcombe*		1
Preface		5
I	The Scope of Administrative Procedure	9
II	Analysis by Function	17
III	Analysis by Units of Organization	26
IV	Analysis by Administrative Sequence	37
V	Organization and Procedure	49
VI	Administrative (Program) Planning	68
VII	Administrative Execution—Purchasing	84
VIII	Administrative Execution—Personnel	99
IX	Administrative Control—the Concept of Control	112
X	Administrative Control—a Pattern of Control	121
XI	Management Planning	135
XII	Management Execution—Work Distribution	154
XIII	Management Execution—Timing and Scheduling	165
XIV	Management Control	176
XV	Possibilities of a Rational Technique of Administration	185
	Bibliography	202
	Index	205

Chapter I

THE SCOPE OF ADMINISTRATIVE PROCEDURE

ADMINISTRATION is the word we use to signify the performance of any task which is too big for one worker. It begins as soon as someone has too much to do and gets someone else to help him; it becomes fully developed in the large corporation or government agency. It has various phases, of which the most important are: *planning*—deciding what is to be done; *execution*—giving orders, instructions, and supervision; and *control*—seeing that the work is actually done according to plan. These phases are basic, existing even in simple administrative relationships such as those of a housewife and her maid. They become complex when large numbers of people are involved. There is also the problem of *coordination,* or seeing that individuals do not work at cross-purposes, which extends into all three phases of administration.

This book deals with administration as such, rather than that of any particular activity. It is specially concerned with the problems which arise in large organizations. Administration on a large scale is not so different from administration on a small scale—there is just more of it. The Red Queen stumped Alice by asking: "What's one-and-one-and-one-and-one-and-one-and-one-and-one-and-one-and-one-and-one-and-one?" It was not that Alice could not add—she simply got tired. The reason why administration is often thought to be a ponderous subject is that people like to take it in large mouthfuls, thinking first about the biggest problems. There are some who talk glibly about merging this and that bureau or setting up a department of so-and-so, without thinking too much about the actual operations going on inside the offices concerned. The reorganizers seldom get down below the level of divisions; sections and units remain as unfathomed as the Aldrich Deep.[1] If one really wants to learn about administration, he should begin on the ground floor—the place where the direct work is done. There the first level of administration is to be found.

---
[1] The deepest place in the Pacific Ocean (30,390 feet).

ADMINISTRATIVE PROCEDURE

Another reason why administration is an obscure subject is that so much writing about it is specialized, dealing really with the subjects that are administered rather than administration itself. We have books on public works, police, fire, welfare, and health activities. But they are discussions of policy in the particular fields, and tend to emphasize differences rather than likeness.[2] Actually, it is mainly the techniques of the direct activities (*purposes* of administration) that vary; the *processes* of administration are far more uniform. In the following chapters there will appear many specific practical problems arising in different kinds of activity. They will never be introduced for their own sake, but only to illustrate principles and methods applicable to all administration. This is entirely a book on administration in *general*.

ADMINISTRATIVE ORGANIZATION

Administration requires *organization*, or the existence of a definite system of working relationships, so that each individual has one supervisor (or occasionally more) from whom he receives orders and instructions and to whom he is responsible. There are many types of organization, all deriving from a common ancestor, the *scalar (hierarchical)*. Scalar organization is the simplest kind; in it individuals are distinguished only by rank and are arranged in a pyramid from the top to the bottom. As soon as there is specialization, scalar organization has to be modified, the result being one or a combination of several more complex types of organization. There is organization by *purpose*, as in a city government divided into police, health, buildings, schools, and other departments. There is organization by *process*, in which workers are arranged by the particular tasks they do—as in central stenographic pools, file rooms, and supply depots. Then there is organization by *area of operation*, which may be simple in a company having branches in different cities reporting directly to the home office, or complex in a company made up of regional and state offices and perhaps a special department for colored clients. Most large modern companies and governments are combinations of the several types of organization.[3]

Two important features of administrative organization are *delegation* and *cumulative responsibility*. The administrator has a large

---

[2] A notable exception is Marietta Stevenson's *Public Welfare Administration*, which deals extensively with general administrative problems.

[3] The merits and defects of these types are discussed in Gulick and Urwick (ed.), *Papers on the Science of Administration*.

THE SCOPE OF ADMINISTRATIVE PROCEDURE

job to do; he cannot do it all, so he delegates most of it to his immediate subordinates, who in turn delegate to their subordinates, and so on down the line. The reverse side of this is cumulative responsibility, which makes each individual answerable for the work of his subordinates. But a person may perhaps have two or three supervisors, each of whom is partly responsible for his work. An arrangement of this sort was advocated by Frederick W. Taylor, who called it "functional foremanship." [4] Under this system an employee might report to a different supervisor on each of several duties or even on various aspects of the same task, such as quality, speed, and care of equipment. In an unmodified state "functional foremanship" means that a worker is directly answerable to several bosses. This means that one of them often has to be given some authority to overrule the others, and even so the arrangement only works well where fields of work can be easily separated.

The work which a large organization has to do is usually complex enough to require several kinds of administrative arrangements in different branches, including some degree of "functional foremanship." It is therefore necessary for those in charge to think very clearly about the administrative framework and the division of work and responsibility. To secure adequate planning, execution, and control, the facts must be clear in the minds of all employees. Each individual must be sure where he stands, what he has to do, and who his boss is. In some organizations these matters are far from certain. When this is the case, it sometimes takes an "outside" investigator to unravel the problem.

ADMINISTRATIVE PROCEDURE

A fundamental distinction is that between the *purpose* and the *process* of administration—between the direct work which is being undertaken and the business of managing it. It is the difference between *what* you administer (purpose of administration) and *how* you administer it (process of administration); between program and procedure. An administrator can not give all his attention to his direct activities and let his organization run itself. Both must be managed. The job of administering involves both *direct administration*—determining *what* shall be done—and *administrative management*—determining *how* it shall be done.[5] In both cases determina-

---
[4] Frederick W. Taylor, *The Principles of Scientific Management*, p. 123; *Shop Management*, ¶¶234ff.
[5] The field of administrative management includes not only procedure in the narrower sense but also organization and the demarcation of fields of work. These are all *hows* of administration and are closely related. "Procedure work" cannot be

ADMINISTRATIVE PROCEDURE

tion (planning) is followed by execution and control.

Administrative procedure is the aggregate of the *hows* of administration; its study is the examination of administrative method. Of course the *hows* are greatly affected by the *whats* with which an office deals, but most *hows* appear in one form or another in all organizations, the special problems being variations of the general. To show what this means, let us walk into any large office without looking at the gold letters on the door, so that we do not know whether it is an insurance company, a publishing house, or a government bureau. Let us watch what the people are doing. Here comes a messenger boy loaded with papers and envelopes of all sizes. He darts into a large room, and threads his way among the rows of clerks sitting at desks and tables or bent over file drawers, until he comes to a central stand on which are two boxes, one marked "in," the other "out." The messenger drops some papers in the "in" box, takes a few from the "out" box, and is on his way. Then someone comes and empties the "in" box, passing some of the papers to the clerks, and some to the important-looking gentleman in the corner, who has a brass name-plate and three telephones on his desk. This person digs away at the papers in his "in" box, scribbles on them or passes them to his clerks for further scribbling, and does his best to get them into his "out" box as quickly as possible. Every few minutes one of his telephones rings, and sometimes all three ring at once, and in between he makes calls himself and converses with a steady flow of people who come up to ask him questions. Once in a while he gets called to the "front office" and when he comes back there is a sheaf of little notes on his spindle and a great pile of papers in his "in" box. Such is the life of any executive—reading and writing letters, memoranda, and reports, constantly conferring and telephoning. Such is administration in general—a continuous round of written and verbal contact between workers and with outsiders.

Now the way in which papers and people circulate through an office is seldom purely haphazard. It is determined by patterns of administration which prescribe, for instance, that papers regarding X must go to A, B, and K for initialing and then be signed by M, and that all inquiries about Y must be referred to Q. These patterns, collectively, are called administrative procedure.

The rules of administrative procedure have many sources. Some are established customs of long-forgotten origin, and some are specific orders appearing in official documents. Others are laid down by

---

effective unless it deals with organization structure and specification of administrative tasks as well as with "routines."

THE SCOPE OF ADMINISTRATIVE PROCEDURE

statute. But however it may arise, a certain kind of rule or habit will usually produce the same results, wherever it appears. By studying like things and different things in the procedure of various organizations, there can be discovered common "cause and effect" relationships. From these can be derived principles for planning the most efficient sort of procedure.

Like the health of a human being, that of an organization depends on good circulation. The blood in this case is the business or *substance* of administration, which flows from one organ to another. A stoppage at any point will prevent other organs from functioning, and its effect may spread so that a whole limb or the entire organism may become paralyzed.

The flow of business is inherent in administration, arising from the division of a large job into tasks and the need for relating each task to the next. Its channels are determined by the way in which the whole concern is organized,[6] and by the habitual or planned patterns of procedure. Since good administration does things not only well but with the least lost motion, good procedure is that which allows business to circulate smoothly and rapidly, and with the fewest interruptions.

THE "SCIENTIFIC" APPROACH TO ADMINISTRATION

Since administrative procedure is not self-determining, but conditioned by such factors as organization structure, the division of authority and responsibility, and the arrangement of fields of work in a scheme of functions, it follows that its study must include all these things. To avoid becoming a branch of political theology, it must stick closely to observed facts, and be systematic in its analysis of them. The study of administration in an exact and, so far as possible, scientific way is comparatively new, and is a stepchild of the "scientific management" school in industry. Some of Taylor's followers carried his techniques, which were originally developed to deal with machine operations, into the field of "office management"—the planning and supervision of clerical work. The step from here to scientific management of *administration* is not an easy one. Instead of manual operations directed at pieces of metal, we must deal with brainwork on business, social, and engineering problems. Instead of routine clerical work such as filling orders, acknowledging and recording

---

[6] As we shall see further on (Chapter III), the real organization structure—the way a concern actually operates—may be quite different from the scheme drawn up on paper. In many offices which have theoretical systems carefully constructed and nicely dovetailed, the actual organization may be very hazy.

ADMINISTRATIVE PROCEDURE

payments, etc., we have the making of discretionary decisions, often in professional fields such as law, economics, sociology, and medicine. The essence of administrative work is its variability; no two problems are the same.

We should like to make our administrative organizations work as smoothly as well-engineered industrial plants. Yet the operators are not dealing with physical things which can be weighed and measured, but with non-physical "situations" and all too often with problems of people. Work which requires imagination and personality cannot be analyzed with tape measure and slide rule. It must be treated in some other way. We have to recognize what administration is—the making of decisions and the necessary preparations; research, reporting, analysis, and discussion. We want to encourage creative ability and initiative in the individual worker, therefore we must avoid oppressive rules and regulations. Yet the work of hundreds of people must be co-ordinated, so that they will all move in the same direction. It is this conflict between the individual's need for freedom in his work, and the social need for regimentation that forms the nub of many a procedural problem. Good administration requires that both these needs be satisfied.

Because administration contains so much of the "human element" and because its problems are so often psychological as well as mechanical, the analyst in this field must, to a large extent, observe and reason like a social scientist rather than a natural scientist. The chemist or physicist must see a thing or touch it before he will agree that it is there; the economist or political scientist, on the other hand, deals readily with abstractions such as "demand," "supply," "sovereignty," etc. The social scientist makes use of concepts as short-cuts in analyzing group behavior. The student of administration must do the same, and likewise he must make sure that his concepts are grounded in reality.

While for the most part we are to deal with administrative procedure from a technical point of view, let us never forget that it is, among other things, a pattern of human behavior, and as such has psychological and social implications. Procedure may be dictated by the actual ways in which things have to be done. On the other hand, it may be nothing more than a remembrance of past needs preserved through ritual. To give an illustration: in some of the older Government bureaus the field stations used to be operated without very specific budgets, expenditures being made out of the appropriations for various activities according to relative necessity. Since the only

THE SCOPE OF ADMINISTRATIVE PROCEDURE

financial control was in the Washington office, field stations had to send all their purchase orders to Washington to avoid the possibility of spending over the appropriations. With the development of the federal budget in its present form, bureaus found it necessary to amplify their internal budgeting, so that today the chief of a field station usually knows in advance what he can spend each fiscal year. Most field stations can and do keep track of their allotments for supplies. Yet in many bureaus all purchase orders, even for purely routine materials available on term contracts, still have to be cleared through Washington—for no apparent reason.

In all phases of our life we have customs and procedures deriving from conditions which no longer exist. But it should be remembered that the difference between social and business procedures is one of subject matter and not of essential nature. John Smith the administrator is psychologically identical with John Smith the Rotarian, Elk, and Methodist. He is as likely to be shocked if you tell him he should completely change the way he keeps his accounts as he would be if you ordered him to crease his trousers on the side. Thus the administrative analyst must consider not only the requirements of the work to be done, but also the habits and reactions of those who do it. It is not enough to plan the best and simplest procedures—they must be introduced so as to hurt people's feelings as little as possible.

ADMINISTRATIVE MANAGEMENT

The foregoing may serve to indicate the nature and ramifications of administrative procedure, which, in short, is the sum of the working habits of an organization. Since people seldom adjust themselves to changing conditions without leadership, it is obvious that here is a field for intensive management—the development of new organization and procedure, and establishing it.

There are two distinct fields of administrative leadership: *direct (or program) administration* which deals with the *purposes* of administration, and *administrative (or procedural) management* which deals with its *processes*. Direct administration deals with *what* is to be administered; it formulates basic programs and policies, it gives the orders for executing them, and it exercises controls to assure the desired results. Administrative management [7] deals with *how*

---

[7] The term *management planning* is sometimes used loosely to indicate administrative management, because planning is one of its most important phases. As used in this book, *management planning* and *procedural planning* mean the planning phase of administrative management. There are also management execution and control, although in most Government agencies these have not been as highly developed

ADMINISTRATIVE PROCEDURE

the program is to be administered; it plans organizational structure and the division of work, and it arranges the routes for administrative business. Administration is the responsibility of line and operating staff officers [8] and, on the top level, of the head of the organization. All of these are primarily experts in the subject matter they are administering. Administrative management is a staff function, and is most effective when assigned to an *administrative analyst*,[9] subordinate to the administrative head and primarily an expert in administration.

Of course, it is possible for an organization to get along without systematic administrative management, or for that function to be a sideline of the administrator. But in a large organization, particularly one which has to get things done on schedule, procedural and other management problems constitute a full-time job, often for a sizeable group.[10]

The visible result of administrative management consists for the most part of written procedure—plans of organization, regulations, and instructions for routing business and doing specific jobs. This procedure is often codified, as in the manuals issued by Federal agencies and certain large companies. It is hardly necessary to argue that it should be consistent, and based on objective analysis of administrative problems.

---

as the planning. *Program planning* and *administrative planning* will be used to mean planning as a phase of direct administration.

[8] For definition of line and staff see Chapter II, "Line and Staff Functions."

[9] The term *administrative analyst* is used to mean an official whose field is administrative management. These officials have also been called procedure analysts, and procedure planners. They are found in "Procedure Divisions" and sometimes in "Planning Divisions" or occasionally in "Organization" or "Management" Divisions. The Civil Service Commission has accepted the term *administrative analyst* as standard for this class of position and gives examinations under this title.

[10] On the development of procedure divisions in the Federal Government, see Chapter XI.

Chapter II

ANALYSIS BY FUNCTION

WE HAVE indicated the general scope of administrative procedure—the way in which business is distributed, performed, and passed on in an organization, as determined by habits, rules, and orders. We have also suggested the need for administrative management—the planning of organization and procedure, their adaptation to changing situations, and control to see that they are working properly. Planning is only possible when we have facts, known as exactly as the circumstances require. The housewife planning her shopping should know the prices of what she is going to buy, and how much she has to spend. She is not safe in assuming that butter is 30c a pound because it was so the previous week, and guessing that there is a dollar in her purse. Likewise, the engineer planning a bridge must have facts. He must know the width of the river to be crossed, the elevations on each side, the consistency of the soil, and the amount of traffic expected. The more elaborate the work which is being planned, the more detailed and accurate the data must be.

Management planning, like any other sort, must be based on facts. These must be drawn from the problem itself, from the organization for which procedure is being planned; or, if it is a new one not yet set up, from relevant experience. The facts must be analyzed—classified and expressed in comparable terms, and, so far as possible, measured. This is an order hard to fill, since administration deals with problems which are often thought of as intangible. Yet, if we cannot be quantitatively exact, we must at least be rigorous in qualitative analysis and avoid guesswork.

In each field, the methods of analysis are based on the subject matter, the phenomena observed. In administration, we encounter three kinds of facts—the fields of work or functions in which a concern operates, the organizational framework and the units set up for each function, and the sequences of individual operations which

ADMINISTRATIVE PROCEDURE

make up the larger undertakings.[1] There are thus three methods of administrative analysis: by function, by units of organization, and by administrative sequence. If given an actual problem to deal with, it would of course be possible to proceed in all three ways at once, since the phenomena are really different aspects of the same subject matter. But the types of analysis can be more easily explained one at a time.

Analysis by function means examination of the fields of work of an organization, and of the branches of each. But what is a field of work (a function) or a branch of it (a sub-function)? A function is generally defined as a sphere of activity dealing with definitely limited subject matter, and having both a definite purpose and at least a moderately specialized technique. Within each function there are sub-functions [2]—limited and more specialized branches—and within these are individual duties.

Functions, sub-functions, and duties are determined by means of classification, which is the systematic observation of similarities and relationships. Since classification is a mental process, it may seem that this way of specifying a function is not objective enough. But it is the kind of answer given to almost every question of the sort. What is a rabbit? It is a mammal, a quadruped, a rodent; it belongs to a species, a genus, a family, an order. All of the terms given are classifications. Now if classifications of functions or animals were just arbitrary arrangements of words, they would be meaningless. But they are always used to indicate common characteristics, so that the designation of a sub-function or animal as class A, type 1, not only shows what it is like but also reveals what other sub-functions or animals are similar in various respects.

Classification is a fundamental phase of analysis. Linnaeus made modern botany possible by classifying all the known plants. Chemistry is based on a classification of the elements, and physics on systematic arrangement of mechanical principles, thermo-dynamic laws, etc. Scientific method, consisting largely of reference of the particular to the general, depends upon a usable classification of data. Likewise, analysis of administrative functions must begin with classification.

---

[1] The problems and working methods related specifically to the subject matter are not administrative phenomena, although they necessarily have an important effect in determining administrative problems.

[2] These are usually called "activities" in municipal budgeting and accounting.

ANALYSIS BY FUNCTION

LINE AND STAFF FUNCTIONS

The first classification of an organization's functions is into two groups: *line* and *staff* functions. The line functions represent the *purposes* of administration; the staff functions embody administrative *processes*. The difference between them varies between different organizations, for what may be purposes in one concern may be processes in another, and vice versa.[3]

The organization charts of large companies and government agencies usually show units set up for both kinds of function. There are departments and divisions of corporations, and bureaus, divisions, and sections in government departments, set up to administer "line" activities such as milling flour, making spark plugs, or building roads, killing pests, etc. Each of these has more or less complete control over the operations (sub-functions) which are integral with and inseparable from its main function. But other operations, which have their own special techniques not closely related to that of the line function, are often done by staff offices serving all the line units

---

[3] The purposes of an organization are the basic things it is set up to do, including everything in the direct line of operation. To perform these direct operations we have to employ certain administrative processes. The direct operations are the line functions, the administrative processes are the staff functions. For instance, in a woolen mill picking, carding, combing, spinning and weaving are line functions. These are processes in the making of woolen cloth but administratively they are purposes; it is the purpose of woolen mills to perform some or all of these processes of manufacture. To facilitate its purposes, a mill must employ certain administrative processes, such as accounting, auditing, time study, personnel work, and research. These processes are common to many kinds of business.

Whether an activity is a purpose or process (line or staff function) depends on the way it relates to the general scheme of work. For instance, in many businesses buying and selling are line functions (basic purposes) because firms can make as much money by intelligent market operations as by efficient production. In other businesses, and as a rule in government, they are processes conducted not for their own sake but merely to facilitate other operations which are the main purposes.

The word *staff* is used to mean a function based on an administrative (or quasi-administrative) process, and as an adjective, is applied to one who performs such a function, as a *staff* officer. In modern organizations many processes, such as hiring and firing, planning, accounting, and reporting, are taken away from the line units and centralized in the hands of specialists. These are then *staff* officials and as such serve all or a number of line departments.

Some authors (such as Mooney and Reiley, Urwick, etc.) have used the word *staff* in a more limited sense to mean the function of assisting a line officer in observation and planning, or "serving as an extension of his personality." When *staff* is used in this sense, the term *auxiliary* is often used to cover functions based on processes. The usage carries the undesirable implication that the processes are in some way inferior to the purposes, and that the officials in charge of them can operate only indirectly, through the medium of their superiors who also have supervision of the line officials.

Observation of almost any Federal agency for a very short time will bring out the fact that staff officers *do* give orders; that they are directly responsible for the processes within their jurisdictions. To call a budget officer or a director of personnel "auxiliary" is to give a wrong impression of their places in the scheme of operations.

ADMINISTRATIVE PROCEDURE

in the concern. Centralized accounting, personnel, purchasing,[4] and public relations divisions are almost universal. These staff units are as much operating agencies as are the line divisions. The main difference is that their activity is defined in terms of process (kind of administration) rather than purpose (program of operation).

The two kinds of function could be charted as interlocking in a cross-pattern, since each line function has its staff aspects and each staff function exists only in relation to particular line functions. A portion of such a chart, showing some of the line and staff functions of a typical manufacturing concern, appears in Figure 1. The diagram suggests the fact that quite different purposes may require identical or similar administrative processes. This is why business men are able to transfer from one industry to another, and why government officials can enter private employment without much trouble in adjusting themselves to their new jobs.[5]

A particular executive act (as distinguished from the formation of a policy) involves not a line or staff function all the way across the chart but only the intersection of a line with a staff function. The area within the intersection is large or small according to the scope of activities covered by the decision. From the point of view of the line official, the matter is a staff aspect of a line function; the staff official thinks it is a line phase of a staff function. This situation always contains the seeds of conflict. Within themselves, staff functions present the same administrative problems as line functions, each having staff aspects of its own. For instance, there must be personnel to do personnel work, supplies for the supply officials, and cost accounting on the cost of cost accounting.

Since programs to be administered always involve both line and staff functions, some pragmatic basis is needed for dividing the work between line and staff units. The one usually applied, though not too systematically, is whether the technique dominant in the situation is most closely related to the line or the staff activity.[6] For instance, in purchasing, general knowledge of the market and of business methods may be more important than familiarity with the activity for which the supplies are bought. On the other hand, some specialized materials, like scientific apparatus, can be bought only by or with the close consultation of the person who is going to use it. Other activities which are usually thought of as staff functions, such as informational work and research, may also be at times inseparable

---

[4] See footnote 3 of this chapter.
[5] See citation of Fayol's views in the opening of Chapter XI.
[6] The procedural phase of this problem is discussed in Chapter V.

ANALYSIS BY FUNCTION

from line operations. That is why concerns which set up research divisions (except for purely scientific research) often find the work of these units being duplicated in line offices. It is hard to take research for line programs away from the line units, because such research is a sub-function of program planning which, in turn, is the first major phase of direct administration.

CLASSIFYING FUNCTIONS

A prerequisite for administrative analysis, and therefore for management planning, is an adequate classification of the functions of the organization being studied. The development of such classifications has long been a concern of public administrators, particularly those concerned with budgeting and accounting. Classifications were first developed for use in setting up appropriation bills and the accounts kept pursuant thereto, but they had to be administratively workable, since budgeting and accounting are but the fiscal aspects of the larger administrative program. Since 1910, when the President's Commission on Economy and Efficiency (Cleveland Commission) began to lay the groundwork of the present Federal budgetary system, the tendency has been in the direction of setting up appropriations by functions and sub-functions (or activities, as they are sometimes called) rather than objects (things and services to be purchased), as was formerly the general practise. The Federal budget as we know it today is mainly arranged according to a classification of Governmental functions, although there persist a few appropriations by objects, such as those for printing and binding and for motor vehicles. The functions tend to reflect a departmental breakdown, since functions are mostly kept within particular branches of the Government, but there are some functions and appropriations for those functions which are distributed among several departments.

Functional classifications are also maintained for the use of administrative officials within departments. The Department of Agriculture, for instance, maintains a "uniform project system" in which the major fields of activity of each bureau and office are listed as "financial projects" (equivalent to function if we consider the term to mean *one* of the purposes of an organization and not its whole field of work). The "financial projects" are broken down into "work projects" (equivalent to sub-functions) which in turn are divided into "research line projects." For each project financial information is supplied and for financial and work projects a description of the work, including "perspective (historical background), object (why),

ADMINISTRATIVE PROCEDURE

and plan (how)." The data are supplied by the bureaus and compiled in the Department's Office of Budget and Finance.

The uniform project system superseded separate bureau systems maintained under a Department of Agriculture regulation which stated:

> Each bureau should maintain in its own files project statements in considerable detail, so that the data will be readily accessible whenever information in regard to a particular line of work is desired by the Secretary.[7]

The keeping of project records by bureaus proved unsatisfactory because of the lack of uniformity, and the present system was inaugurated in 1937. Its objectives are described as follows:

> Its principal purpose is to make immediately available to the Secretary's Office, and to chiefs of bureaus and other interested persons and agencies, uniform statements of the work done in each bureau. It is closely integrated with the financial data required in preparing the annual budget and with the informational material required in preparing the annual reports of the chiefs of bureaus and the annual report of the Secretary, and forms the basis of the Department's program of work.[8]

Classifications of functions have also been developed in the field of municipal government: like those in the Federal establishment they have had their origins in the fiscal zone. A classification which has gained wide acceptance is that developed by the National Committee on Municipal Accounting as part of a "Model Classification of Municipal Revenues and Expenditures". This classification was designed to serve as the basis for (1) municipal accounting, budget making, and reporting; (2) municipal cost accounting and administrative control; and (3) the compilation of financial statistics by state and Federal agencies.[9] The part on expenditures includes a listing of "functions" (broad fields of municipal activity such as fire protection, police, libraries, etc.) and "activities" (equivalent here to sub-functions). This classification, like the Department of Agriculture's uniform project system, was designed not only for fiscal use but also as an aid in assembling the information needed for administrative purposes and for reporting.

Systematic classification and division of administrative work has long been practised by the German ministries. Their code of administrative procedure states:

---

[7] U. S. Department of Agriculture, *Administrative Regulations* (now obsolete).
[8] U. S. Department of Agriculture, *Revised Manual of Uniform Project System*, Washington, 1937. P. 1.
[9] National Committee on Municipal Accounting, *Model Classification of Municipal Revenues and Expenditures*, Bulletin No. 9, Chicago, 1937.

ANALYSIS BY FUNCTION

The distribution of business among the Divisions and Principals' Units is regulated by the "plan for the distribution of business". In this plan the spheres of work are to be marked off clearly and precisely according to objective criteria. This is the foremost prerequisite for rapid and frictionless work.[10]

As a further means of classification, the German ministries also employ a "systematic classification of files," which serves not only to show where various papers may be found but also to whom incoming business should be routed. Each incoming letter is given a reference number indicating the function and sub-function. Because the whole work of the ministry has been precisely divided, this number serves both to guide the letter to its proper recipient and to show where it is to be filed for reference. That a classification of files (also a classification of work) was no task to be done haphazardly was well understood by the writers of the German code, who stated:

> The value of this classification is as fundamental for good clerical management as it is for the practical usefulness of the files. Therefore, the classification is to be compiled, on the basis of the data supplied by the Filing Rooms and Principals,[11] by the Division Directors themselves or under their direction by officials who understand the internal development of the individual fields of work and their relation to the whole work of the Ministry and of the Government. The Principal in Charge of Simplification [12] and, wherever advisable, also the Chief Clerk of the Ministry are to be consulted.[13]

A classification for use only in finding filed papers may be entirely mnemonic. But one intended also for general use in management, as is the German classification, must be systematic and reflect the true framework of functions. Therefore, the administrative analyst in charge of making one should consult extensively with the officials in charge of each function, with similar officials in other organizations, and with outsiders versed in the subject matter. Finally the classification should be sanctioned by the top administrator so that it may be accepted as a basis for planning and action by everyone.

It is not within our province to discuss in detail the principles of classification. This ground has already been covered by Dewey [14]

---

[10] Arnold Brecht and Comstock Glaser, *The Art and Technique of Administration in German Ministries*, Part Two, "General Code of Administrative Procedure in the Reich Ministries," p. 50.
[11] A Principal is an official having a rank approximately equivalent to an American section chief. See Brecht and Glaser, *op. cit.*, Glossary.
[12] Official dealing with efficiency, procedure, etc.
[13] Brecht and Glaser, *op. cit.*, Part Three, "Filing Room Code," pp. 131-132.
[14] Melvil Dewey, *Decimal Classification and Relative Index*. The principles of classification given in the preface of this book may be found valuable. Dewey's arrangements of business, government, and office subjects are not, however, suitable for administrative use.

and other authorities. The most suitable arrangement for an organization will depend on the purposes and basic operations of its line activities, and on the environment in which it operates. It is sufficient here to sound two general warnings. The classification should not be too greatly influenced by the titles of functions or operations, such as "administrative audit," "review," "control," "liaison," and so forth. These words may mean anything or nothing, and the classifier must probe behind them to find the real function, if any. Nor should classification necessarily follow the organization structure. It should be a guide to more efficient grouping of administrative units rather than a crystallization of existing arrangements. For these reasons budgetary and file classifications will usually require considerable adaptation before they can be used for administrative analysis. While they often provide useful suggestions for the classifier, they do not as a rule present a balanced picture of an organization's work. They are particularly deficient in showing the relationship between line and staff functions, which is one of the important things a classification for administrative analysis should do.

ANALYSIS OF A FUNCTION

Having determined what an organization's functions are and how they are related to each other, the administrative analyst may proceed to analyze them one at a time. It is best to begin by surveying a main function, and then to work down to sub-functions and duties. At each level, enough information should be gathered to give a comprehensive picture of the activity, including at least the answers to the following questions:

1. *Purpose:* What is the direct activity (purpose of administration)? How does the administrative function facilitate the accomplishment of the direct work?

2. *Necessity:* Could the administrative activity in question be eliminated or curtailed? How essential is it?

3. *Co-ordination:* Are the direct operations and the administrative work consistent within themselves and with each other? Do they conflict in any way with other functions or with the major objectives of the organization?

4. *Method:* What operations are involved in the direct work? Specifically, how are these operations supervised?

5. *Assignment:* What unit or units carry on the function? What are the channels of supervision? How is the work divided—by sub-function, or by area of operation, or both? Are two or more units,

ANALYSIS BY FUNCTION

which could be combined, doing the same or similar work? Is any work being done twice?

6. *Work Load:* How much working time, and of what type and grade of employees, is required? What is the unit of output? How many such units are produced?

7. *Accomplishment:* Does the function, as carried on and administered, serve its purpose? What improvements are needed?

The assembling of all these facts on any major area of administration is bound to be a long job. But in the course of gathering them, the analyst will secure the familiarity with operating problems and their implications which is essential for sound executive management. He will have provided himself with a major part of the factual background which is the basis of planning for better administration.

Chapter III

ANALYSIS BY UNITS OF ORGANIZATION

IN THE first phase of analysis, the work of an organization is separated into its component functions and sub-functions, then the purposes and processes of each branch of the work, its relationship to other work and to the whole program, and how and by whom it is administered and executed, are considered in turn. The second phase is, in some degree, the reverse of this process. Attention is first directed to the units of administration and their organizational relationship. Then each unit is scrutinized, and the method and flow of its work studied. The relation of this work to the scheme of functions comes last.

It might seem at first as though analysis by units of organization were merely a rearrangement of facts previously discovered, but this is only partially true. While the classification of functions is used to sort tasks and duties as the operations of each unit (or worker) are observed, it is here not an end in itself but only a springboard to more precise observation and analysis. Procedure can only be discussed in an abstract way if the organizational framework of the company or agency in question is not known. The administrative analyst must have organization charts showing the divisions and sections both in their formal power relationships (lines of authority) and in their actual operations.[1] These charts should not be thought of as photographs of an unchangeable structure, but as working diagrams, to be changed as need arises. Organizations should be built so as to permit the simplest and most direct procedures. The common habit of planning organization in the abstract and then parceling out the business is inexcusable.

The organization charts of two large agencies of the Federal Government appear, as examples, in Figures 2 and 3. They will be used further on to illustrate some procedural problems. In order to safeguard the neutral viewpoint of this book and, at the same time,

---

[1] That there may be a considerable difference between formal and actual organization will be shown a few pages further on.

ANALYSIS BY UNITS OF ORGANIZATION

permit free discussion of administrative technique, they have been left unnamed, being designated simply as "Agency A" and "Agency B." The charts for both agencies have been somewhat condensed for the sake of simplicity.

The "General Administrative Officer" of Agency A, who is intermediate in rank and line of contact between the administrator and the division chiefs, is found only occasionally in American government offices, and then usually in those headed by boards. Such an official is most useful when the head or heads of the agency have highly professionalized or quasi-judicial functions or are called upon to participate extensively in national politics. He may be compared with a *Staatssekretär* or Permanent Undersecretary in a German or British ministry. By attending to all matters of housekeeping, he permits the politically responsible head to devote himself to charting and developing broad policies and to conducting liaison with the legislature and the public. As can be seen, "Agency B" does not have such an officer.

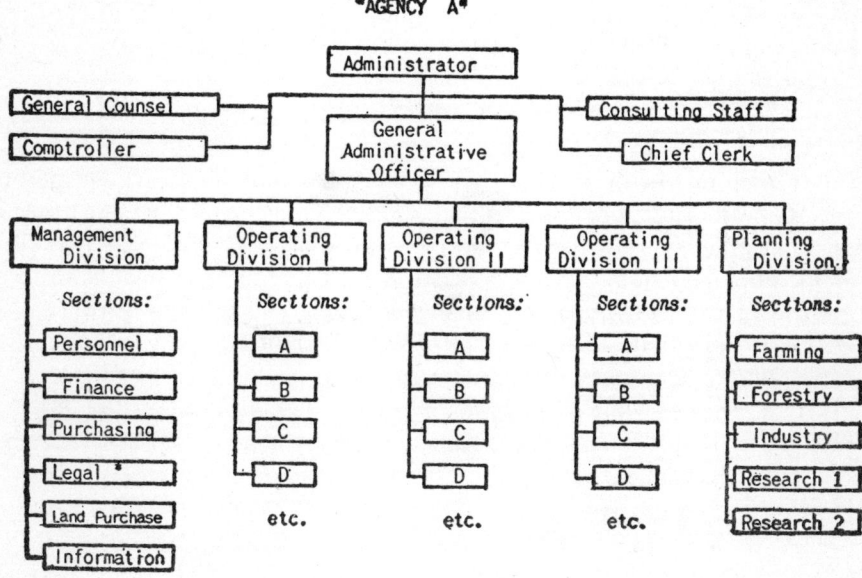

Figure 2

* Handles minor legal matters, prepares contracts, etc., as well as performing clerical work for the General Counsel in the Administrator's office.

ADMINISTRATIVE PROCEDURE

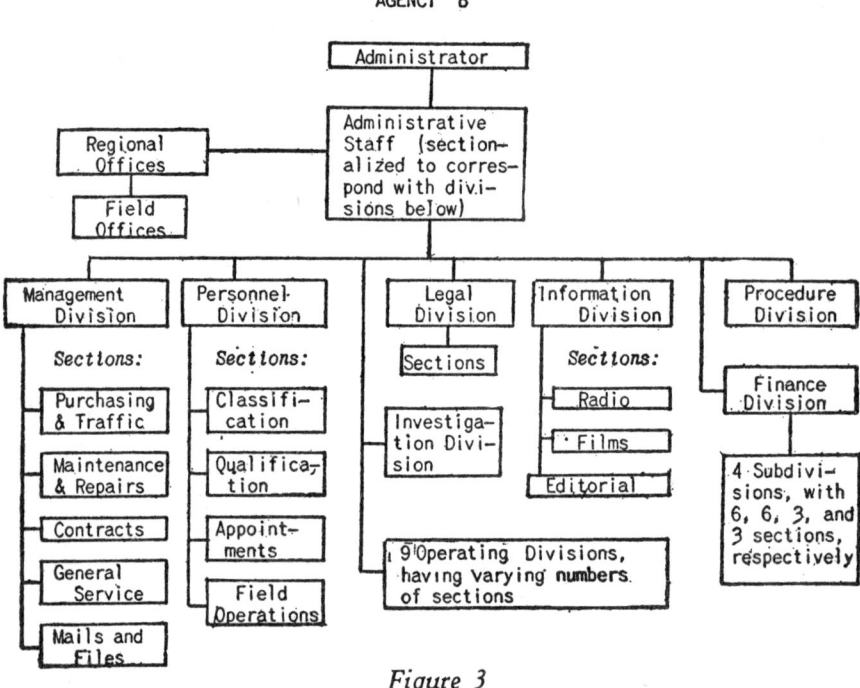

Figure 3

It will also be noted that "Agency A" has one division for operating staff functions (the Management Division) and one for planning, while "Agency B" has 6 operating staff divisions and a Procedure Division. The "Agency A" Planning Division is concerned mainly with program planning, while management planning is carried on under the direct supervision of the General Administrative Officer. Curiously enough, almost the reverse is true in "Agency B." This agency's Procedure Division has a fairly broad responsibility for administrative management within the organization, while program planning takes place in the line divisions and in the Administrator's office. It is obvious from the charts that the operating staff work of "Agency B" is much more elaborate than that of "Agency A." Most of the actual decisions on personnel and financial questions in "Agency A" are made in the line divisions, the Management Division serving mainly as a facilitating channel. In "Agency B," on the other hand, the staff divisions exert a real control within their jurisdictions. The consequences of what turned out to be an overdevelopment of staff operation are discussed in Chapters VII and VIII.

ANALYSIS BY UNITS OF ORGANIZATION

In "Agency B" each section is divided into units, the number depending on the volume and complexity of the work. Some sections have as many as 100 employees in Washington. As shown by the chart, contacts with the field offices are, in theory at least, centralized in the administrative staff, which is a whole division in itself. The field offices are organized as miniature replicas of the central organization. The Administrator's office is, to a large extent, occcupied in "clearing" material passing between Washington divisions and their counterparts in regional offices, a number of people doing little else. This arrangement has at times caused considerable delay in communication.

ORGANIZATION AND FUNCTIONS

Having obtained an organization chart of the agency or company we are going to study, we may begin to analyze the operations of units, beginning with the major divisions and working down to sections and sub-sections. There should already be at hand a classification of functions. The distribution of these functions and their sub-functions to units of organization was covered by the analysis suggested in the previous chapter. This material becomes a tool for further analysis. We may also have before us documentary evidence in the shape of written procedures, assignments of duties, authorizations, and job descriptions. Piecing these together will yield an approximation of what each unit is doing.

It will usually be found that for the most part organization and functions will correspond. There will be divisions responsible for major fields of work and sections within them performing the sub-functions. In fact, the entire aspect of an organization chart, with names of units suggesting the fields in which they operate, may lead one to suppose that the structure was conceived to fit exactly a set of functions. On the other hand, if the observer begins by studying functions independently of organization, he may be greatly mystified by divergence from what seems to be a common-sense rule; namely that organization should correspond exactly to function. Yet there may be reasons against full compliance with the rule.

In the first place, the classification of functions may be open to dispute. Even if there is agreement on the nature and relative significance of basic purposes and processes, no two analysts are likely to divide the fields of work in exactly the same way. There is also the border line of activities in which line and staff techniques seem of equal importance, and which are hard to locate definitely. If such questions can provoke debate among academicians, they are bound to do so among operating officials whose interests are at stake.[2] In spite of these uncertainties it is usually possible to get a fairly good idea of the relation between functions and organization by comparing the functional arrangement of fields of work with the formal organization chart and the official statement of duties for each unit. Discrepancies should be noted, and referred to again when an operating organization chart is made.

Formalized and second-hand data are not sufficient for real administrative analysis, because they tend to dwell on theoretical and ideal ways of doing things rather than the actual methods. Stated procedures usually tell the employee what to do in a general way; they seldom tell him how to do it. Like cook-books, they ignore the possibility of error. Actual methods, particularly where the work load is variable, can only be learned by direct and detailed inquiry from workers and supervisors or, far too often, only from personal experience.[3] And operating methods are very important, not only for the individual unit, but for all other offices associated with it in the chain of administration. The way in which each group works—its speed of production, the quality of its results, and the errors it makes or corrects—have far-reaching effects.

The analyst must therefore visit each division, section, and unit the work of which he is studying. He must sit down with the chief, with the administrative assistants, research workers, and clerks, and let each describe the job as he sees it. He must gain the confidence of each by showing a sincere and unprejudiced wish to learn: he should particularly avoid expressing any conclusions before he has had time to digest *all* the facts. While it is essential to let each interviewee talk freely, the questioning should be such as to cover the unit thoroughly. The following points should be included:

1. *Purpose:* What, briefly, is the job that is being done? What is the transition from the raw material to the finished product? What are the criteria of satisfactory accomplishment?

2. *Relationships:* How does the job fit into the classification of functions? Into the administrative sequence of which it is a part? What are the preceding and following operations and where are they done? How does the job relate to the larger objectives of the organization?

---

[2] The common tendency to give too much weight to the number of subordinates in classifying positions makes officials loath to give up activities, even unnecessary ones.

[3] A staff official should be assigned to a line office every now and then, so that he may see problems from "the operating man's angle."

ANALYSIS BY UNITS OF ORGANIZATION

3. *Method:* What are the processes in doing the work? If the job is one of supervision, what are the methods of observation and control?

4. *Work Load:* What is the unit of work? Are the items or "cases" uniform or variable? How long does it take to dispose of a unit? Does the work come in evenly; does it pile up?

5. *Personnel:* How many people, and of what type and grade,[4] are assigned to the work? Are they overworked, or the opposite? When is overtime necessary?

6. *Conditions of Work:* Are the office arrangements and equipment suitable? Is incoming material in the proper shape? What improvements would help?

7. *Channels of Contact:* Who supervises the job? Who is supervised in connection therewith? What regular operating contacts are made with other offices? Directly or through intermediaries?

Some of the points covered in analysis of units of organization are carried over from analysis by function. Insofar as functions and units correspond, data once gathered may be used again. But the second type of analysis is much less theoretical than the first kind, and depends for its success on a closer observation of people at work. There is particular need for carrying the inquiry to the smallest units and, wherever a unit is doing a number of things, to the individual duty.[5] For instance, it may be found that the duties assigned to an individual or group are of uneven quality,[6] that is, requiring varying degrees of skill and judgment, and being of unequal importance. When the work load contains items covering too great a range in quality, the worker either is faced with some tasks too advanced for him or he wastes some of his time on things which could be done by someone of lesser ability. This situation is perhaps more frequent in the case of the higher and intermediate executives than in that of clerks; it is often the result of failure to delegate.

A complete or extensive set of answers to questions such as the foregoing would provide a good picture of operations, and would provide the necessary background for solving problems turned up by the analyst. For, needless to say, he would find some things which could be improved, even in the most nearly perfect office. An intelligent outsider looking in can always help, but he cannot do so by

---

[4] Grade in terms of salary classification.
[5] The term "duty," as used in a technical sense here and further on, means an integrated assignment of work repeatedly performed by the same person or unit. The idea of repeated, or at least continuous, performance is inherent in the term. Writing a single report is a task; writing a weekly report is a duty.
[6] A more precise definition of quality appears in Chapter IV.

ADMINISTRATIVE PROCEDURE

general or abstract consideration. He should get the facts, as well as all possible figures.

MEASURING WORK LOAD

In surveying units of organization, thought should be given to the possibilities of measuring the work. Techniques have been developed for evaluating clerical and stenographic tasks in terms of units; these may be found in use in a number of offices.[7] For executive work the problem is more difficult, partly because the operations are mental rather than manual, and partly because of the non-uniformity of the subject matter. Yet measurement of executive work load is possible. Such measurement must not try to dodge the variability of the tasks by subjecting them to a Procrustean system of units, but must accept differences in bulk and importance as a basic condition. In fact, it must even assay the non-uniformity.

Several methods of measuring executive work, including two that have been *successfully applied* in government offices, are described in Chapter XIII, which deals with "Timing and Scheduling." There would be no more than a reference to measurement here, were it not that one particular technique has special value in determining what the "actual" operating organization of an office looks like, as contrasted with the formal "official" organization chart.

The method here described was developed to meet a specific problem in a government office. Over a number of years both the volume of business and the number of personnel of this office had increased steadily, but there had been no elaboration of the organization structure, nor extensive delegation of administrative authority. The result was that the major executives became bogged down with routine and were unable to give time to constructive planning and broad observation. It was desired to relieve them of some of their load. But first it was necessary to determine just what this load consisted of. It would then be possible to decide which duties could be delegated and what amount of time could be cleared for each official. The plan required each executive, during a test period, to enter on a daily report card a running record of his activities. The record showed the time consumed on each item of work, the physical process (writing, telephoning, etc.), the person contacted, and the subject matter. The brevity and simplicity of entries is indicated by the sample form in Figure 4.

---

[7] Tennessee Valley Authority, Office Service Department, *Office Method Bulletins*, Especially numbers 24, 25, 37, 38, 43, 46, 60, 78. Also Public Administration Service Bulletin, *The Work Unit in Federal Administration, 1937*.

ANALYSIS BY UNITS OF ORGANIZATION

U. S. DEPARTMENT OF..
BUREAU OF ....

EXECUTIVE WORK LOAD SURVEY DATA

Name: *William Burgess* Date: *9-17-40*
Position: *Ass't Chief, Fiscal Section*

Item	Type of Work	Begun	Ended	Contact With	Subject
1	R—M	9.00	9.15	Davis, Development Div.	Purch. order, bldg. mat'ls
2	Ph—1	9.15	9.18		
3	W—M	9.19	9.25	Jordan, Purch.	"
4	W—M	9.25	9.38	Davis	"
				Walden, Field Survey Div.	Budget est. for F. S. Div.
5	Ph—2	9.38	9.43	Brown, Acc'ts	Susp. of voucher
6	Ph—1	9.43	9.52	King, GAO	"
7	Ph—1	9.53	9.58	Brown, Acc'ts	"
8	R—Docs	9.59	10.25	———	"
9	Ph—1	10.26	10.30	Brown, Acc'ts	"
4	W—M	10.31	10.54	See above	See above
10	R & S—L	10.55	11.01	Jordan to TVA	Purch. fert, TVA
11	C—1	11.02	11.46	J. H. Bennett	Applic. for job
12	Ph—1	11.46	11.50	Jackson, Pers.	J. H. Bennett
13	C—1	11.52	12.21	Williams, Beale, Elph'stone, Accounts	Errors in allotment ledgers
14	C—2	12.22	12.40	Bur. Chief	Budg. Wisc. Proj.
15	Lunch	12.40	1.15		
16	R & S—L	1.15	1.18	Lewis to WPA	Laborers, Acc'ts
17	R & S—M	1.18	1.19	James to Pers.	Req. appointment
18	Ph—1	1.20	1.33	Proc. Div.	Purch. Office Sup.
19	C—2	1.34	2.07	Same as 13	Same as 13
			and so forth		

Abbreviations:

    C—conference   (1—my office; 2—other office)
    Ph—phone call   (1—I called up; 2—he called up)
    R—reading   Rep.—report (regular)
    W—Writing, dictating   Sp. Rep.—special report
R & S—reading and signing   CF—case file
    L—letter (outside department)   Doc—documents, laws, etc.
    M—memorandum (inside)

Figure 4

It can be easily seen that this kind of study, if conducted over a long enough "typical" period, would produce a detailed cross section of an official's work, and would permit the singling out of elements

ADMINISTRATIVE PROCEDURE

for delegation or distribution to other officials. For instance, the items of work could be tabulated by subject, showing the number of minutes spent on each, with possibly the following breakdown:

    A. all work
    B. telephone calls
    C. conferences
    D. reading
    E. reading and signing
    F. writing or dictating.

The work could also be distributed by officials contacted, under the following subheads:

    A. by subject
    B. by physical process
    C. by process and subject.

This information would make it possible to tell how much time could be saved by having certain subjects handled by subordinates, by having certain officials deal with each other directly instead of through the officer in question, and by various other specific rearrangements. It would also show what combinations of duties would constitute normal work loads for newly set up positions. In short, it would provide the data for an equitable distribution of tasks.

By tabulating the work in terms of minutes rather than number of items, the element of variability in the bulk of executive tasks would be compensated for. It would still be possible to measure the variation itself by finding the average, maximum, and minimum times, and the distribution of tasks in various subjects. This might also show differences in the production rates of various executives; for instance Mr. A. might handle cases of a certain type in an average of twelve minutes while Mr. B might consistently take twenty minutes to perform essentially the same work. Such findings, while they should not be used for jumping to conclusions about relative merit, might be helpful in shifting particular duties to those best fitted for them.

The time spent by each official in contacting other ones would provide the means of showing in quantitative terms the operating relationships between members of the organization. If extended to all officials regularly making contacts outside their own offices, the data would show the operating relationships between units. The information could be shown graphically in a very simple way by drawing a line of a certain thickness for each number of minutes of

ANALYSIS BY UNITS OF ORGANIZATION

communication and superimposing these lines on the organization chart. By way of illustration, this has been done in Figures 5 and 6. The first of these diagrams shows the organization chart of an imaginary division. The second shows the same chart with the lines indicating minutes of communication added.

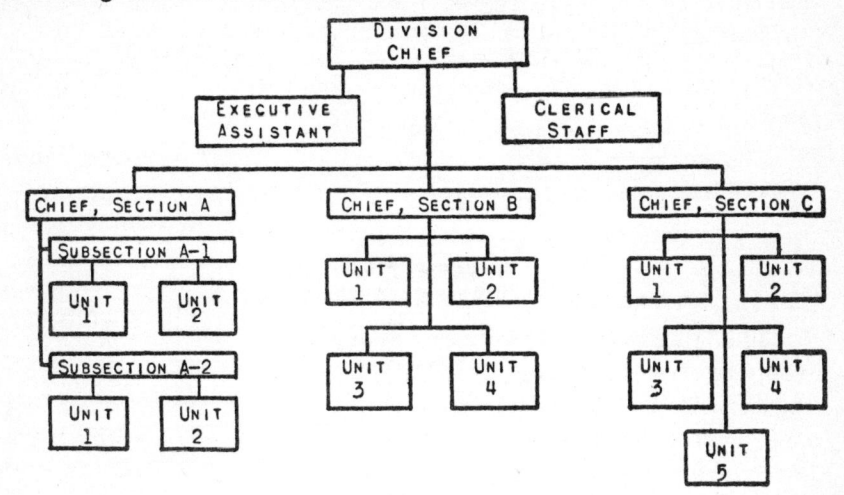

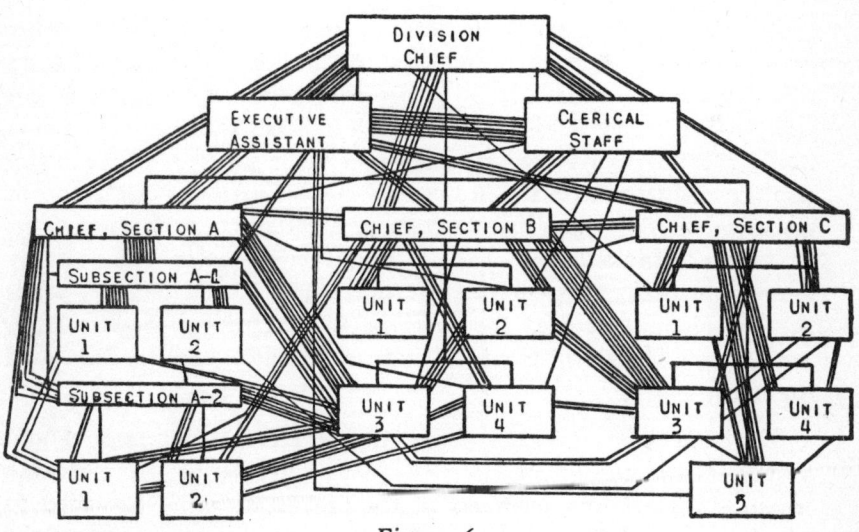

Figure 5.

Figure 6
Each line is equal to one hour of communication.

On the basis of a factual finding of actual operating relationships, it should be possible to re-allocate functions and the units responsible for them so as to bring closely related activities together. For instance,

ADMINISTRATIVE PROCEDURE

Figure 6 shows that, from a quantitative viewpoint,[8] Unit 3 of Section B in our imaginary division should be transferred to Subsection A-2 of Section A. Likewise, Unit 3 of Section C belongs in Section B. A major objective of administrative management is to reduce the volume of inter-office traffic to the minimum, because doing business across sectional or divisional lines is inevitably more complex than doing it in one's own bailiwick. This end may be furthered by changing the design of the organization so as to keep continuous processes within the same offices as long as possible.

Analysis by units of organization, especially if quantitative methods are used, may well lead to a revision of the classification of functions, which was originally a product of qualitative thinking. This is as it should be: science begins with axioms which are used as bases for planning programs of observation; then, as a result of the observation, it revises the axioms. Each succeeding step utilizes accumulated knowledge and is, at the same time, a means for correcting its defects. Although analysis by function would seem logically to precede that by units of organization, the two should react upon each other freely. For it is possible that experience will show that the order should be reversed.

---

[8] There are of course factors other than the volume of business which must be considered.

Chapter IV

ANALYSIS BY ADMINISTRATIVE SEQUENCE

THE two methods of analysis already introduced focus attention on the work or structure of an organization. They can be used on various scales—in a bureau, division, or section. But within the limitations they are all-inclusive, covering all the functions or all the units in the area surveyed. Analysis by administrative sequence, an intensive rather than extensive method, covers both functions and units, but only as they relate to a single connected series of operations. The processes leading to a desired result are studied in turn, and each considered in its relation to that end. The objective is to arrange the tasks and the transfers between them (including consolidation or elimination where desirable) so that the end result is secured with a minimum of time and effort.

A basic element of scientific management as applied to physical processes is time and motion study. The modern engineer plans machinery and layout so that employees work with a minimum of bodily motion, and so that materials travel the shortest distance from one operation to the next. By analyzing the course followed by a piece of work, unnecessary travel of men and material can be cut out and the job as a whole simplified. The same process is applicable, in part, to administration, particularly to the problem of moving the work rapidly to those who do it and getting it disposed of promptly.

But industrial methods can not be transplanted wholesale to administration. Administrative management cannot, for instance, improve the technique of *thinking,* which is an essential part of each executive act. Better thinking is a product of education and mental training.[1] It is not implanted by a set of standard instructions. What management can do is to simplify and expedite the mechanical phases

---

[1] Proper thinking in administration, with constant reference to basic objectives and policies, is to some extent a product of indoctrination (inculcation of basic principles on which the organization operates), concerning which see Mooney and Reiley, *The Principles of Organization,* pp. 10-13, 175-178.

ADMINISTRATIVE PROCEDURE

of administration, cutting the amount of clerical detail the executive must deal with and enabling him to use his powers of thought, whatever they may be, to the best advantage. The most important time and motion economies in administration, however, are made not in the actual performance of particular tasks but in the transfer of business from one worker to the next—in the chain of *communication* which is integral in the administrative process.

The administrator of a large organization does not himself handle much of the routine work; at least he should not. He is essentially a ringmaster, not a performer. He is responsible for dividing up the work, assigning areas of operation to subordinates, and regulating the order in which things are done and the way in which work moves from unit to unit and division to division. All of these functions, and particularly the third, fall within the province of administrative management. The administrator, who is responsible for results, must satisfy himself that these matters are being handled correctly. While he should take a hand in developing the general frame of organization and the basic procedures, he should delegate the details to administrative analysts, because the exact analysis needed for proper definition of functions, development of work assignments, and setting up of routines is too voluminous and too technical for him to do alone.

Each distinct executive or clerical operation performed by an individual is a task; repetitions of the same task are a duty. Nearly every task belongs to an administrative sequence, which is a series of tasks leading to a specified end. Not all the tasks in a sequence need belong to the same function; some objectives require the co-ordination of a number of functions. Within one line function, several staff functions may be involved.[2] For instance, answering a letter, the subject matter of which stays within a line function, might involve tasks in three staff functions. The first, getting the necessary information, is research. The second, writing the letter, might be editorial or executive. The last, typing the letter, is stenographic.[3] Even a more complicated sequence can be divided the same way; the only difference is a greater number and diversity of tasks. Larger sequences are more likely to spread over several line functions. Thus, the developing of a public housing project may include finance, legal work, construction, and social work, which are all line functions since they involve different

---

[2] Supra, Chapter II, "Line and Staff Functions."
[3] In a highly "functionalized" organization these tasks might be performed by different divisions.

ANALYSIS BY ADMINISTRATIVE SEQUENCE

kinds of direct operation.[4] The tasks in such undertakings fall into groups according to functions and distribution to divisions, sections, and units.

After a task or group of tasks is performed by an individual, the work must be passed on to someone else. These transfers of work (or, more exactly, of the pieces of paper on which the work is recorded) may be spoken of generally as "administrative traffic." All the transfers needed to accomplish a given administrative sequence may be called the "motion" of that sequence and each transfer of the matériel [5] from one worker to another a "move." The first operation in analyzing an existing or proposed administrative sequence is to divide it into steps or individual tasks. Then it must be seen how many "moves" are needed. In the interest of efficiency, the number of moves and their distance (physically and organizationally) should be kept as low as possible.

ADMINISTRATIVE MOTION TAKES TIME

An administrative move may take anywhere from a few seconds to a few weeks. The time it takes, which can be called "motion delay," consists of three elements: (a) the time required for the physical transfer of the work from one person to another, (b) the time before the recipient gets around to acting on the matter, and (c) the time it takes him to decide what he should do about it. For example, an executive may have to get his superior's approval before he puts a certain plan into operation. He writes a memorandum outlining the proposal. This may reach the superior in a few minutes if he is in the next room or in a week if it must go across the country by mail. There may be other matters on hand which must be dealt with first, so the plan may rest in a desk drawer for several hours or several weeks. When the superior finally reads the memorandum, he may have to spend some time securing the information he needs before passing judgment on it. These three elements of time constitute the motion delay in the particular case.

The motion delay caused by any transfer of work is a variable quantity which can only be predicted within approximate limits. Each administrative move, however, does have a real cost in time and money, both in the operations needed to accomplish the move itself

---

[4] It will be remembered that direct operations are the purposes of administration. The direct operations have their own purposes too, but the purpose of *administration* is always in a sense secondary—to facilitate the direct operation in question.

[5] This term is used to indicate the papers covering any administrative sequence or "case."

and in the effect on the time when the end-result is obtained. In general the time required for any move and the cost of handling the matériel increase with the physical distance. They also increase with the organizational distance. This is, within a section or unit papers may be passed directly between workers, between sections they are usually carried by messengers, while between divisions, particularly in large offices, they are often assembled and sorted out by mail rooms. In the latter case, three hours is a reasonable average time for an interdivisional transfer within the same building, assuming normally good messenger service.[6]

To make any administrative move worth-while, its direct and indirect time and money costs must be compensated by (a) increased efficiency through specialization, and (b) prevention of possible costly mistakes through supervision and control. When introducing moves in an administrative sequence, other than the absolute minimum needed for doing the executive work in the most direct way, it should be ascertained whether the gains from improved operation and control will outweigh the probable expense and delay.

Different classes of work demand various degrees of specialization, hence varying quantities of motion. For example, the job of tuning a piano can be done best by a single workman. A move, or the turning over of a half-tuned piano to someone else to finish, would cause an actual loss of efficiency. The making of an automobile is exactly the opposite. The only efficient way to make one (or rather to make thousands) is to divide the work up into a great number of specialized tasks. Because automobile manufacture necessarily requires that each car pass to a long succession of workers each of whom adds something, its engineers have minimized the elements of delay by setting up production lines with exact timing of each step. This is only possible when the work is completely standardized, and there is always the danger of a complete tie-up when any machine breaks down or its operator sits down.

The motion requirements of administrative work are as variable as those of mechanical operations. There are some jobs of research or specialized supervision which can best be carried on by a single official with little reference to outsiders. There are other projects which by their nature require the collaboration of hundreds of people. Two elements are always open to judgment. First, granted that the

---

[6] Officials of an agency whose buildings are located in different "zones" in Washington, and whose inter-building mail is carried by the consolidated messenger service operated by the Post Office Department, have told the writer that it frequently takes a whole day to get a paper to an official in another building.

ANALYSIS BY ADMINISTRATIVE SEQUENCE

nature of an undertaking determines in a general way that there must be a certain amount of specialization, how far should one go in dividing it up? Should each particular task be done by a different worker, or are there combinations which can be assigned to the same individuals or units? Second, granted that a definite number of operating steps (those concerned only with the actual performance of the work) are necessary, how many control steps are needed to assure that the work has been properly done and that no irregularities have taken place? These are questions that the administrative analyst will have to answer.

As has been pointed out the most noticeable thing about administrative traffic is its lack of uniformity. Except for some kinds of clerical and fiscal operations, the work is "brain work" and can not be standardized in full detail. The flow of business is uneven, and the three elements of motion delay tend to be at a maximum. While scheduling of administrative work is quite feasible, and can be much more accurate than many people now believe, it can work only if the factors of variability are recognized, since industrial "production line" methods can not be used. Motion delay can be reduced but not eliminated. It is thus desirable to keep the number of moves in any sequence down to the minimum which will provide the necessary expertness for particular tasks and will inhibit unco-ordinated or improperly supervised actions.

To show how all this applies to an every-day problem, let us take the case of a construction superintendent on a highway project who finds that he needs an additional steam shovel. The purchase of this engine is an administrative problem of some importance, particularly if there are salesmen with good political connections in the offing. The simplest way in which the superintendent could get his steam shovel would be to go out and buy it. However, the rules of all public agencies and most private concerns require that materials (except minor items) be purchased through established channels, the reason being: (1) to make sure that supplies bought are for reasonable and legitimate needs, (2) to see that they are appropriate for the uses to which they will be put, (3) to prevent "rake-offs," and (4) to secure the lowest prices through centralized purchasing and competitive bidding. So the superintendent, instead of buying the shovel, fills out a requisition stating exactly what he wants, accompanied by a memorandum explaining why. The requisition is approved by the District Superintendent, and probably by certain other officers, and forwarded to the purchasing agent. This official

ADMINISTRATIVE PROCEDURE

has the specifications prepared or checked by a consulting engineer and then advertises for bids. Then he buys the shovel and has it delivered to the project. All these administrative steps and the consequent moves take time and cost money, both directly and indirectly by holding up work on the project. Whether the result is a net gain or loss depends on a number of intangible factors including individual quotients of honesty and ability. One superintendent could perhaps buy machinery as well as the procurement officer, while another might spend twice as much and not get the right thing. But whatever the channels are for purchasing (or any other sequence), they should operate with the fewest and shortest moves for the necessary administrative operations.

CHARTING AN ADMINISTRATIVE SEQUENCE

The first step in analyzing an administrative sequence is to list the individual tasks and the units which perform them. It is always a good thing to present this information graphically, so as to make clear the number and distance of moves and to throw into relief any

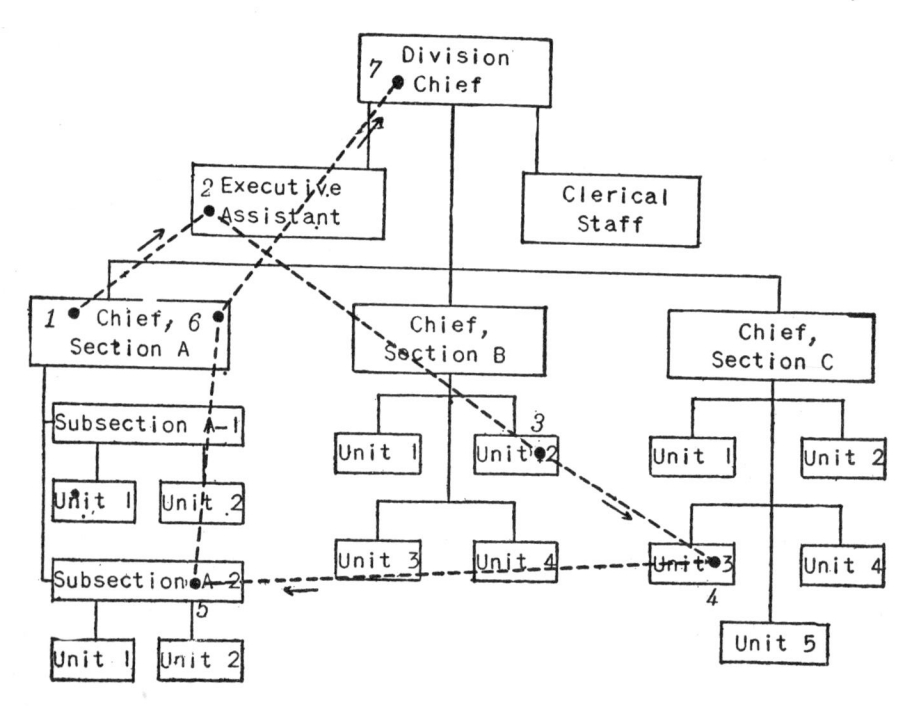

Figure 7

ANALYSIS BY ADMINISTRATIVE SEQUENCE

back-tracking. A simple way to illustrate a short sequence is to superimpose the lines of flow on the organization chart. Let us suppose that a sequence carried on entirely within the imaginary

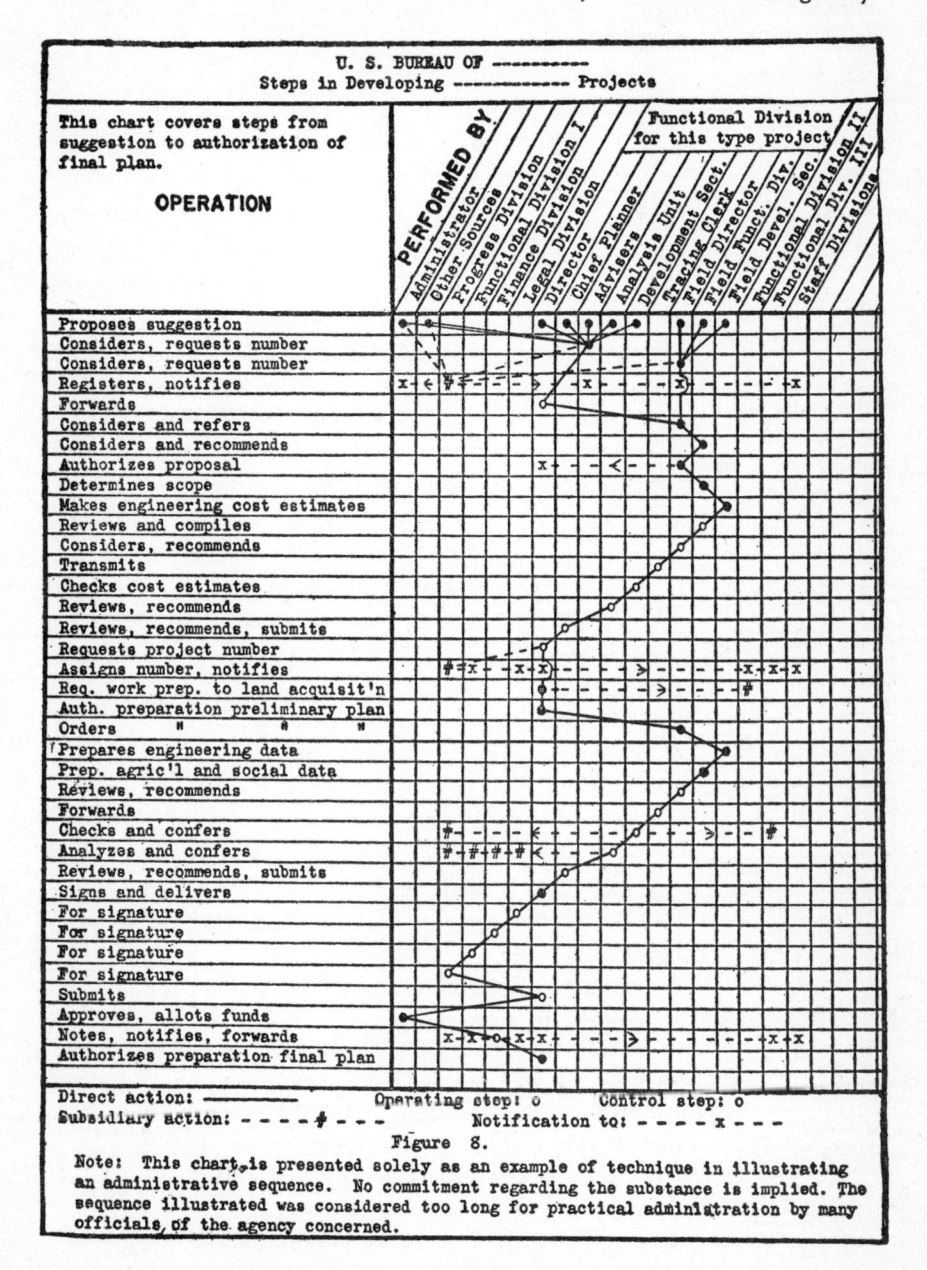

U. S. BUREAU OF ----------
Steps in Developing ------------ Projects

This chart covers steps from suggestion to authorization of final plan.

OPERATION

Columns (PERFORMED BY): Administrator, Other Sources, Progress Division, Functional Division I, Finance Division, Legal Division, Director, Chief Planner, Advisers Unit, Analysts Unit, Development Sect., Tracing Clerk, Field Director, Field Devel. Div., Functional Div. Sec., Functional Division II, Staff Divisions III

Operations (rows):
- Proposes suggestion
- Considers, requests number
- Considers, requests number
- Registers, notifies
- Forwards
- Considers and refers
- Considers and recommends
- Authorizes proposal
- Determines scope
- Makes engineering cost estimates
- Reviews and compiles
- Considers, recommends
- Transmits
- Checks cost estimates
- Reviews, recommends
- Reviews, recommends, submits
- Requests project number
- Assigns number, notifies
- Req. work prep. to land acquisit'n
- Auth. preparation preliminary plan
- Orders   "   "   "
- Prepares engineering data
- Prep. agric'l and social data
- Reviews, recommends
- Forwards
- Checks and confers
- Analyzes and confers
- Reviews, recommends, submits
- Signs and delivers
- For signature
- For signature
- For signature
- For signature
- Submits
- Approves, allots funds
- Notes, notifies, forwards
- Authorizes preparation final plan

Direct action: ─────   Operating step: o   Control step: o
Subsidiary action: - - - - ≠ - - -   Notification to: - - - - x - - -

Figure 8.

Note: This chart is presented solely as an example of technique in illustrating an administrative sequence. No commitment regarding the substance is implied. The sequence illustrated was considered too long for practical administration by many officials of the agency concerned.

ADMINISTRATIVE PROCEDURE

division introduced in Chapter III (Figure 5) has the following steps:

1	(initiates)	Chief, Section A
2	(approves)	Executive Assistant
3	(compiles statistics)	Unit 2 of Section B
4	(additional data)	Unit 3 of Section C
5	(writes up)	Subsection A-2
6	(reviews)	Chief, Section A
7	(finally approves)	Division Chief

The way this sequence would look drawn on the organization chart of the division is shown in Figure 7.

Another way of showing the progress of a sequence, particularly a long one, is a cross-analysis chart, sometimes referred to as a "flow chart." Brief descriptions of the various steps are given in columns running across the paper, and the units or officers which perform them are listed at the head of columns running down. Usually the sections of a division are grouped together, and other offices are placed according to "organizational" distance. A cross-analysis chart used in a Federal agency is given in Figure 8. This chart is in the form in which it was circulated to the agency's officials except for changes in certain titles and for the use of symbols to distinguish operating steps (those strictly necessary to the actual doing of work) from control steps (those reviewing work done tentatively by others).

The cross-analysis chart does not go into the details of operations nor does it cover the clerical steps in transferring and recording papers. It does not in itself provide a basis for concluding that any step or move is unnecessary. It is only a graphic index of the steps in a sequence and of those who do them, and an indicator of where thorough investigation may prove most fruitful.

In tracing the course of a sequence, care must be taken to include every move and not merely the principal ones. Though this might seem a superfluous warning, it is surprisingly easy to make a chart which seems to be complete and then find, upon persistent inquiry, that there are operations which had eluded earlier observation, of which those responsible for preceding or ensuing steps are not even aware. It is not sufficient to rely on written instructions or even on descriptions given by executives. These are useful as starting points, but the facts must be verified by actually following the sequence around. Attention should be paid to customary ways of handling papers: for instance, if it is a written or unwritten rule that all papers passing from one division to another must clear through the divisional offices, the chart should not show them going directly from a section in one division to one in another division. It is essential to account

ANALYSIS BY ADMINISTRATIVE SEQUENCE

for even the most perfunctory steps, because each move introduces some expense and delay.

ANALYSIS OF INDIVIDUAL TASKS

The first step in analysis of an administrative sequence is, as we have seen, the making of a chart showing the time and place relationship of operations. This may be supplemented by a "time table" showing the average times between key steps if the files will yield the data. It is then necessary to consider each task both as an entity and in its relation to the whole purpose of the sequence. The questions to be asked about each task may to some extent follow the outline suggested for analysis of a function. Particular emphasis should be placed on the question, "why?" Lack of a definite answer from those responsible for the task indicates that it may perhaps be eliminated.

The information about each step should include an estimate of its qualitative character, or, as we shall use the word, simply its "quality." This is a summing up, preferably in numerical terms, of the answers to three questions:

(1) How much skill and experience are required for performing the task?

(2) How important is the subject matter; what are the consequences of omission or improper performance; and

(3) How much discretion, judgment, and authority are inherent in the work?

Tasks should not be rated by the grade or salary of those who perform them, or even by the qualifications they happen to possess. On the contrary, positions are classified and filled according to the nature and grade of their duties and tasks, and this is a function of personnel workers rather than administrative analysts. While tasks may for convenience be classified in terms of salary grades,[7] their evaluation should be based only on the aptitudes strictly necessary for doing them and not those pertaining to the positions of which they constitute fractional duties. Tasks are only raised in quality by outstanding workers if they can succeed in changing the tasks themselves. For instance, a procedure may call for "tabulation of prepared data, under close supervision," which is assigned to a junior statistical clerk and becomes the major part of his job. If the clerk learns to interpret the data in their raw form so they need not be pre-digested, and if he learns to produce the desired results with little or no super-

---

[7] There are disadvantages in doing this if resultant demands for reclassification cannot be met.

ADMINISTRATIVE PROCEDURE

vision, he may be entitled to a re-classification upward, not directly because of his abilities, but because the job has changed. There are many tasks, however, which no degree of aptitude or initiative can change. The administrative analyst is interested in the quality of tasks because he wants things administered as economically as possible. He does not, for instance, want to see a division chief assigned duties which a section chief or administrative assistant could do satisfactorily. He will compare his estimates of the quality of tasks with the personnel expert's analyses of entire positions so as to work out the most economical and sensible assignments. Job descriptions should always be made available to the analyst for use as guides to the best utilization of human resources.

Besides evaluating the quality of a task, the administrative analyst should determine its "functionality," or its exact place in the network of line and staff functions. With this information, with the general data on sequence and assignments in the form of a flow chart, and with reference to material previously gathered on functions and units of organization, he may proceed to determine whether the sequence, as it stands, is the best way of accomplishing the objective, or whether it could be done more simply and economically. The exact methods of interpretation and criticism must necessarily depend to a large extent on the subject matter and environment of the undertaking. There are, however, a few general criteria which will work in almost any instance if intelligently applied. They are quite unspectacular, for the best administration is simple.

EVALUATING AN ADMINISTRATIVE SEQUENCE

An administrative sequence should, in general, conform to the following standards:

1. *Each task should contribute positively to the basic purpose.* Every step should fit into a logical pattern and should have definite and essential results. If the need for a step is doubtful, the presumption is in favor of eliminating it. Care should be taken that work is never duplicated, particularly in the field of control.

2. *Similar tasks should be combined.* Doing so will reduce the number of administrative moves and will permit preliminary work, such as familiarization with the background of the particular case, to be done once instead of twice.

3. *Administrative moves should be as few and short as possible.* The time and cost of motion [8] make direct routing essential. Formal

---

[8] See material under "Administrative Motion Takes Time" in this chapter.

ANALYSIS BY ADMINISTRATIVE SEQUENCE

signatures and clearances should be kept down to the minimum; the matériel should travel as rapidly as possible between those who do the actual work.

4. *Each task should be well-balanced.* The three elements which make up the quality of a task should be well adjusted. For instance, skill and authority should not be wasted on unimportant subject matter. Nor should a task which requires experience and judgment include a lot of unessential detail.

USES OF ADMINISTRATIVE ANALYSIS

These criteria, particularly 1, 3, and 4, are restatements of the common-sense proposition that energy should be reserved for the most essential work and then utilized as completely as possible. This rule would, for instance, indicate the elimination of steps which are mere formalities or which embody such administrative fictions as the concept that the department head or the bureau chief does all the acts which are in fact done by his subordinates. It is a symptom of faulty planning when high executives have to sign a multitude of miscellaneous papers which they have had no hand in preparing and often do not even have time to read. It would be better if such documents were rubber-stamped, issued over the signatures of subordinates, or signed "impersonally" in the name of the organization.[9]

This method of analyzing an administrative sequence is frankly qualitative and based upon the judgments made by the analyst. It is not a substitute for objective factual analysis based on operating statistics and cost accounting. It is designed to reach activities to which these more precise methods can not be applied. In the "intangible" sphere of higher administration we must necessarily use qualitative and perceptive data, but if we proceed with caution and constantly check our mental process, we can make practical improvements in administrative technique.

We have to develop ways and means of dealing with the phenomena of administration; with functions, units of organization, and processes. We have to classify and evaluate the vast and mystifying assortment of facts observed in a large establishment. It may appear at first that the concepts and ways of thinking suggested are too abstract—not readily applicable to everyday problems. But

---

[9] The last practice is followed extensively by European governments but has not been adopted in the United States. The Tennessee Valley Authority, however, uses a modified form of this device by signing its letters: TENNESSEE VALLEY AUTHORITY—John Smith, Executive Assistant, etc.

administrative theory (as distinguished from experience) is like economic theory; it begins with the abstract and works down toward the concrete. Before the economist can hope to deal with the complexities of current problems he must sharpen his "tools of thought" against imaginary problems which are deliberately over-simplified to bring the method of attack into the clearest relief. The same is true of the administrative analyst.

Administrative science is still in the stage where economics was at the time of Adam Smith and Ricardo; it is still necessary to spend time inventing and testing concepts and terminology, and there are still no guaranteed ways to solve problems. Yet administrative technicians in many government agencies and private companies are even now applying rational management to administrative problems. They are using tools in experimental ways and improving them as they go along. The methods of analysis covered in these three chapters were introduced in terms of imaginary cases so as to avoid confusion over particular objects of administration. But they are intended for use in dealing with concrete problems, in understanding existing functions, organizations, and procedures, and in planning improvements. To test their validity, they must be applied to real situations in real organizations.

Chapter V

ORGANIZATION AND PROCEDURE

THE PREVIOUS chapters have set forth ways of observing the phenomena of administration from three points of view. We may analyze by *function*, observing the purposes and processes of administration and arranging them in a cross-pattern of line and staff functions so that a field of work can be seen as a staff phase of a line function or a line phase of a staff function. We may analyze by *units of organization*, studying the power relationships between offices and employees, seeing how their specific duties and tasks are delimited, and discovering the channels of formal and informal contact between them. We may analyze by *administrative sequence*, following a whole job through from beginning to end, tracing the administrative moves and seeing whether each operation makes a positive contribution toward the objective. The three types of analysis are complementary.

Applying the three methods to the same organization will not produce three isolated sets of facts. The results will consist for the most part of the same facts, but interpreted in three different ways. And from this there can be drawn the obvious conclusion that the functions, organization, and procedures of any agency or company are highly interdependent. One may not be changed without corresponding changes in the others. If a function is abolished, the people who perform it must be laid off, transferred, or given some other function. If the organization is shaken up, and units, sections, and divisions moved around, administrative sequences will automatically be rearranged and business will flow in new channels. If changes begin with a revision of administrative sequences, the operating organization (in terms of actual channels of contact) will change too, even though the formal structure remains the same.

If all three of the foregoing factors and their interrelationships are not taken into account in management planning, the results may sometimes be far from those anticipated. For instance, if a change

ADMINISTRATIVE PROCEDURE

in the assignment of functions and in the routing of sequences is undertaken without due thought on the matter of organization, it may be found afterwards that the duties in question have not been moved but duplicated. One of the Federal departments some time ago centralized certain types of accounts in a departmental accounting office. The units which had kept these accounts in the subordinate bureaus were not disturbed, as the departmental authorities were loath to interfere with the bureaus' internal management. Later, they were much surprised to find *two sets of accounts* being kept; the bureau accountants went right on doing what they had always been doing. For they had to do something!

CONCENTRATION VERSUS DEVOLUTION

To illustrate fully the interrelation between organization and procedure it is necessary to examine certain ways in which administrative groups tend to behave and to show the effects of this behavior on the flow of business. Of primary importance are two conflicting impulses: that toward concentration (centralization) of administrative power and that toward its devolution (decentralization). When the first is dominant, the central authorities reach out for greater and greater control over the subordinate units, often snuffing out intermediate offices in the process. Rules are issued ordering that communications between geographical or functional divisions be routed through the central office for review. The power of division chiefs, plant managers, etc., to plan and control is in large measure transferred upward to the main office, which reserves all important decisions to itself. The result is that subordinate executives and field officers are reduced to the status of clerks since they have to wait for approval before doing anything.

Concentration of authority is frequently self-defeating, because the central officials become snowed under with reports, requests, complaints, and inquiries; they are so plagued with telephone calls and visitors that they cannot work. There is a natural reaction to this in the opposite tendency toward devolution—the desire of subordinates to operate with a minimum of interference and the tendency of certain personalities to ignore or sabotage the policies of the central group. These people hound the officials in the main office, protesting and arguing, until finally there is a frantic wave of delegation. A period of over-concentration is frequently followed by extreme devolution, which leads to duplication of work and often to conflict, there being no central policy but an assortment of policies pursued by

ORGANIZATION AND PROCEDURE

different groups. This situation in turn brings corrective measures on the part of the central officials, who begin co-ordinating and setting up new controls. The history of many public agencies and corporations shows a series of pendulum-swings between the extremes of concentration and devolution. Few and happy are the organizations which enjoy a sustained period of balance.

There is no "one best" degree of concentration of authority which will fit all organizations. The proper adjustment always depends on a number of factors, including the nature of the work administered, the environment (physical, political, legal, and socio-psychological) [1] in which the organization operates, and, particularly, the caliber of the personnel and the mutual feelings existing between them. Where there is distrust and suspicion, due to lack or ability or integrity on the part of officials, or to a tense political situation, particularly one involving open or tacit dislike of governmental policies by a substantial number of people, there is bound to be a high degree of centralization, as in Russia, which is afflicted by both these evils. Where there is mutual confidence, manifesting itself in trust by high officials in their subordinates and willingness of the latter to adhere to policy, there can be and usually is wide decentralization. Thus, in organizations such as the British Colonial Service, and the American Forest and Indian services, local administrators are given wide discretion. The German civil service has occupied more or less of a "middle" position in regard to concentration of authority, there being a particular lack of detailed control on the departmental level. In spite of a long period of political turbulence and, more recently, an intense centralization of over-all policy-making, this has been possible in Germany because of the general excellence of personnel and a long-established unwritten code of administrative ethics.[2] The adminis-

---

[1] See Chapter XV, "The Environment of Administration".

[2] An atmosphere of political tenseness makes concentration of authority within executive departments necessary because of diversity of political belief and consequent hostility among the personnel. Insofar as the civil service is immune to political strife the necessity for strict control does not arise. It is not necessary that there be political unity among the populace at large, but only among the classes from which civil servants are recruited. The German civil servants had a tradition of political neutrality and were thus able, as Finer points out (*Theory and Practise of Modern Government*, pp. 154, 803) to carry over into the Republic the administrative methods and *esprit de corps* developed under the Monarchy. The rather large number of new officials brought in by the Socialists and Republicans after the World War were gradually assimilated, and adopted the prevailing conservatism of the service. These conditions enabled the National Socialists to inaugurate their program, so far as old-line agencies were concerned, with a very small turnover of personnel and no changes in the prevailing moderately decentralized system of procedure. This does not apply, of course, to the Nazi "New Deal Agencies" such as

ADMINISTRATIVE PROCEDURE

trator and the administrative analyst must in each case judge how much centralization is necessary on the basis of the factors enumerated. They had better err in the direction of devolution, since it is easier to set up controls than to remove them.[3]

If the channels of contact in an agency are drawn on its organization chart (as in Figure 6), the more concentration of authority there

ADMINISTRATIVE SEQUENCE SUPERIMPOSED ON
ORGANIZATION CHART

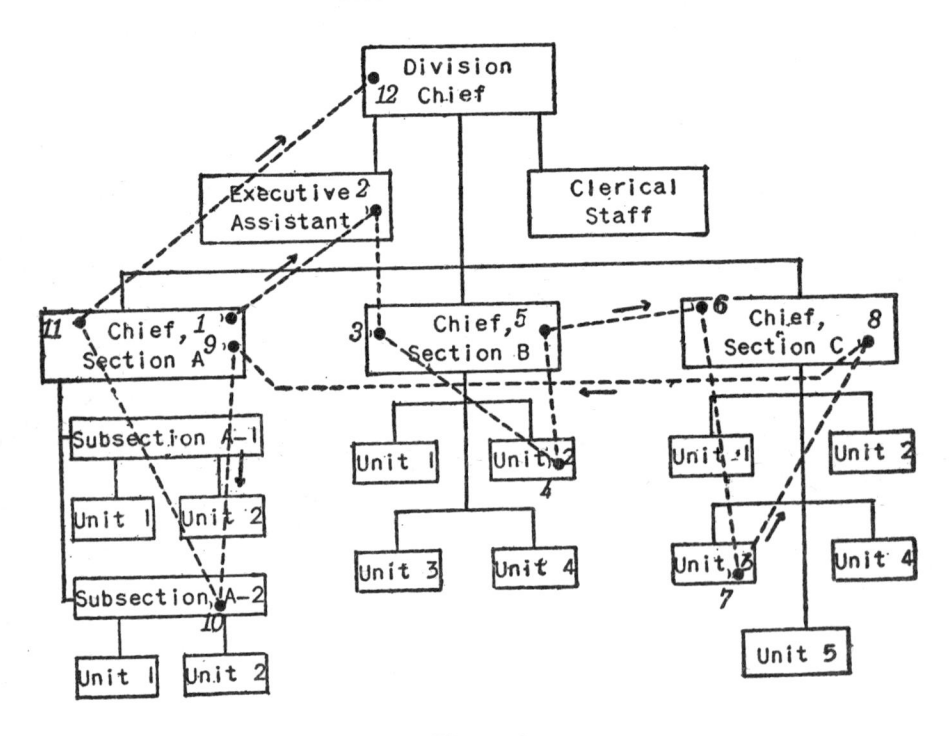

Figure 9

Same sequence as in Figure 7, but with all inter-sectional business clearing through offices of section chiefs.

---

the Propaganda Ministry, the Labor Front, and the Hitler Youth, nor to the party organization.

It may be concluded that, in dictatorships and democracies alike, old-line organizations about which there is little actual or potential controversy can operate on a decentralized basis, whereas new agencies and those carrying out radical programs of action require tighter control to secure unity of action.

[3] Anyone who has tried to get administrators to give up controls which have once been established will attest to the truth of this statement.

is, the more the lines will run vertically; the more devolution, the more horizontal and oblique lines there will be. Under complete centralization there would be contact only along the formal lines of authority; units could only contact each other through the section chief, and sections only through the division chief. Actually such a situation seldom exists, although in many organizations it is customary for a section in one division to clear with the appropriate division chiefs before approaching a section in another, except on a routine matter. In numerous cases, "blanket" clearance is given covering functions or duties and the formal lines of authority come to life only when changes in routine or policy are in order. Under the opposite extreme of complete devolution any unit may contact any other unit at any time and on any subject without external check. The problem is how to manage things so that the higher officials are duly consulted on important cases and in the formation of policy, and yet not bothered with a multitude of minor matters.

The relation of the concentration-devolution question to procedure may be illustrated by a simple example. Under a degree of centralization requiring clearance through section chiefs of all inter-sectional business, the administrative sequence described on page 9 and illustrated in Figure 7 would have twelve steps instead of the previous seven. It would then appear as shown in Figure 9.

As a general rule, authority concentration brings about increases in the number of moves contained in administrative sequences, while devolution reduces the number. This is an argument for having as much decentralization as the circumstances of each case permit.

ORGANIZATION BY LINE AND STAFF FUNCTIONS

Of equal importance with the general degree of concentration of authority in an organization is the extent to which its branches are set up in terms of line and staff functions, respectively. In other words, how complete is the authority of line executives over all phases of their programs, and to what extent have staff functions (which are also staff phases of line functions) been transferred to staff offices? And in case of dispute between line and staff officers, whose decision prevails?

It is theoretically possible for an organization not to be divided by function, if all its members are participants in all its purposes and processes. Such was the case in the medieval guilds of shoemakers, smiths, and other craftsmen, in which the apprentices and journeymen learned all the phases of the art, the only distinctions being those of

ADMINISTRATIVE PROCEDURE

rank and seniority. But in modern organization, which rests on the premise of specialized division of work, there must be functional organization of one sort or another, so that the pure scalar organization [4] is today practically non-existent.

When large-scale corporations and government agencies first appeared upon the scene, the administrative hierarchies were usually arranged by line functions or by distinct areas of operation. In one sense administrative line functions might be thought of as staff phases or processes necessary for achieving an organization's total objective. For instance, surveying, mining, transportation, smelting, casting, packing, and sales are staff aspects of the business of making and selling pig iron. But these direct operations dealing at first hand with things and with people outside the organization are purposes of administration. That is, administration exists in order to plan, execute, and control these activities. So, from our point of view, branches of administration concerned primarily and directly with conducting these basic operations are line functions, while branches concerned mainly with providing *ways and means* for direct activity and primary administration are staff functions.

This distinction may be applied in a generalized way to the several kinds of activity which are found in a manufacturing concern. Henry Fayol, the French industrialist, lists the following kinds of business operations: [5]

1. *Technical*—Production, manufacturing, etc.
2. *Commercial*—Purchase, sales, and exchange.
3. *Financial*—Finding and controlling capital, using funds the best way, avoiding dangerous liabilities.
4. *Security*—Protection of goods and persons, including avoidance of strikes.
5. *Accounting*—Stocktaking, balance sheets, accounts, cost accounting, statistics, etc.
6. *Administration*—Prevoyance (forecasting and planning), organizing, co-ordinating, commanding, and controlling.

In a business enterprise, technical and commercial [6] activity are clearly line functions. Competition may cause the technical activity to become subordinate to the commercial, so that production depart-

---

[4] See Chapter 1, "Administrative Organization".
[5] Henry Fayol, *Industrial and General Administration*.
[6] In government organizations, commercial activity is largely a staff function, since it mainly consists of purchasing for use and not for manufacture or resale. However, there are agencies in which purchasing is a line function, such as the Surplus Marketing Administration, and, from an internal point of view, the Treasury Department's Procurement Division.

ORGANIZATION AND PROCEDURE

ments are constrained to manufacture articles which can easily be sold rather than those which, from an objective point of view, might best serve the consumer, or which represent the best utilization of materials and labor. Financial activity is a staff function if it confines itself to providing the fiscal means for production and distribution. However, it may be partly or wholly a line function if the corporation enters into speculation or investment as a major source of revenue, or is a holding company. Security and accounting are staff functions, since one is concerned with providing the proper environment for line activity and the other with evaluating and controlling it. Administration is not so easily accounted for; sometimes it is a line function, sometimes a staff function, and sometimes both. For practical purposes, administration is a line function when it deals with purposes, programs, policies, and particular cases of direct activity—the *whats* of administration. It is a staff function when it is concerned with administrative processes and methods, with organization and procedure—the *hows*.

Under pure line organization each primary division of a concern has certain direct operations which it is wholly responsible for administering. It also has complete control of its administrative methods and procedures, and does its own "housekeeping." The chief is responsible for hiring and firing, subject to the direction of the higher administrator. Secondary divisions and subordinate units have their particular fields of work to supervise, but their authority and responsibility are more limited. The degree to which heads of these minor units have to obtain specific consent from their superiors before acting or are free to proceed on their own initiative is directly related to the degree of simple concentration or devolution of authority. In pure line organization there is no separation of staff from line functions, no operating distinction between administrative purposes and processes.

To show how all this would work out in practice, let us refer back to our imaginary division, making it more real by clothing it with functions; let us assume that it is a state department of public welfare. Such a department, consisting entirely of line units, is shown in the part of Figure 10 above the broken line.[7]

---

[7] For actual organization charts of state public welfare departments see Marietta Stevenson, *Public Welfare Administration*, pp. 138-171. There is no standard structure for such departments.

ADMINISTRATIVE PROCEDURE

State of ------------------
DEPARTMENT OF PUBLIC WELFARE

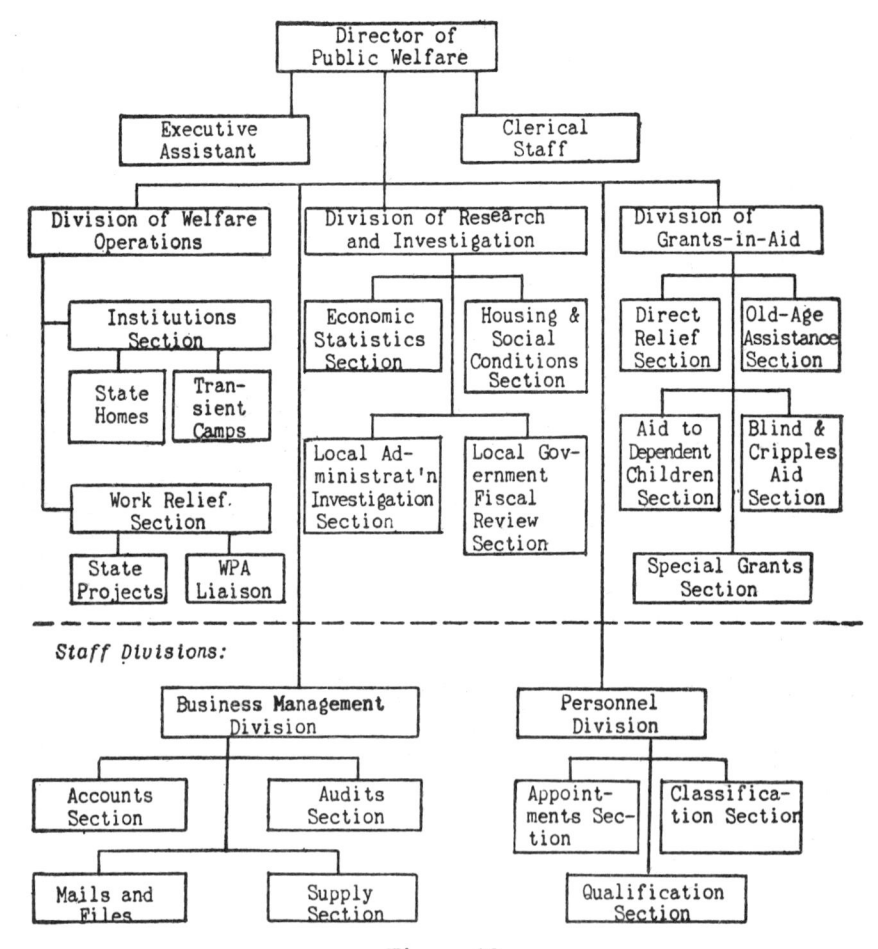

Figure 10

The staff divisions shown here represent the minimum which is likely to occur under modern practise. Possible additional staff divisions or sections might be responsible for information, library facilities, maintenance, and management planning.

In this type of organization, which has no staff units, routine matters coming within a single section's jurisdiction would be handled entirely by that section; more important questions would be referred to the division chiefs or the director. The line dividing routine and important matters would result directly from the degree of concen-

ORGANIZATION AND PROCEDURE

tration of authority. The director might issue a list of questions to be referred to him for personal decision; such a list would then become a part of the *procedure* of the department. Each matter which involved several fields of work would have to pass in turn to the proper sections and divisions. There would thus arise administrative sequences, the routing of which would also depend on the relative centralization of authority. Each sequence would have its operating steps—those necessary for the actual performance of work and the making of executive decisions in the first instance. The number and order of these would be largely determined by the characteristics of the thing administered and by the definition and assignment of functions. But the control steps, consisting of the review of other people's work and the confirming of their decisions, would depend on whether authority were retained or delegated in the particular cases.

A typical sequence occurring within our department of public welfare would be the issuance of a grant-in-aid to a city for direct relief. The administrative objective is to make a grant commensurate (in terms of the total sum available for such grants) with the known needs of the community, and to assure proper administration by the local authorities. For these purposes the Direct Relief Section of the Grants-in-Aid Division, which receives applications and awards grants, must secure a number of reports. It must have usable information on general economic conditions in the city (unemployment, wage levels, rents, prices, etc.), on social conditions affecting the need for relief, on the state of the municipal finances, and on the competency of city welfare officials. It will therefore request data, simultaneously, from the Economic Statistics, Housing and Social Conditions, Local Administration Investigation, and Local Government Fiscal Review sections of the Research and Investigation Division. On the basis of the information received, the Direct Relief Section will evaluate the city's need, determine the amount of the grant, and issue instructions to the State Treasurer as to the way it shall be paid.[8] These are only the *operating* steps: they represent the minimum quantity of direct administrative work needed to accomplish the objective.

It is quite improbable however that any such direct administrative sequence having no control steps would exist in a public agency. Nor should there be a complete absence of administrative review in the grant-in-aid procedure, the results of which are important not only

---

[8] Although the department has been pictured as a pure line organization so far, we have to admit a staff officer (for all departments) in the person of the State Treasurer, unless we make the unrealistic assumption that each department assumes direct custody of the money appropriated to it.

ADMINISTRATIVE PROCEDURE

technically but politically. A more probable procedure based on a normal concentration of executive authority [9] would be somewhat as follows. The city's application for a grant, addressed formally to the Director of Public Welfare, would be opened in the Office of the Chief of the Grants-in-Aid Division, perhaps given a cursory inspection there, and forwarded immediately to the Direct Relief Section for preliminary study. This section would prepare a memorandum, requesting the necessary data, to be signed by the division chief and addressed to the Chief of the Division of Research and Investigation, who would relay the request to the appropriate sections. When each section had prepared its part of the material, the whole would be reviewed and correlated into a single report by the divisional office. This report would be signed by the chief, who would thereby assume responsibility for the work of his subordinates. The determination made by the Direct Relief Section as to the amount of the grant would be reviewed in some detail by the Chief of the Grant-in-Aid Division, and then probably sent up to the Director for formal award of the grant.

The introduction of the controls and clearances described, which represent typical administrative practice, increases the number of administrative moves from five in the original procedure to twelve in the new one. The comparison is illustrated in Figure 11. Under hyper-concentration of authority, the application might be originally considered by the Director and referred to him again during the intermediate stages, which would increase the number of steps still further. It may be asked how many of the steps introduced in a "normal" concentration of authority are really necessary to assure proper administrative review. The answer is apparent in the steps themselves:

---

[9] By a "normal" concentration of authority is meant the more or less standard practice which allows each unit to communicate directly with other units within the same superior unit, but requires communications to outside units to "clear" through the officer in charge of the superior unit. In other words, a section may communicate directly with any other section in the same division, but two sections in different divisions must communicate through their respective division heads. It is also customary under such "normal" concentration for formalized decisions, such as the promulgation of regulations, judgments, allotments of funds, etc., to be made by the head of the establishment.

"Normal" concentration is frequently (and desirably) modified in practice by cutting out the control steps in repeated sequences. Thus, if two sections in different divisions communicate regularly on the same subject, they may be allowed to do so directly instead of through the division heads. It is best that this freedom be extended to cover non-recurrent subjects, provided that sections can be counted on to inform division heads of matters which merit their attention.

ORGANIZATION AND PROCEDURE

ISSUANCE OF A GRANT-IN-AID FOR DIRECT RELIEF IN THE PUBLIC WELFARE DEPARTMENT, STATE OF ....

OPERATION	DONE BY: CITY	STATE TREASURER	DIRECTOR OF PUBLIC WELFARE	CHIEF, GRANT-IN-AID DIVISION	DIRECT RELIEF SECTION	CHIEF, RESEARCH & INVESTIGATION DIVISION	ECONOMIC STATISTICS SECTION	HOUSING & SOCIAL CONDITIONS SECTION	LOCAL ADMIN. INVESTIGATION SECTION	LOCAL GOV'T FISCAL REVIEW SECTION

A. Under extreme devolution of authority (no control steps)
1. Applies for grant
2. Receives application; requests data
3. Prepares data; submits report
4. Reviews reports; determines amount of grant; notifies
5. Is notified

B. Under normal concentration of authority
1. Applies for grant
2. Receives application; inspects, forwards
3. Studies application; prepares request for data
4. Signs request for data
5. Transmits request for data
6. Prepares data
7. Reviews & assembles data; prepares & transmits report
8. Forwards report
9. Analyzes, makes preliminary recommendation for grant
10. Reviews, makes recommendation for grant
11. Awards grant; notifies
12. Is notified

Figure 11

ORGANIZATION AND PROCEDURE

numbers 4, 5, 8, and perhaps number 2 are really only formalized clerical treatment of the subject matter, and therefore could easily be dispensed with. Numbers 7 and 10, on the other hand, represent substantial review, with a probable improvement of the end-result. Concentration of authority should never be generalized to cover all business in a preconceived way; it should be adjusted to suit the subject matter of each particular case. When control steps enable the higher officials to make a positive contribution to the administrative process; when the result of their handling a case personally instead of stating a policy and letting their subordinates carry it out is an *important job better done*—then concentration of authority is a good thing. When this is not so, it begets only useless red tape.

ENTER STAFF ORGANIZATION

The procedures just described were predicated on an organization arranged solely by line functions, in which each unit managed all the staff phases of its own sphere of activity except what was separated from the organization altogether. Under this scheme each of the sections, or at least each of the divisions, would keep a set of budgetary accounts and each would schedule vouchers for payment directly to the State Treasurer. Each would buy for itself whatever supplies it needed, would provide its own messenger and file service, and each division head would have independence in hiring and firing employees (subject to civil service rules, if any), with important posts at the disposal of the Director or the Governor. But simple line-functional organization, although the progenitor of modern line-and-staff frameworks, has today almost disappeared from the scene, particularly in public agencies.[10] Our department of public welfare, if it has kept abreast of modern trends, will have taken certain staff phases common to all or several line functions away from the line divisions and placed them in charge of departmental staff units. We must then add to the department a Business Management Division, with sections for accounts, audits, mails and files,[11] and supplies, and also a Personnel Division containing classification, qualification, and appointment sections and possibly others.[12] These staff divisions are shown in the part of Figure 10 below the broken line.

---

[10] Line functional organization, in respect to the larger units, tends to persist in multi-plant manufacturing corporations.

[11] The Mails and Files Section will not necessarily operate an exclusive centralized file-room; it may concentrate on developing standard methods to be used in divisional or sectional file units.

[12] The exact functions of a department's personnel office will depend among other things on whether the state has a civil service department and what services this department offers.

ADMINISTRATIVE PROCEDURE

The introduction of a staff division has an immediate effect on procedure. The Direct Relief Section will no longer send vouchers in payment of grants directly to the State Treasurer but will instead route the necessary authorization, through established channels, to the Business Management Division, where the Accounts Section will make an encumbrance on its books and prepare the vouchers, which will perhaps be pre-audited by the Audit Section before going to the Treasurer. Also, during the preliminary stages of making grants, the Local Administration Investigation Section may sometimes ask the Audit Section to examine the books of municipal governments,[13] particularly if it suspects irregularities in the spending of previous grants.

Staff organization not only affects the flow of line procedures, but it radically changes the way "housekeeping" functions are carried on. All appointments, promotions, and terminations of employment will be made by the Personnel Division which, if it has real authority within its jurisdiction, will act on its own judgment and not merely at the behest of other divisions. The same principle will apply to procurement of supplies; it is unnecessary to repeat the details.

As staff functionalization progresses, additional phases of activity are removed from line divisions and entrusted to staff units. There follows a gradual "professionalizing" of the staff functions, and an elaboration of their details. Staff units not only take over work which might otherwise be done by line offices, but they add new functions of their own. For instance, the British Machinery of Government Committee, in recognizing the staff function of information, suggested that the duties of an intelligence (information) division include the following:

The conduct of special enquiries into, and the preparation of reports upon, matters affecting the business of the Department;
The care and maintenance of a Departmental library;
The continuous study of the methods of administration prevailing in regard to the same subject-matter in other parts of the United Kingdom (where a separate system of administration prevails), in the Empire, and in foreign countries; and
The scrutiny and circulation in the Department of statements of general interest bearing upon the Department's work, whether from particular branches of the Department, from other Departments, from the Press, or from other sources.[14]

---

[13] This would still be a line activity so far as the local government was concerned; it would only be a staff activity within the State agency.
[14] Lord Haldane of Cloan and others, *Report of the Machinery of Government Committee*, London, 1919.

ORGANIZATION AND PROCEDURE

The third of these duties would today be assigned to a procedure (administrative management) division rather than to an information division. But this does not detract from the point illustrated, which is the elaboration of staff functions under the modern trend of organization. From one point of view this lightens the load of the line officer by relieving him of duties not inseparably associated with his particular subject matter. But doing so inevitably increases the number of administrative moves in sequences involving the staff functions which have been detached from the line offices. Staff organization which becomes too elaborate may in fact impede the line officer by making it impossible to do anything without reference to somebody else, and by introducing complications and delays into what would be simple undertakings if the line officer could do them undisturbed.

The setting up of operating staff officers frequently involves a departure from strict scalar organization in which each officer takes orders from one superior. As a practical matter the line officer is often directed by the personnel officer with respect to employment matters, by the purchasing agent so far as supply questions are concerned, etc. To preserve the fiction of scalar organization, some agencies require staff officials to issue instructions over the signature of a line administrator. But others frankly recognize divergent delegation [15] and allow staff officers to issue instructions on their own responsibility.[16]

There is a school of thought called "functionalism" which holds that organization should go entirely by staff functions or processes, and that each process should be performed by a single unit for the whole organization, no matter what line function is involved. Under complete functionalism the line units are divested of all duties, except those which exist only in their special fields of work. All operations

---

[15] See Chapter IX, "Types of Control Devices."
[16] In this connection there should be noted the distinction which White *(Public Administration,* Chapter 5) makes between "staff" and "auxiliary" agencies. Both types are classified as staff agencies by the writer if they are mainly concerned with administrative *processes*: with ways and means. Of the "staff" agency, White says:

"The staff agency is outside the direct line of the administrative hierarchy . . . . [It] stands somewhat apart, an adjunct to the office of the chief executive or of a major operating executive. Its special status invites misconception of its true function and value.

"One danger is that the executive will assign to the staff operating functions which belong to the departments. . . . .

"There is also a tendency for a staff agency to become a control agency in its own right, acting in the light of what it knows or believes are executive policies . . . . an active staff may be tempted to follow the line of direct intervention."

White indicates that it should be restrained from doing so. Of "auxiliary"

ADMINISTRATIVE PROCEDURE

which overlap two or more fields, including not only the staff functions previously mentioned but also stenography, filing, clerical and statistical work, drafting, planning and research, and even dictating correspondence (except the most technical) are centralized. Because of its proclaimed virtues of improving performance and avoiding wasted time caused by slacks in work, functionalism will be more fully discussed in the chapter on "work distribution." [17]

BALANCING LINE AND STAFF ORGANIZATION

As with concentration and devolution of authority, there is no uniformly desirable compromise between pure line organization and the more advanced phases of staff organization. The "best way" is always determined by the nature of the line functions and the form taken by their staff aspects. Operating staff divisions can justify themselves only by proving that their specialists can do their share of the work better—sufficiently so to compensate for additional administrative moves caused by shifting the sequences concerned from division to division. The end-result, considering not only the performance of the operation in question but that of the *entire administrative job,* must be an improvement in quality and speed and a reduction in the cost of administration.

The problem of line versus staff organization must be solved with specific respect to each situation, that is each intersection of a line function (purpose) with a staff function (process).[18] In this con-

---

agencies White says in part: "They exist to serve and within limits to control the primary agencies. . . . . The auxiliary agencies are usually not difficult to identify, but confusion arises at times because they are incidentally employed by chief executives for staff and sometimes for control purposes as well as their own specific function. This does not destroy their essential nature."

The tendency of "staff" agencies to assume control functions within their fields (which White admits is proper for "auxiliary" agencies) is a natural one which the writer believes should be guided but not suppressed. The distinction between "staff" and "auxiliary" agencies appears to break down in practice. The essential difference is one of subject matter rather than administrative relationship. The Budget Bureau, a "staff" agency, has operating functions in the field of budgetary administration and clearance of legislation. Within these spheres, particularly in detailed matters, its relationship to the line Departments is similar to that of the Procurement Division or the Civil Service Commission. *Pari passu,* the "auxiliary" agencies do considerable advisory work.

It would seem most realistic to designate all agencies or units whose functions are based on administrative processes as staff organs, admitting their authority to give orders or make determinations having the effect of orders within their proper fields, and recognizing that differences in their work will cause variations in their operating methods and their relationships with line units.

[17] See Chapter XII, "Functionalism in Administration."

[18] Some organizers make the mistake of thinking of the staff function in the abstract instead of in its relation to line functions. For instance, some concerns have "perfect" filing rooms which are infernal nuisances so far as the line officials are concerned.

ORGANIZATION AND PROCEDURE

nection, there could be asked a few questions which are simple enough but which require thorough analysis of the situation to get the right answers. These are:

(1) Which technique is dominant in the situation—that of the line function or that of the staff function?

(2) Can the staff function be more economically performed by the line office or by a specialized staff unit? Is the volume of business from line offices sufficient to justify such a unit?

(3) Will transferring the work to a staff unit delay the work of the line unit excessively? Will it result in "administrative pyramiding"—that is, will the work, in whole or in part, be done twice? Will the net result be a lifting of burdens from line officers or a complication of their duties?

(4) Is the staff function so closely interrelated with the line function in question that line officers must exercise close technical supervision if they do not do the work themselves? Or can they forget about it?

(5) Are there administrative dangers (such as the possibility of graft in purchasing or political influence in personnel work) which make a staff unit useful as a means of control?

The problem of the amount of staff organization, like the amount of concentration of authority, can only be solved by objective study and thought, from a viewpoint of the major purposes of the organization rather than the particular processes involved. Considerations based on formalism must not be allowed to enter the picture. By asking, and then answering on the basis of practical observation, a set of questions which get at the root of the matter, showing the nature and techniques of administrative operations, and the controls necessary to assure sound over-all accomplishment, the administrative analyst can determine the proper organization structure and distribution of duties to meet particular needs.

ADMINISTRATIVE COMMITTEES

A factor in modern organization as significant as the operating staff division is the administrative committee.[19] Committees, even more than staff units, are products of complexity of function; they are created to deal with problems which overlap the jurisdictions of several

---

[19] For a fuller treatment of administrative committees, see the author's article, "Managing Committee Work in a Large Organization," *Public Administration Review*, Spring 1941, pp. 249-256.

ADMINISTRATIVE PROCEDURE

units of organization or which require the joint consideration of a number of officials. It is significant that a large organization like the Department of Agriculture has well over one hundred inter-bureau committees of various sorts, and at least that many more intra-bureau groups. The Federal Government as a whole has about four hundred inter-departmental committees concerned with everything from social welfare to specifications for blotting paper. Private concerns seldom have as many committees, largely because their functions are simpler, but they are gradually turning to them as means of dealing with complex problems and of giving more officials the opportunity to participate in the formation of policy.

There are four main types of administrative committees. The executive committee operates within its sphere much as an individual would: it has direct responsibilities, makes definite decisions, and gives orders. The policy forming or planning committee has no immediate responsibilities, but is expected to analyze a problem or field of activity and develop a long-range program of action. Such a committee's determinations are best submitted as recommendations to the chief administrator—to give it direct authority often leads to organizational confusion. The fact finding committee gathers and classifies information, usually in more detail than a policy forming committee, but does not as a rule make definite recommendations. Finally, there is the discussion committee, which does not have any set task to perform but exists mainly for exchanging information and ideas. In practise, many committees which begin as one type take on characteristics of others, and some are hybrids from their inception.

Within a large organization there are certain to be some jobs which call for committees, particularly when discordant interests are to be reconciled. In evaluating existing committees or planning new ones, however, it is wise to watch for certain pitfalls which may destroy their usefulness. It has been found, for instance, that once an organization is accustomed to using committees, there is a tendency for them to multiply out of all reason with the result that they interfere with each other and encroach on the fields of operating units. Another difficulty is that committees tend to bog down if their instructions are not specific and if their chairmen are not capable organizers. But the worst problem is the tendency on the part of those setting up committees to choose as members the most important (and hence the busiest) officials. At one time in the Department of Agriculture, 43 of the "key men" each belonged to 10 or more committees, 21 belonged to more than 15, and one official, who also held a very exacting coordinating assignment, belonged to 33.

The tendency of administrative committees toward self-frustration obviously calls for systematic management. In each organization there should be *one* official with final authority over committee assignments. This person should keep, or superintend the keeping of records of the membership, duties, and accomplishments of all committees. He should be responsible for applying certain common-sense rules designed to get the most out of committee work. To begin with, he should forestall the establishment of any committee which is not needed. He should then see that each committee which is established has a definite and limited assignment which neither duplicates the work of other committees nor hampers operating units. He should work out a time budget for the committee, indicating the approximate number of hours per month required of its members, including work between meetings. He should control the selection of members, so that no one has so much committee work that it interferes with his regular duties, and he should arrange for temporary assignment of research men, investigators, etc., if the committee's functions require this. He should see that as many officials as possible, particularly the junior executives, are given an opportunity to participate, not only to avoid overloads but also as a means of in-service training. Finally, he should obtain brief but informative progress reports from each committee, so that the work of committees may be accurately taken into account in planning and coordination.

Administrative committees are to be considered in any study of procedure, both as centers of policy formation and planning, and as participants in administrative sequences. Their existence has definite effects upon the channels of authority and communication, on the time required to accomplish sequences which involve committee action, and on the work loads and capacities of organization units whose members participate in them. Proper organization planning includes analysis of the situations in which committees will prove most valuable, specification of the right kinds of committees, including their authority, membership, duties, and work loads, and provision of adequate controls to see that committees function properly.

Chapter VI

ADMINISTRATIVE (PROGRAM) PLANNING

PLANNING is inevitably the first phase of administration. Back of every order given, every letter dictated, and every conference called there is a plan, be it an organization-wide progam developed over a long period or an individual project thought up on the spur of the moment. Sound administration recognizes the function of planning and provides for assembling a unified plan (rather than an assortment of individual plans) by setting up channels through which plans, wherever they originate, flow to a central authority which co-ordinates [1] them in a general plan. If there are planning units in a department's bureaus or a corporation's subsidiaries there must be an over-all organ to integrate their efforts in a master plan for the whole organization.

Planning, administrative or otherwise, is not a purely reflective process nor does it consist of drawing charts and diagrams "out of the blue." Its operations require a highly developed ability to observe. Harlow S. Person [2] has suggested that planning consists of the following successive steps: (1) definition of purpose, (2) formulation of policies, determining the exact limits of projected activity, (3) formulation of program, arranging ways and means in a tentative program of action, (4) design of plan, bringing ways and means into exact quantitative, qualitative, and functional relationships,[3] and (5) differentiation of projects, making each as independent as possible.

Each step in planning must take into account the possibilities and limitations of men and materials and the relation of the organization

---

[1] Some might prefer to use the term "integrate" exclusively in this connection, reserving the word "co-ordinate" for execution rather than planning.

[2] Harlow S. Person, *On The Technique of Planning*, Bulletin of the Taylor Society and the Society of Industrial Engineers, November, 1934, pp. 14ff.

[3] As applied to the planning of administrative work, "quantitative" might include the number of personnel required for a certain operation and the time it would take them to do it. "Qualitative" would refer to the *degree* of skill, and "functional" would mean the *type* of skill, in its relation to complementary skills.

ADMINISTRATIVE (PROGRAM) PLANNING

to its environment. The first three listed here constitute the field for administrative or program planning—determining *what* is to be done. The fourth and fifth steps involve management or procedural planning—deciding *how* programs are to be carried out, and more particularly how they are to be administered. Dr. Person goes on to differentiate between the several planes or levels of planning, as follows: (1) directive planning—the making up of a program, its division into major projects, with lump-sum budgets for each, and control of broad policies by the administrator; (2) administrative planning (Dr. Person uses the term here in a sense different from ours)—the assignment of tasks to specific working units, and control by comparing actual accomplishment with the plan, and (3) operative planning, carried on within each working unit.[4] These levels cut across our line dividing administrative from management planning, including some of each, as shown by Figure 12. As the terms are used here, administrative planning means planning the activity which is to be administered, while management planning means planning the administration of the activity. Both types occur on each of the three planes, though in varying degree.

Neither administrative nor management planning should go too far into the technical details of operations. "Detailed specification," says Dr. Person, "is a function of the technological methods necessary for the achievement of the objective, not of planning itself. Planning does not seek detail in arrangement for its own sake. It seeks rather to discover the least pre-arranging which the technology of achievement of the particular objective requires." This is not to say that planning should ignore technique. It only means that methods of operation should not be specified in more detail than necessary to insure execution of the plan. In management planning, particularly in the field of office work, it is often necessary to go further into detail than would be desirable in laying out programs of direct activity.

A plan begins with an idea, and anyone can have an idea. So when we talk about the initial responsibility for planning we mean the responsibility for gathering ideas, sifting them, and putting the good ones in usable form. No individual can ever have enough ideas to keep a large organization moving. The good planner is the one who goes out looking for ideas, who gets many people all over the

---

[4] The distinction between administrative planning and managerial planning discussed in Dr. Person's article, "Research and Planning as Functions of Administration and Management," (*Public Administration Review*, Autumn, 1940) will be of interest to those who care to go further into the subject of planning.

ADMINISTRATIVE PROCEDURE

AREAS OF PLANNING

ADMINISTRATIVE (WHAT)   MANAGEMENT (HOW)

Directive (Top Level)

ADMINISTRATIVE (WHAT)	MANAGEMENT (HOW)
1. Major objectives	1. Frame of organization
2. Basic scheme of operations	2. Assignment of major fields of activity
3. General policies and criteria of accomplishment	3. General channels of responsibility and coordination
{With respect to major functions}	4. Administrative procedures (in broad terms)

Administrative (Middle Level)

1. Breakdown of operations into specific functions and projects	1. Specific assignment of duties to subordinate units of organization
2. Standards of accomplishment: quantity (including time, money) quality	2. Procedures (more specifically)
	3. Timing and scheduling operations
3. Assignment of priorities within organization and major divisions	4. Means of observation and direction

Operative (Bottom Level)

1. Division of functions and projects into tasks	1. Assignment of tasks to individuals
2. Assignment of priorities within units	2. Operating procedures
	3. Flow and timing of tasks
3. Specification of individual and group jobs	
4. Planning of unit production (work budget)	

Figure 12

organization to tell him how they think things could be done better, and who never fails to give credit for the ideas that he uses.

In private business, program planning centers in the controlling officers. With the help of research staffs, technical advisers, and line officials, they map out what they are going to do, and lay the broad

ADMINISTRATIVE (PROGRAM) PLANNING

outlines before their boards of directors and stockholders. In public affairs, these preliminary plans frequently take the form of drafts of authorizing laws, which are submitted to legislatures by interest groups, by legislators themselves, and by the agencies concerned. Following legislative or directorial approval of the basic plans which determine the general scope and limitations of activity, definitive administrative planning begins.

Both pre-legislative and post-legislative program planning are basic responsibilities of line officials. Although planning and the various phases of execution may be delegated to different divisions, the responsibility of evaluating the plan in its broad aspects and determining whether it can be practically carried out is one the top administrator cannot delegate. And each division chief must likewise, within the limits of the over-all plan, decide what he is going to do to carry it out. He will also contribute his share in making the major plan, which must be based on known possibilities of execution. If program planning is centered in a division set up for that purpose, it might, from an exclusively operating point of view, be considered a staff function. But, from an administrative standpoint, it is a line function because it is concerned with *what* is to be done (administrative purpose), and because planning is an integral part of administration.

Management planning—the planning of administration—has in the past been done co-ordinately with program planning, or at least by the same people. Recent tendencies, however, place it increasingly in the hands of administrative analysts, who are staff officers concerned with *how* administration is to be carried on, and who are specialists in administration itself rather than in the subject administered. More will be said about this in the chapter on management planning.[5]

Planning, as a continuous process, begins with the assembling of data needed to determine objectives and means of accomplishment. In the case of new businesses and public undertakings which have no precedents, this information is necessarily somewhat academic. In an established agency it is culled from operating experience. The channels which bring it to the planners are in large part the administrative controls through which they check on the execution of previous plans —that is, clearances, inspections, reports, accounts, and the like. There is thus a continuous cycle of planning, execution, control, and

---

[5] See Chapter XI.

ADMINISTRATIVE PROCEDURE

re-planning. This cycle appears in each plane and in both administrative and management planning.

PROCEDURE IN ADMINISTRATIVE PLANNING

The creation of a program of operations is an administrative sequence. The speed and efficiency with which it is carried out depend, among other things, on the number and kind of administrative steps, the motion delays, and the work loads of participants. Before any large scheme of action gets under way, each group which takes part must have its operating plan and all these must fit together under the master plan. An administrative problem of the first order exists in the setting up of planning machinery to meet the particular objectives of the case. Must the plan be made ready on short notice? Or are detail and technical accuracy more important? What different groups of people must approve the plan? With what other plans must it be integrated?

There are alternative ways of planning, the choice depending on administrative need. When time is short, but the fields of activity do not need to dovetail too closely, it is best to have an individual or small group prepare a plan for each operating division, with direction only in terms of major policies. If close co-ordination is also vital, then there must be a central planning authority for the whole organization, but care must be taken lest it become too involved. Where acceptability to the maximum number of people is more important than speed, it may be preferable to have planning done by line executives, either step by step upward, or through a network of committees which may include outside interests with which the organization deals. This machinery is slow, and occasionally its product is inconsistent. But sometimes this kind of planning is essential, particularly when the resulting action is to be carried out co-operatively by agencies under different political controls, such as the Federal Government and states, or states and counties, etc. A compromise must always be made on the basis of the relative importance of different objectives. It is seldom that we find a planning procedure which embodies high speed, perfect technical accuracy, extreme acceptability, and complete co-ordination all at once.

The program of integrated land-use planning recently started by the United States Department of Agriculture, with the active co-operation of the land-grant colleges, is an example of a multiplex procedure set up to provide flexibility (a different plan for each type-of-farming area) and maximum acceptability. A broad agricultural

ADMINISTRATIVE (PROGRAM) PLANNING

plan, embodying the work not only of all bureaus of the Department and of co-operating Federal and state agencies but also of the individual farmers who carry out the plan in their own communities and counties, is being worked out for each of the 3,000-odd farm counties in the United States. The program has been elaborated in extra detail for 300 of these counties, and is now being placed in experimental operation in at least one county of each state.[6] Since the element of compulsion is altogether repugnant to both Federal and state agricultural authorities, it is necessary to have a planning procedure which will not only produce agreement on details but will sell the whole idea of planning. And the best way to do this is to have the farmers, who are the ultimate arbiters, do much of the planning themselves.[7] For this and other practical reasons, leadership in basic planning has been entrusted to the County Extension Agents, who organize local planning committees of farmers and local representatives of state and Federal agencies. These committees, which represent the various kinds of farming in the area, work out the initial agricultural plans for each

---

[6] *Planning for a Permanent Agriculture*, Miscellaneous Publication No. 351 of U. S. Department of Agriculture. Washington, 1939, Government Printing Office.

[7] Another reason for having democratic planning by the people directly concerned is that the results are more likely to be workable. The transition from concentrated emergency planning to decentralized permanent planning is well illustrated by the following excerpts from *Planning for a Permanent Agriculture*:

"In the emergency period that began in 1933 the need for quick action made it necessary to rely on specialists in planning national farm programs within the authorizations of the Congress. It was apparent at once, however, that specialists could not do the job alone. Agricultural planning proved to be too complex a task and the responsibility too great to be left wholly in their hands. Administrators agreed that it was essential for farmers themselves to take a dominant role in determining the broad outlines of such programs. It was but a step farther to the realization that local help was needed in adapting national programs to the great variety of local situations.

"Even after the immediate emergency phases had passed there remained a persistent tendency, however, to rely on expert opinion alone in the preparation of programs. .... The Department made an effort early in 1935 to have more farm people take part in the planning.

"The development of the idea for community and county land-use program-planning committees grew out of this effort which began four years ago. The experiences of these older committees indicated plainly the need for full farmer participation in program planning. They proved that a satisfactory national plan cannot possibly be developed by Federal and State officials acting alone. . . . .

"Differences between expert and farmer opinion as to needed agricultural adjustments are generally due to differences in available information upon which the opinions are based. This does not necessarily mean that the farmer has less information than the expert. It may mean only that each has different kinds of information. Both the farmer's information and "expert" information are needed in building an adequate program. The expert is often a specialist with vision for only one aspect of a problem. Though the farmer may not see that particular aspect so clearly, he is likely to see other pertinent phases of his problem that the specialist overlooks. Beyond this, policy judgments might differ for reasons no more tangible than differences in social philosophy." *Planning for a Permanent Agriculture*, pp. 7-10.

ADMINISTRATIVE PROCEDURE

county, compiling the necessary statistics and land-use maps to go with them. In this work they can call on public agencies for technical and scientific assistance.

The county plans are reviewed by a state planning committee, the secretary of which is the State Representative of the Bureau of Agricultural Economics, the Department of Agriculture's central planning agency. This official is always a planning technician. Together with a representative of the state experiment station and one from the Extension Service, he also serves on the Joint Committee of the Land-Grant College and the Bureau of Agricultural Economics, which acts as an executive committee to keep the planning work going. The state planning committee includes representatives of all Federal bureaus engaged in programs affecting land use, and of state agricultural agencies, and farmers from each type-of-farming area in the state. This committee and the representative of the Bureau of Agricultural Economics together work out a flexible state agricultural policy, which is kept abreast of changing conditions, and forwarded periodically to the Bureau in Washington. As the central program planning organ of the Department of Agriculture, the Bureau integrates incoming state plans with regional and national governmental objectives. This is done through inter-bureau committees, so that the planning process in the Department is as co-operative as it is in the states. The result is a series of plans for co-ordinate action of whatever agencies are most appropriate to deal with farm conditions in particular areas. Although plans flow into the Bureau from state offices, the action programs that come out are frequently interstate in scope, as are the majority of farm problems.

For those plans which are for joint execution of several bureaus, the Office of Land-Use Co-ordination, a staff agency attached to the Secretary of Agriculture, takes the lead in getting the work under way. This is the fourth step in planning—design, which means deciding who does what, when, and where. It could also be viewed as the first step in execution, for the dividing line between planning and execution is often indefinite. The translation of plans of action into definite schedules of things to be done usually takes place in series of interbureau conferences for which the Office of Land-Use Co-ordination acts as a secretariat, preparing agenda and working up information requested by conferees. The representatives at these conferences are both technical advisors and negotiators; they are expected to criticize the plans laid before them as to feasibility, and to indicate definitely what their bureaus are prepared to do. Naturally the con-

ADMINISTRATIVE (PROGRAM) PLANNING

ferees have to consult with their bureau chiefs and with operating officials at various stages. During the resulting intervals between meetings, the Office of Land-Use Co-ordination prepares minutes summarizing the conclusions and points remaining at issue. In due time a schedule of operations is agreed upon, which is then drafted in exact form by the Office and promulgated by the Secretary.

The products of the sequence of actions just described are plans which are probably as good as could be made for the purpose. They are based on first-hand experience with operating conditions. Initially formulated by county and state representatives of the people concerned, they have been checked by field experts and Washington technicians, and fitted into the national agricultural program.

The only reason why this method of planning "from the bottom up" should not be used for all administrative planning is that it takes a long time. A county committee can develop its plan for a one- or two-year period in three or four months if information is reasonably accessible and there are no feuds to compromise. But then its time in transit to Washington and its realization in action programs laid before interbureau conferences may vary between six and nine months, and it is usually a month from the beginning of conferences to the submission of the finished plan before the Secretary. Clearly this extended sequence will not serve when plans are needed quickly to meet a natural or social emergency.

Whenever the Department of Agriculture is faced with a situation demanding immediate and positive action, a short-cut planning procedure is used. In this case planning begins in the Bureau of Agricultural Economics, which sends investigators to examine the problem in the field. It also engages in consultations if necessary, but keeps the essential work within its own hands. By thus controlling the time element (not getting in a situation where the action of someone else must be waited for) a complete operating plan can be worked up to meet a close deadline. This was done, for instance, in 1938 when the New England hurricane made it necessary to start immediately on the job of clearing and salvaging timber. Except in cases of extreme haste all interbureau programs are cleared, according to their province, either through the Office of Land-Use Co-ordination or the Office of Marketing and Regulatory Work. These offices ascertain, by the conference method or otherwise, that operating bureaus will accept the plans, with agreement as to their meaning. The number and kind of steps in the planning procedure is in each case adjusted to the

ADMINISTRATIVE PROCEDURE

relative importance of speed, technical accuracy, acceptability, and co-ordination.

PLANNING IN BUREAUS OF THE DEPARTMENT OF AGRICULTURE

The planning machinery just described functions only in the field of program planning. Management planning on the Departmental level has generally been divided, and more or less restricted. The Secretary, his immediate staff, and a small group of line executives who are referred to loosely as the "key officials" of the Department, have for a period of years studied the larger administrative problems and as a result have brought about a general reorganization corresponding more closely to the scheme of basic functions than did earlier arrangements. Detailed management planning has been confined to the writing of regulations and procedures on such subjects as personnel, procurement, and accounting (covering these fields from a Departmental point of view only), and the rendering of a limited amount of technical advice by operating staff offices. There has generally been no attempt to prescribe procedures or techniques for use within bureaus, even for common business operations. This lack of technical control stems from the long-standing tradition that the Department should not interfere with the internal administration of bureaus.

Recent changes, however, have pointed to a greater interest on the part of Departmental officials in the improvement of bureau organization and procedure. A Division of Organization has been established in the Office of Personnel, with responsibility for reviewing organization plans and making general analyses of bureau operations. Co-operating closely is a new Division of Fiscal Management in the Office of Budget and Finance, which is undertaking to improve and simplify business procedures. And, finally, there has been set up an "administrative council" which meets periodically and is to be an over-all arbiter on management problems. Within each bureau of the Department both administrative and management planning are found. The two types may or may not be separated. In the "management-conscious" bureaus there are usually distinct facilities for each, whereas in others there may be no attempt to distinguish between the two or even to set up well-defined planning mechanisms.

It is not always necessary to have special planning officials to have good planning. It is necessary, however, to have people somewhere in the organization who have the ability to plan, the authority to plan, and the time to plan. Both administrative and management planning

ADMINISTRATIVE (PROGRAM) PLANNING

may be done by line executives, either singly or in committee, if they have sufficient understanding of the functions, organization, and processes of their concern. But to make this possible, the time of these officials must be cleared by taking away parts of their work loads or by extensive delegation to subordinates. If neither is done, one of two things will happen: either the planning will be done very slowly, inadequately, or not at all—or the executives' routine work will pile up.

The Bureau of Biological Survey [8] holds to the principle that planning should not be separated from line administration. Consistent effort to clear the time of executives for planning is made through systematic delegation of as much detail as possible. There is no systematic distinction between administrative and management planning. The general phases of both are normally handled in conferences, but detailed studies are assigned to line officials concerned with the subject matter. For example, when it was decided to decentralize administration by setting up regional offices, the Chief of Bureau called a series of conferences to plan the areas and headquarters of regions, the regional organization structure and personnel, and the distribution of supervisory duties between the field and Washington. Afterward, the business manager and his assistant, who had attended the meetings, wrote a "Regional Director's Manual" which translated into working procedures the broad plan agreed upon at the conferences. The Bureau of Biological Survey has no regularized channels for planning. When new work is undertaken the responsible line administrator is expected to analyze the job, outlining what is to be done, and how. He considers the relations between the new function and existing ones, the effect on jobs, the flow of papers and work loads in Washington divisions, and prepares a combined administrative and management plan taking these factors into account.

An informal system, in which plans are made by individual line officials or are created through contacts and occasional meetings, works well enough in a comparatively small and simply organized agency. It depends for its success on wide delegation of routine executive work by those in authority, and on the absence of a large

---

[8] The information presented here was gathered while the Bureau of Biological Survey was still in the Department of Agriculture, and before Reorganization Plan Number 1, which moved it to the Department of the Interior, had been announced. The transfer (July 1, 1939) and the later merger of Biological Survey with the Bureau of Fisheries into the Fish and Wildlife Service (June 30, 1940) do not affect the value of this case material, which was recently pronounced "Still up to date" by a bureau official.

ADMINISTRATIVE PROCEDURE

volume of fluctuating business. Under the right circumstances it is efficient, because few administrative moves are involved and because plans are always acceptable to those who have made them. But in a large and complex organization, particularly one which has to lay out in detail a great many local projects, the absence of predetermined channels for planning would prove a source of confusion.

The Farm Security Administration, another bureau of the Department of Agriculture, presents a very different picture. Farm Security is a large organization; it has 18,500 employees compared with the 1,050 in the Bureau of Biological Survey,[9] and it has been even larger. It administers a multiple program, the major branches of which are its rural and suburban (subsistence homestead) resettlement projects; rural rehabilitation, which involves loans for farm equipment, animals, and supplies combined with farm management supervision to assist needy farm families in becoming self-sufficient; and the tenant-purchase program to promote farm ownership through long-term loans. The three activities overlap considerably (for instance, many resettlement and tenant-purchase families also have rehabilitation loans) and must be co-ordinated with other Department of Agriculture activities, such as soil conservation, agricultural adjustment, crop insurance, and forestry. There is need for continuous and detailed administrative and executive planning.

The Farm Security Administration has always distinguished between the two kinds of planning, and has definite channels for each. Management planning, which includes planning for administrative planning, centers in a Procedure Division, which reviews and coordinates the proposals of line officials and is charged with perfecting the routings and administrative steps for planning as well as for operating and control sequences. The work of this division, which will be described more fully in Chapter XI, includes the maintenance of an "Instruction Manual," which explains organization and procedures.

The procedure to be outlined here, that of planning resettlement projects, is being held in abeyance, since Congress has not made appropriations for new projects for several years. This circumstance detracts only slightly from its value as an illustration. It is used here because it is a good example of planning on a recurrent (project) basis, and because it represents the kind of planning which has to solve simultaneously a number of different problems. The procedure is described as set forth in the manual; there was, of course, some

---

[9] In round numbers, as of June, 1939. The number of employees fluctuates from month to month.

ADMINISTRATIVE (PROGRAM) PLANNING

variation in the way individual projects were developed, as required by the circumstances in each case. The planning of resettlement projects had the objective of ascertaining that the projects actually established would be economically and socially sound, legal, and within certain other policy limitations. Because reasonable speed was also an objective, the procedure underwent considerable simplification after it was put into operation. The number of operations was finally reduced to what was thought to be the minimum by which project plans would conform reasonably to the standards.

The process starts when a Regional Director receives a "suggestion," either from the Washington office, from members of his own office, or from interested persons in his district. If he thinks the suggestion has possibilities, and if funds to finance a project are within reach, he superintends the compiling of a "proposal," which is a simple preliminary plan designed to show whether the cost of developing a complete plan is justified. The proposal contains social and economic data sufficient to show that the project is needed, and gives gross estimates of the cost. Detailed estimates must be deferred until land has been optioned, for the physical characteristics of the particular tract are important in determining the cost of land conditioning, engineering, and construction. The proposal is prepared in the regional Resettlement Division, the appropriate technicians working on it simultaneously. After review by the Regional Director (which need not be extensive since he has probably kept in close touch with the work) the proposal is sent to the Administrator's Office, which forwards it to the Washington Resettlement Division. The proposal is then reviewed and recommended for acceptance, modification, or rejection by the technical sections, each considering the proposal from a specialized point of view. It then goes to the Director of the Resettlement Division, who evaluates it in relation to the resettlement program as a whole, and submits his recommendations to the Administrator. The Administrator, if he approves, immediately authorizes the use of funds to cover the cost of appraising and optioning the land needed to carry out the proposal and the cost of preparing the final plan for the project.

The final plan, which is prepared in the regional Resettlement Division, contains more detailed justifying data, preliminary house plans, maps, and specifications, and budget estimates for land purchase

ADMINISTRATIVE PROCEDURE

and acquisition work,[10] architectural and landscape planning, construction and inspection, and administering the completed project. The Regional Director reviews the plan and forwards it to Washington, where it passes through the same sequence as did the proposal. The examination of the final plan is naturally much more thorough than that of the proposal. The proposal is general in its scope, and usually formulated only with reference to the general location, whereas the final plan has been developed to fit a specific tract of land, and must be considered in relation to that land's particular characteristics. Upon approval by the Administrator, funds for the purchase of lands under option are authorized, and land acquisition is begun. Funds for other purposes are made available as projected in the budget, as the need for them arises.

A number of offices participate in the planning process, in both the "proposal" and final stages, and each has an opportunity to contribute something. The approved plan, which may differ in a number of ways from the proposal, has been checked for technical soundness from a number of angles, and has been co-ordinated with the Administration's program.

The number of steps required to put a proposal and a final plan through the customary reviews is considerable. It may properly be asked whether the degree of improvement afforded by detailed scrutiny of plans by the Washington office is worth its cost in time and money, particularly since the regional offices of the Farm Security Administration could easily be equipped to operate independently. This question, in one form or another, arises in every regionalized organization. The answer in this case lies in the fact that resettlement is a fairly new activity of the Government, without sufficient time to develop standard criteria. During the years when the program was expanding, each project was largely an experiment, and the chances of failure due to mistakes in social or economic planning were so great that the Administrator could not afford to take chances. The political pressures in some localities also made it necessary to go slowly in giving more authority to local offices.

The Farm Security Administration, however, is progressively decentralizing responsibility for execution both within the Washington office and from Washington to the regions, as fast as the development of policies and criteria and the training of field officials will

---

[10] The Attorney General is required by law to approve the title to land acquired by the United States, if public funds are to be expended thereon. It is necessary to trace the ownership back to the original grant or patent, and to correct any infirmities in the title, before the acquisition can be completed.

ADMINISTRATIVE (PROGRAM) PLANNING

permit. The execution of the rural rehabilitation program (a large volume of widely scattered small transactions) has from the beginning been largely decentralized. Likewise, the execution of the more recent tenant-purchase program was begun on a decentralized basis, after careful initial planning and the development of operating techniques which could be assimilated by a going organization. If the resettlement program is continued, its operating techniques may be perfected to a point at which detailed planning and execution can be left to the regions. In this case the Washington office would confine itself to program and policy planning, broad-scale administrative supervision, inspection, and analysis of results. In the last few years the Farm Security Administration has arranged for increasing participation by field personnel in planning and in developing standard operating practices, so that they will be prepared to take greater responsibility when it is given to them.

A third type of planning is predominant in the Forest Service.[11] Here the emphasis is on a long-range program in which preliminary plans are made years in advance and gradually shaped into final form. There is, as a rule, no hurry about planning, for adherence to a schedule eliminates the need for haste. Plans are produced regularly each year, and are integrated with the budgets submitted through the Department and the Budget Bureau to Congress.

The operating divisions of the Forest Service are responsible for preparing master plans for the full accomplishment of their functions.[12] Within these plans, priorities of projects are established, according to which funds are allotted as they become available. Allocations are first made to cover existing work loads on projects already under way. This work is re-planned as it goes along by means of annual work-load analyses, in which tasks are classified both by function (activity) and by unit of organization.[13] The analyses are always divided into two parts, as follows:

Section I—Recurrent Work
Embracing all operative and maintenance work of more or less constant volume and of a recurring nature.

Section II—Non-Recurrent Work
Embracing all construction and development projects, surveys and special project work of a non-recurring nature, and certain operative jobs, the volume and frequency

---
[11] The activities of the Forest Service are outlined in Chapter X.
[12] Within many fields of public endeavor the amount of possible activity is limited only by the amount of money available. It is a common practice to plan ahead of expectations so that "windfalls" may be turned to the best advantage.
[13] The classification of activities is that used in the cost accounting system of the Forest Service. *Forest Service Manual*, Volume 2, page FC-F2-1.

ADMINISTRATIVE PROCEDURE

of which fluctuate so sharply from year to year as to require special organization or financial consideration.[14]

The analyses of existing work and the "project work budgets" for proposed work are initiated in the Ranger Districts and National Forest offices,[15] and reviewed in the regional offices by Boards of Review, each of which has a "regional planning officer" as executive secretary. The Boards of Review are expected to counterbalance undue pressures from operating divisions and to "exercise necessary co-ordination, correlation, and determination of essential priorities." Summaries of present work load and of "project work" are forwarded to the Washington office in time to arrive before April 1 of each year; they provide the basic material for preparing the annual budget estimate for submission to the next session of Congress.[16]

The planning mechanism of the Forest Service, which combines the flow of plans upward through line units with review and co-ordination by special planning officers, provides thorough technical accuracy and integration, and enlists the co-operation of officials in each field unit. It functions slowly, but there is sufficient time to permit adherence to a schedule, so the planning can always keep ahead of operations.

PLANNING PROCEDURE AND ADMINISTRATIVE URGENCY

Planning, as a procedure, behaves in the same way as any other administrative process. The more it is subdivided into a great number of steps assigned to different units of organization, the longer it will be before plans are completed. Yet concentration of program planning in a single unit will frequently diminish the soundness of detail and the plan's acceptability to operating officials. At the same time letting each line office plan its own work without centralized review weakens co-ordination and leads to waste and duplication of effort. The administrator necessarily has to judge the effect of these tendencies on his organization and to choose between evils in laying out his planning machinery.

The method of planning must be fitted to circumstances; if plans are needed quickly, it is well to concentrate planning in a central office. This office should have immediate access to every unit of the organization, and its inquiries should receive preferred attention, so

---

[14] *Ibid*, Volume 1, page GA-C3-3, 9.
[15] See Chapter X, first section.
[16] Bureau budget estimates are presented to the Department Budget Officer in May; they go to the Budget Bureau in September and to Congress the following January.

ADMINISTRATIVE (PROGRAM) PLANNING

that the results will be workable in terms of operating knowledge. If time permits, however, it is better to spread the planning function over the various operating divisions, providing a central co-ordinating body. The delay in this procedure will be repaid by improved accuracy, acceptability, and co-ordination, and will very likely be made up by time saved in carrying out the plans.

If planning is recognized as a part of administration just as important as execution or control, it is possible to find time for it. Moreover, any planning procedure, even a complex one, can be speeded up by setting and maintaining a schedule of operations. It is always preferable to spend ample time in planning, so that the operations which follow form a systematic sequence leading surely to the desired end, rather than to plan in a hurry and then waste time and money correcting mistakes and replanning. The most thorough planning permits the greatest decentralization of power to execute, and provides the means whereby projects may be carried out with the fewest control steps and the least administrative delay.

Chapter VII

ADMINISTRATIVE EXECUTION— PURCHASING

THE essential fact about administration is that no two problems are alike, much less two programs or two organizations. If the form and content of administration could be exactly foreseen and standardized, planning would be its beginning and end, and robots could do the executing and controlling. It would then be possible to write an administrative textbook which would teach the solution of the limited number of problems. If such were the case, many interesting jobs would become dull chores and intelligent people would become truck drivers rather than executives.

Fortunately, administration is not a stereotype. Its principles can only be stated in general terms, and it is left to the administrator's common-sense and imagination to apply them to specific situations. Yet it is desirable to illustrate these principles, particularly the newer and more experimental ones in the field of procedure, by application to a few typical problems so as to show how they may be used in a practical way. In picking the operations to serve as our "guinea pigs," it is logical to look for those which occur in every administrative organization rather than in just a few. The best common denominators in administration are the staff functions (which occur everywhere), and the most suitable for procedural study are purchasing and personnel.

Although line functions vary enormously from one organization to another, and their arrangement differs greatly, even between concerns engaged in the same general field of activity, the handling of staff functions is far more (though by no means completely) standardized. As explained in Chapter V, staff functions were originally treated as incidental phases of the line functions to which they were related. It was only as their specialized techniques developed that they became established as separate fields of operation. Today, every large company and public agency has its purchasing agents, its personnel managers, its lawyers, and its accountants—men who have

ADMINISTRATIVE EXECUTION—PURCHASING

learned their skills in special schools or through apprenticeship, and who belong to recognized professional associations.

The specific techniques of administrative staff activities are covered in a multitude of textbooks and technical journals, mainly from the introverted or professionalized point of view. Professional zeal is not to be deprecated, but it is at times neglectful of the needs of the people served: a man may be so intent on doing a good job that he forgets those who are waiting for him to do it. The procedural side of staff work is that most easily ignored by the technicians, because the effects of good or bad procedure [1] are felt mostly outside the staff unit. Yet the way in which business comes to the staff officials, the administrative sequences within the staff office, and the channels through which papers are returned to the line officers are as vital to the organization as the quality of the staff work itself. A thing must be done in the right way at the right *time*. If an organization can avoid tripping over its own toes in its staff operations—if it can get the right kind of personnel and the right kind of materials when and where they are needed, and if its legal and fiscal operations proceed without delay—it is going a long way toward efficient management.

OBTAINING SUPPLIES FROM STOCK

The administrative sequence which most closely concerns the greatest number of workers is that of obtaining ordinary materials from stock. In private concerns the usual procedure is to have a shop requisition filled out and signed by the foreman and taken directly to the stock room, the same messenger bringing the supplies back if he can carry them. Private business can not afford to have its employees lose time waiting for materials—its very existence is dependent on elimination of waste time. In public agencies the incentive to simplify and expedite is less immediate, and the desire to avoid making mistakes (or at least to avoid being blamed for them) is more pronounced. The supply procedures of government offices vary in accordance with the differing personalities and habits of thought of their organizers. Two contrasting sequences are those of "Agency A" and "Agency B," the agencies introduced in Chapter III.

The procedure in "Agency A" emphasizes directness. A section which requires supplies fills out a requisition, which is signed by the chief or by someone to whom he has delegated authority to order

---

[1] The term procedure refers here not to the content of the work so much as to the arrangement of operations, and the factors which determine motion delay.

ADMINISTRATIVE PROCEDURE

supplies, and is then sent directly to the warehouse. It is received there by an Accounting Clerk who checks the prices of the items ordered and, after crediting the warehouse and debiting the ordering office, sends one copy to the supply room to be filled and the other to the Finance Section for entry on the books.

This procedure, which reflects the expressed desire of the officials of "Agency A" to make it as efficient as a comparable private business, calls for only two moves and one control step (the checking of prices) before the supplies are actually forwarded. A considerable responsibility is placed on the officer who signs the requisition. He must see (1) that the supplies are of the right kind and for a legitimate purpose, and (2) that he does not exceed his budgetary allotment. This is a proper responsibility, for the head of a section should know what he needs and how much money he has got. The acceptance of this idea makes it possible for each working unit to get what it needs as soon as it needs it, without external controls.

The supply procedure of "Agency B" is very much longer. A section requiring materials fills out five copies of a requisition (instead of three as in "Agency A") and forwards four to the Divisional Supply Officer ("Agency A" does not have such officers). This official checks the prices of the supplies ordered and forwards three copies to the division chief, who signs them and sends them on to the Finance Division. This division pre-audits and encumbers funds for the order and returns it to the supply officer, *via* the division chief. As inter-divisional mail is received by a central distributing station in each division, recorded, and then re-routed, the "motion delay" is considerable, sometimes aggregating two days or more for the round trip. Each division has a small stock of supplies, and if the items ordered are on hand the supply officer sends them as soon as the requisition has been received back from the Finance Division. If they are not in stock the requisition is forwarded to the warehouse.

The supply procedure of "Agency B" involves four or five administrative moves, two of which are complex since they pass through divisional offices and mail distribution centers. Responsibility is divided among a number of people, in fact there is no certainty as to who is really responsible for an order. The result is frequent confusion, delay, and "buck-passing." The officials who planned this procedure, which fails to short-cut the normal weaving in and out of line business, evidently did not think of the time required for administrative motion or of the need for giving definite responsibility to one individual.[2] Whether the basic responsibility for orders from stock rests with the ordering official or with the manager of the stock room is not fundamental. The important thing is that it should be given, wholly and unquestionably, to one or the other, and that there should be direct communication between the parties concerned.

OPEN MARKET AND CONTRACT PURCHASES

Before an item can be placed in stock it must be purchased, and frequently articles are needed for current use which can not be practicably stocked in advance. Efficient administration depends, among other things, on a workable purchasing procedure: one which will function quickly and yet avoid paying higher prices than necessary. It is axiomatic that purchasing for an organization will be *to some extent* functionalized in a staff division. It remains to be decided whether it should be completely centralized or partly done by branch purchasing offices serving line divisions or geographical units, how flexible the policies and procedures will be, and to what extent purchasing may take place outside the regular channels.

An organization scattered in small units over a wide territory usually allows its branches some leeway to buy for immediate needs. This may vary from a general permission to buy anything which can not be issued through a field warehouse or obtained under a term contract, down to the narrow prerogative of purchasing in an emergency.[3] It is common, however, to allow purchases up to a certain amount; in the Government the limit for direct purchases by minor field units is generally based on the size of purchase which may lawfully be made without advertising for bids.[4] In large organizations the procedural advantage of direct purchasing and the economic benefit of centralized buying can both be obtained by the use of "term contracts." Under these transactions, the successful bidder undertakes to supply at a fixed unit price as many of the items in question as may be needed over a definite period of time. Service to field units is at its best when the contractor has suitably located sales branches or dealers who can give immediate delivery. The Procurement Division of the United States Treasury Department negotiates

---

[2] The ordering of routine supplies (pencils, paper, etc.) does not warrant the administrative review which might be desirable for large orders, such as automobiles, steam shovels, etc.

[3] The concept of an "emergency" has been rather narrowly defined so far as the Federal government is concerned, being limited mostly to floods, fires, accidents, etc.

[4] The amount varies between Departments and bureaus. Legislation has been introduced to standardize it at $100, allowing purchase without bids in exigencies, with the approval of the Department head, up to $500.

hundreds of such contracts for the entire Federal Government, and issues a "General Schedule of Supplies" which lists the contracts and articles available thereunder. This arrangement provides excellent economies, but is subject to the disadvantages of inflexibility. In order to provide the greatest inducement for bidders to offer low prices, many contracts are "mandatory." That is, Federal agencies can purchase the items in question *only* from the contractors, unless specific clearance from the Procurement Division is obtained. This causes excessive delay when materials listed on the schedule do not meet a particular operating requirement and it becomes necessary to wait for permission to buy exactly what is wanted. This type of case occurs fairly frequently. It has also been found that complaints against general schedule contractors do not always receive prompt attention, but this situation will doubtless be corrected in time.

Small open market purchases and buying under term contract are procedurally alike in that the scope for purchasing technique is limited in both cases. In small scale open market buying, the ratio of possible savings to administrative cost is not such as to warrant more than a limited "shopping around" and in purchasing from contract the bargaining has already been done. The problem in either case, as with issuance from stock, is to get the goods in the hands of the user as quickly as possible. In geographically centralized offices it is usually necessary, for mechanical reasons and to avoid confusing vendors, to issue all purchase orders and receive all deliveries at one point; it is important to provide channels through which that point may be reached in the most direct way. If the procedure for drawing a purchase order is complex—which is unfortunately the case in many Government agencies and in some private concerns—it may happen that field units will obtain supplies more rapidly than subordinate sections of the central office.

If the flow of requisitions is subjected to the routing indicated by a "normal" concentration of authority, it is likely to be slow. Such routing, which follows the formal lines of authority, except in communication between units of equal rank within the same immediately superior unit,[5] is quite proper for sequences involving the laying out of major programs and policies, and the making of important decisions. But it is quite unnecessary for the mere procurement of supplies to carry out activity already authorized, particularly if the character of the supplies is predetermined by the program of operations. That

---

[5] See Chapter V, particularly footnote 9.

ADMINISTRATIVE EXECUTION—PURCHASING

is, if you direct your subordinate to construct a building according to certain plans, you have by implication authorized him to obtain lumber, cement, hardware, plumbing materials, and whatever else is called for. Why insist on repeating the authorization piecemeal by reviewing each order for material which is merely a logical consequence of your previous instructions? The absurdity of subjecting all requisitions, indiscriminately, to detailed administrative clearance is not appreciated by a great many Government bureaus. It is common practice to require each requisition originating in a subordinate unit to be approved by the division chief (in whose office considerable delay may be encountered) and then by the business manager, before it is sent to the purchasing officer. Much time can be saved by allowing each operating unit headed by a responsible official to send requisitions directly to the purchasing office or via the appropriate accounting unit when advance encumbrance of funds must be made. It is still possible to route unusual orders or those over a certain amount to the higher administrative officials without imposing upon them a volume of unnecessary detail.

PURCHASES THROUGH BID PROCEDURE

Larger purchases are usually made by advertising for bids. In the Government this is mandatory (except in emergency) for transactions over a certain amount ($50 in most cases, $300 for emergency relief funds). Private concerns often have varying amounts, usually somewhat higher, above which bids are obtained. Their procedure is of course less formal and they do not have to make the bids public. If the organization is very large and contacts flow up and down the lines of authority without short cuts, the bid procedure may be very slow, particularly if the bids received are referred back to the requisitioning office for recommendation as to which bid should be accepted.

In some Federal departments, bid transactions are largely centralized in departmental contracting offices. Observations made of the time between the issuance of a bureau's requisition and the acceptance of bids in one such department indicated that the interval averaged 22.5 days, during 8 of which the opened bids were in the requisitioning bureau for recommendation. To this there must be added the time which it takes for the bureau to issue its requisition and the

ADMINISTRATIVE PROCEDURE

PURCHASES THROUGH BID PROCEDURE
FLOW OF BID TRANSACTIONS IN A TYPICAL
FEDERAL DEPARTMENT

Washington Solicitation and Award

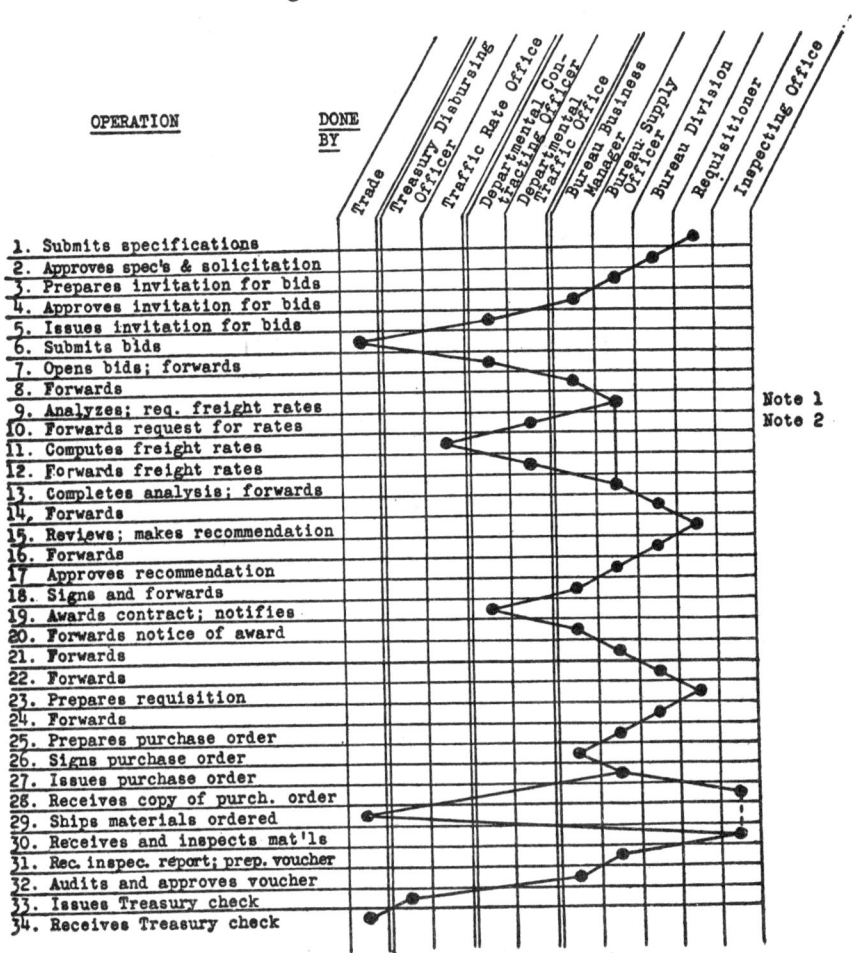

OPERATION	DONE BY	Trade	Treasury Disbursing Officer	Traffic Rate Office	Departmental Contracting Officer	Departmental Traffic Office	Bureau Office Manager	Bureau Business Officer	Bureau Supply	Bureau Division	Requisitioner	Inspecting Office
1. Submits specifications											●	
2. Approves spec's & solicitation										●		
3. Prepares invitation for bids						●						
4. Approves invitation for bids										●		
5. Issues invitation for bids						●						
6. Submits bids		●										
7. Opens bids; forwards						●						
8. Forwards										●		
9. Analyzes; req. freight rates										●			Note 1
10. Forwards request for rates						●							Note 2
11. Computes freight rates				●								
12. Forwards freight rates						●						
13. Completes analysis; forwards										●		
14. Forwards									●			
15. Reviews; makes recommendation								●				
16. Forwards							●					
17. Approves recommendation						●						
18. Signs and forwards							●					
19. Awards contract; notifies						●						
20. Forwards notice of award												●
21. Forwards									●			
22. Forwards								●				
23. Prepares requisition											●	
24. Forwards										●		
25. Prepares purchase order									●			
26. Signs purchase order						●						
27. Issues purchase order									●			
28. Receives copy of purch. order		●										●
29. Ships materials ordered		●										
30. Receives and inspects mat'ls												●
31. Rec. inspec. report; prep. voucher							●					
32. Audits and approves voucher						●						
33. Issues Treasury check			●									
34. Receives Treasury check		●										

Figure 13

Note 1. Freight rates (for comparing shipping point and destination prices on an equitable basis) would not be used for smaller transactions.

Note 2. If the Department has a rate file, the traffic office will compute the rates itself instead of forwarding the request. Rate service was formerly furnished most Departments by the Procurement Division, Treasury Department. At present Departments obtain them from various sources. As land-grant freight and express rates are shortly to be discontinued for civil departments, the use of freight rates in evaluating bids will be largely eliminated unless railroads grant other concessions to the Government.

time after acceptance of a bid before the purchase is completed;[6] these times vary between departments and bureaus.

In purchases for field use the procedure is sometimes speeded up by solicitation, opening, and immediate recommendation by local offices, which forward the bids to Washington for award. Some of the larger decentralized bureaus have in their regional offices purchasing officers with authority to make awards up to varying amounts, but even these must send their larger transactions, as well as certain kinds of smaller ones, to Washington. The flow of bid transactions in a typical department, when both solicitation and acceptance are in Washington, is shown in Figure 13.

The reason why Government bid procedure takes so long lies in the number of administrative moves. The best way to make it move faster would be to eliminate some of these moves. But this is easier said than done. Shall the operations to be abolished be those of the central contracting office or the bureau business offices? It would be possible on the one hand to have bureaus advertise for and accept more of their bids in the field.[7] Or the central contracting office could make its awards, on the basis of the specifications, without referring the opened bids back to the bureau for recommendation. Either solution would have potential disadvantages: the first would increase the possibility and perhaps the frequency of "improper" purchasing through unduly restrictive specifications and technically reasonable but legally unjustifiable preferences; the second might cause occasional procurement of unsuitable materials. Both decentralization to the field and centralization at the expense of bureau business offices are thorny subjects. The impasse arises when centralized business operation is superimposed on an organization decentralized in its line operations, and when responsibility for purchasing is divided.

The purchasing organizations of some departments show duplications of available skill and of function. Bureau supply officers, including those in regional offices and large field stations, are usually

---

[6] After accepting a bid the contracting officer issues a "notice of award" which informs the vendor that he has a contract to supply such and such an article. Shipment is not made, however, until the vendor receives a "purchase order" issued pursuant to the contract, usually by the bureau. Why these two documents should not be consolidated has never been satisfactorily explained.

[7] It would probably be impractical to have departmental bureaus accept bids in their Washington offices, as the resulting multiplicity of contracting officers of the same department in the same city would be very confusing to vendors. It would, however, be possible for bureau business managers to review bids sent in from the field and to authorize officials at the field stations in question to accept particular ones. This would amount to the same thing, so far as bids solicited in the field are concerned.

qualified to operate independently within fairly broad limits, although they do not have all the resources of the central offices. The latter could quite as well, save for geographical barriers, serve the individual requisitioners without the interposition of bureau officials. The analyses of bids made by bureaus are often repeated in detail by the central contracting offices, which quite naturally refuse to accept responsibility for the work of others without checking it in detail.[8] This situation arose more or less accidentally and is due to failure to appreciate the factor of administrative pyramiding.

Pyramiding is a bugbear to efficient administration. In its incipient stages it is subtle and hard to detect; once intrenched it is almost impossible to uproot. It usually occurs when an activity originally carried on by operating divisions or their staff branches is transferred to a central service agency. Such centralization is always resisted because of the loss of independence entailed and because of the natural bureaucratic desire to retain as many functions as possible. Basing their position on the supposed need for "administrative control," the operating divisions keep the offices and most of the personnel formerly engaged in the activity for the purpose of channelizing contact with the new central agency. What happens then is that the people in the operating divisions do practically what they did before and the central office does it over again. Pyramiding is universal; it occurs in purchasing, personnel work, filing, accounting, and in line as well as staff activities. There are only two ways to prevent it: either allow the function in question to remain decentralized, or else remove it completely from the line divisions, moving the personnel elsewhere and making sure that they are not replaced. The latter is the more difficult, for functions once abolished often rise phoenix-like from the dust.

Several departments have been exploring the possibility of decentralizing most of their purchasing, so far as possible, to regional offices and field stations. One such plan currently under consideration would constitute the larger field units as "primary" procurement offices with authority to accept bids up to $2500 or even higher, and smaller ones as "secondary" offices with authority up to $1000. The quality and efficiency of purchasing would be maintained by standard practices, systematic inspection, and by department specifications for materials not covered by Federal rules. A number of these have been

---

[8] The officer who signs the contract is liable for loss to the Government in case of error or irregularity. However, enforcement of this liability, where the contracting officer acted in good faith, is extremely rare.

issued by various departments. Most important would be intensive and continuous training of purchasing officers.

Under a scheme such as that just outlined, a central purchasing or contracting office would become essentially a technical agency concerned with standardizing the best practices, and with planning the location, staffing, and facilities of local purchasing offices and warehouses so as to serve all field activities effectively and rapidly. Any such reform would require a period of education, since bureaus and departmental offices are usually unwilling to surrender to the field offices authority which has always been closely retained in Washington.

CONSOLIDATION OF FEDERAL PROCUREMENT ACTIVITIES

By Executive Order 6166 of June 10, 1933, the President granted the Procurement Division of the Treasury Department authority to consolidate within itself all purchasing and warehouse activities of the Federal Government, except those in the War and Navy Departments. The order was so worded as to have the effect of extending the power of reorganization conferred by the 1933 Economy Act,[9] permitting the Procurement Division to take over any purchasing activity whenever it might see fit and to prescribe regulations for the conduct of purchasing left to other agencies.

For several years the Procurement Division confined its direct activity largely to purchasing for the Emergency Relief Program (FERA, WPA, and allotted funds) and to the negotiation of term contracts for materials in common demand. In June 1939, however, it announced its intention to take over all Federal purchasing except that for the Army and the Navy. It has already assumed the purchasing function for the Public Roads Administration,[10] the Social Security Board, and a number of other agencies; further transfers are possible.[11] The prospect of consolidating Federal purchasing and warehousing in a single agency raises some interesting problems of organization and procedure.

The Executive Order opened the way to consolidation of procurement "as a means of economy." Yet centralization of detailed opera-

---

[9] This was accomplished by transferring the *function* of purchasing as of the effective date of the order, leaving the *operations* to be transferred later. This is a nice distinction, but it has not been questioned legally.

[10] The Procurement Division returned to the Public Roads Administration its authority to purchase "General Schedule" items.

[11] The taking over of purchasing for these agencies by the Procurement Division has not been an unqualified success. This fact, together with the heavy load of emergency work thrown on the Procurement Division by the vast "defense" program (which demands a great deal of activity besides the strictly military expansion), has apparently put any further consolidations into the background.

ADMINISTRATIVE PROCEDURE

tions (as distinguished from co-ordination) may bring about the opposite result. There will undoubtedly be a good deal of administrative pyramiding if Federal purchasing is centralized on a Government-wide scale. Bureaus and departments will retain vestigial procurement offices to meet their real or fancied needs, and will continue to give more or less detailed administrative treatment to purchase orders. There will be an increase in the overhead cost of purchasing, for even though the Procurement Division may show a lesser percentage cost, as compared with costs in departments and bureaus which purchase independently, for *its part* of the process, the total cost of purchasing will go up. Comparison of the purchasing offices of organizations which deal through the Procurement Division and ones which deal directly wtih vendors seems to indicate that the number and type of personnel required in a bureau or department is approximately the same for either mode of operation. The cost of centralized purchasing in the Procurement Division does not replace that of decentralized operation in the agencies served, but is incurred *in addition to it,* save for very minor adjustments. Unless the increase in overhead can be compensated for by economies in price and in warehousing costs, the result will be a net loss.

Acceptance of the idea that centralization of all phases of purchasing on a Government-wide scale will be advantageous implies a failure to analyze the administrative processes involved. Purchasing has two basic sides which may be called the internal and the external. The first consists of determining what is wanted, and applying whatever controls are necessary to see that a purchase is justified and in line with program and policy, and that funds are available. The second consists of making contact with vendors, obtaining the most advantageous prices, and placing orders. When purchasing is done by an office which is an integral part of the agency served, these two phases are accomplished simultaneously in one set of operations. Only the external side of purchasing can be transferred to an outside agency, and doing so produces an inevitable duplication of work.

The disadvantages of indirect purchasing would seem particularly obvious in purchases made under the term contracts in the General Schedule of Supplies. In this case the bargaining (which is the most important part of the external side of purchasing) has already been done—prices, terms of delivery, discounts, and servicing have already been agreed upon. The placing of a purchase order is merely a mechanical function. Yet the Procurement Division insisted for a time that the agencies it served should obtain General Schedule items through its channels instead of direct from vendors. The offices concerned found that the operation of preparing a requisition was almost identical with that of making up a purchase order; the forms were similar and called for approximately the same entries. The relaying of these routine orders through the Procurement Division resulted only in extra paper work and delay. It could not, in the nature of the situation, produce any advantage to the Government. After some pressure from the operating agencies, and the accumulation of a large backlog of small orders, the Procurement Division admitted this fact and returned to a number of offices their authority to purchase directly from General Schedule contractors.

The same arguments apply, with slight modifications, to purchases through bids, except in cases in which consolidated orders are practical.[12] The agency needing materials must prepare or designate specifications for what it wants; it must state what, how much, where, and when. The copying of this information on the standard form which is used for soliciting bids is again a mechanical process, which can and should be consolidated with the administrative action. The relaying of all communication between the customer and the trade through an intermediary office results in excessive delay and cost, which cannot, under the more or less formalized Government procedure, be justified on the basis of possible superior technique possessed by a central procurement agency. When an outside purchasing office attempts to exert administrative authority over individual transactions, for instance by changing the specifications, the result is usually intense friction and frequently means the procurement of articles not suitable to the purposes for which they were bought.[13] The administrators and technicians of line organizations who know their jobs must necessarily know what is needed for those jobs and where to get it; indeed, obtaining the right kind of materials is an inherent part of the job itself. While within an organization of limited size a purchasing office can be useful in taking over some of the load of the line officials, it should never be very far removed from them and should always be under the same over-all supervision to preclude any conflict of interests. With certain exceptions to be noted immediately hereafter, the key to effective purchasing lies not in centralization but in decentralization combined with standardiza-

---

[12] Except for materials for which there is constant demand, the consolidation of orders can not be accomplished without excessive delay. In the Government such consolidations are mostly limited to certain bulk commodities.

[13] On the authority of purchasing officers to modify requisitions, see White, *Public Administration*, pp. 77-78.

ADMINISTRATIVE PROCEDURE

tion of the best and simplest practices.

FIELDS IN WHICH CONSOLIDATION IS BENEFICIAL

The Procurement Division can utilize its strategic position to best advantage for both itself and the Government as a whole by concentrating on those aspects of supply work in which consolidation will bring the most obvious benefits. The four most important fields of this kind are: (1) term contracts, (2) pooling of common requirements for bulk commodities, (3) warehousing of items in common demand, and (4) specifications. These activities already represent a major part of the Procurement Division's work, but they are susceptible to wider expansion. They are procedurally alike in that they tend to simplify the procurement process, reducing the total number of administrative steps and hence the time required for accomplishment.

The term contract is a method of shortening the purchasing procedure in individual cases, since the detailed work of obtaining prices and contracting is done once instead of many times. By expanding the General Schedule of Supplies to include as nearly as possible all articles for which there is repeated demand by several agencies, the volume of bid work in departments could be reduced to that needed to procure specialized items. For commodities for which nation-wide contracts are not feasible, the possibility of regional or state contracts should be explored. It is also possible to contract for materials subject to fluctuating prices (for which long-term fixed prices are likely to be too high) by basing the prices on standard market quotations from recognized sources. The term contract is one of the best ways of buying for public agencies with a minimum of administrative detail; the slightly higher prices (as compared with contracts for specified quantities) are generally outweighed by lowered administrative costs and the removal of the incentive to overstock. However, loopholes should be provided to prevent the excessive rigidity which results from a series of mandatory contracts. Either the contracts should be drawn for *optional* use, or clearance to purchase outside them should be given in blanket amounts to be distributed by the agencies concerned instead of separately in each case by the central contracting agency.

For some commodities, price behavior and marketing conditions make term contracts impractical and yet the common demand of a number of agencies justifies consolidated buying. For such materials,[14] wholesale contracting by the Procurement Division is advantageous,

---

[14] For instance, coal.

ADMINISTRATIVE EXECUTION—PURCHASING

provided departments are not forced to anticipate their needs too far ahead. In a few cases, notably the purchase some years ago of an oversupply of tires which became obsolete due to model changes in automotive equipment, waste has occurred because needs were inacurately estimated. Decisions as to what materials and how much of them to buy in large quantities should be based on analyses of market conditions and of the stability of demand in the using agencies, particular attention being paid to the possibility of obsolescence or deterioration.

The warehousing of materials in common demand by a number of Government departments and agencies offers a fruitful field for consolidation. It may even prove feasible for the Procurement Division to render complete warehouse service to some agencies, particularly those whose work is done entirely "on paper" and not with machinery, instruments, apparatus, or specialized equipment. Most bureaus which conduct programs of physical development (such as the Forest Service, Fish and Wildlife Service, Public Roads Administration, Soil Conservation Service, and the Bureau of Reclamation) or the management of property (such as the National Park Service and the Lighthouse Service) combine warehousing of new equipment with the storage, maintenance, and operation of existing equipment in such a way as to render uneconomical the separation of the two functions. But many kinds of material, including office supplies and furniture, building materials, electrical and plumbing fixtures, automobile parts, and the like, could be conveniently supplied to field activities from strategically located warehouses.

The fundamental consideration to be kept in mind by the Procurement Division, in planning its development and its relationships with other agencies, is that it is a service unit and not a controlling organ. It must remember that its own line function is a staff function so far as others are concerned and is not self-justifying. If it plans its program from the point of view of the operating agency, provide short supply procedures and easily available facilities where needed, and avoid encumbering itself and others by trying to do too much, it will succeed in vindicating the President's hope for greater economy and efficiency.

The foregoing detailed considerations have dealt with purchasing in the Federal Government. But the procedural problems illustrated are equally applicable in local government and in private business. It is obvious that the purchasing mechanism of any organization should be planned to permit operating officials to fill their needs

ADMINISTRATIVE PROCEDURE

with a minimum of bother and delay, that is to say, with the fewest administrative moves. At the same time it is necessary to guard against unwise or improper buying, favoritism, or other evils which arise when line units are left too much to their own devices. The best method which will provide good purchasing with a minimum of administrative motion is that of predigestion: term contracts, and standardized specifications and bid procedures. By making the actual purchasing transactions as simple as possible it is practical to decentralize, maintaining control through budgets, reports, inspection, and clearance of particularly large or specialized orders, rather than by putting each requisition through a vast and creaking mill. The central procurement authorities of departments and of the Government should be technicians rather than clerks; they should develop accessible sources of supply and simplified procedures and educate the operating officials in their use. In this way the most can be done with the least administrative effort.

Chapter VIII

ADMINISTRATIVE EXECUTION—
PERSONNEL

THE PERSONNEL function as such is a fairly recent development. It was formerly thought that hiring and firing could not be separated from direct line administration—the power to discharge being equal to the power to control. Specialized personnel offices were made necessary by the commercial and industrial revolutions of the eighteenth and nineteenth centuries. In the relatively small establishments prior to that era, foremen could safely be given authority to hire and fire, because an aggrieved worker could still complain to the employer, who would judge the case from an institutional point of view, since his interest as sole or part owner and that of the "organization" were more or less identical. But as organizations grew larger, it became harder and harder for subordinates to see the heads, and at the same time conflicts between the interests of intermediate executives and those of their companies became more and more frequent.

Since the days when anyone could appeal to the "big boss" were gone forever, unchecked personnel authority on the part of operating officials led to politics, intrigue, and loss of morale. There was a need for some arbitrating force which would have no direct interest in particular cases and which would safeguard the welfare of the whole organization. Thus the original impetus toward the setting up of personnel units came from the fact of bigness itself. There were also more specific conditions, such as: (1) increasing specialization of jobs and the need for exact judgment of mental and physical capacities; (2) the breakdown of recognized insignia of craftsmanship and the rapid growth of new occupations without traditions; and (3) the tendency of workers to organize and the consequent need for well-conceived employee relations policies. Today personnel offices, at least in large organizations, are the rule rather than the exception.

Personnel offices, so far as their functions and relation to other branches of the organization are concerned, fall into two general types. One kind is a "service unit" which does not usually decide who shall be employed, discharged, or promoted; it acts as an advisory body, supplying technical counsel and information to operating officials. It may of course inform the head of the establishment when it thinks that these officials are acting unwisely, but it does not possess any authority on its own account. The other kind of personnel office is a "functional unit" which possesses substantial authority [1] for employment, promotion, and discharge, and which is free to depart from the recommendations of line officers. The exercise of its power is naturally tempered by the need for maintaining cordial relations with operating heads, but in the last analysis such an office has higher authority, subject to control by the top administrator.

Both types of offices provide the information needed for intelligent personnel actions, measuring and rating employees' abilities, receiving applications and keeping lists of prospective employees, etc. Both types also attend to the mechanical functions of maintaining employee records, and processing payrolls, as well as assisting in problems of personal adjustment. The first type of personnel office predominates in private businesses, particularly those small enough to permit the reference of difficult problems directly to the head; the second is more usual in the Government and in very large corporations. A number of special conditions, including laws, regulations, and decisions of accounting officers create an environment [2] which makes it necessary for public agencies to have more elaborate and centralized personnel offices than private concerns of the same size. This is particularly so in agencies operating under a civil service system, where considerable skill is required in "putting through" appointments and in unraveling the many knots which arise therein.

Whether the personnel office is a service or functional unit may depend, among other things, on the relative importance of speed and care in recruitment and promotion. A functional personnel office normally makes its decisions on the basis of objective data, which take time to gather. If haste is not at a premium, it is of advantage to have a fairly complicated system for selecting personnel in order to secure appointees of the highest merit. But if there are major tasks demanding immediate action, especially those requiring large forces of temporary workers, appointment becomes largely a procedural problem to be solved in the shortest way. The need for qualified personnel may be as great as before but there is no time to

---

[1] See quotation from H. P. Dutton on the functional authority of staff officers, Chapter X, "General Principles of Control in the Forest Service."
[2] See Chapter XV, particularly "The Legal Environment."

ADMINISTRATIVE EXECUTION—PERSONNEL

go through the usual procedure of examination and investigation. In this case the best thing to do is to leave the problem of selection up to the operating officials, relying on general administrative supervision to find out whether those chosen are doing their jobs properly. In an established agency, where there is a career service, and the objective is to recruit the most qualified people and to promote strictly according to merit, a functional personnel unit is essential. But in an emergency agency, or one which has to get a large program under way in a short time, it is often better to have a service unit acting automatically on advice from operating officials.

The comparison of personnel procedures in "Agency A" and "Agency B" is a case in point, showing the results of adjustment and failure to adjust to emergency conditions. Both were New Deal agencies, exempted from civil service rules, and obliged to recruit administrative and clerical personnel by the hundred during the first months of their existence. Although each agency had a personnel division, theoretically completely responsible for filling all but the major posts, actually the recruiting was done by the high officials and their newly appointed subordinates. The new administrators were presented with empty offices and full dockets. They had jobs which had to be filled quickly. They were in too much of a hurry to wait for the personnel divisions to examine applications, investigate qualifications, and establish objectively compiled employment lists. So they did what was quite natural: they picked business, professional, and political associates, and personal friends, and asked their personnel divisions to appoint these people to the vacancies. These divisions were thus mainly occupied in "putting through" the appointments of people who were pre-selected. Their actual functions (though not their ostensible ones) were those of service rather than functional units.

In "Agency A" the appointment of administrative personnel, except in the highest grades, was performed in the following manner. An office wishing to fill a vacancy made out an "employment requisition" which was forwarded with a job analysis to the Employment Management Unit in the Personnel Section. For a new position, the Classification sub-unit would allocate a grade and a salary. The Examining sub-unit then referred back to the originating office the applications of persons appearing to be best suited for the position, including by request that of the person indicated by the requisitioner.[3]

---
[3] The Personnel Section could object to the designation of a person obviously unqualified. To this extent it had a functional authority.

ADMINISTRATIVE PROCEDURE

The latter selected the appointee, secured (sometimes by telephone) the approval of the head of the Employment Management Unit, and forwarded to that unit an "authorization for contract." The unit then notified the appointee to report for duty. Two or three subsequent routine steps took place but did not delay the date the appointee began work. This whole procedure involved only five interdivisional administrative moves, accomplished by direct contact, with additional moves inside the Employment Management Unit when new classifications were needed. For appointments to higher grades, the approval of the Administrator was required. While it was expected that division chiefs would be kept informed of forthcoming appointments, there was no hard-and-fast requirement that the papers clear through them. This extremely simple procedure enabled "Agency A" to expand its organization rapidly and to enter upon its work with a minimum of confusion. The high caliber of the principal officials first appointed minimized the tendency toward ill-considered appointments which might otherwise have resulted from the rather personal bases of selection.

The basic operations in the appointment procedure of "Agency B" were similar to those in "Agency A." There were, however, a number of additional steps, and the concentration of authority which required all interdivisional communications to clear through division chiefs tended to maximize motion delay. Requests for personnel were first passed upon by divisional personnel representatives (assigned to operating divisions but under the jurisdiction of the Personnel Division) and then routed through the offices of the division chiefs. There followed a sequence of several steps within the Personnel Division, including "investigation"—writing to the references given by the applicant and filing the answers. As nearly all appointments were "pushed through" at the request of section chiefs, this process was perfunctory and might as well have been eliminated. The requirement of "political clearance" by special officials designated to look over the endorsements of applicants for clerical and sub-professional positions (and to weed out any Republicans in sheep's clothing) added several more moves to the majority of cases during "Agency B's" period of greatest expansion. Contacts with these "political" officers, whose exact status was kept conveniently vague, could be made only through special liaison officers who were completely swamped by the volume of business. Those officials who attempted to circumvent this administrative "bottleneck" or who tried to expedite matters by having

ADMINISTRATIVE EXECUTION—PERSONNEL

Congressmen intervene were severely reprimanded.[4] The number of administrative moves in the appointment procedure of "Agency B" was about double that of "Agency A" and the responsibility for action was distributed among a correspondingly greater number of people. During "Agency B's" period of mushroom growth it was customary to put employees to work before formal appointment (although this was officially forbidden) and some worked as long as three months before they received their first pay-checks.[5]

PROCEDURE UNDER CIVIL SERVICE

In Government agencies operating under Civil Service, the appointment procedure is inevitably more complicated than in exempted organizations. Yet it would be possible, without detriment to the merit system, to simplify and shorten some of the routines by decentralizing to the departments certain functions now performed by the Civil Service Commission. This point is made clear by a review of the sequence of operations now necessary for filling a position in the Federal service.

In operating a civil service system it is necessary to establish registers of eligibles—lists of applicants qualified to fill each type of position, arranged according to an impartial determination of relative merit. This activity is divided along processive lines between the Commission's Examination and Application Divisions. The initial steps are described by the Civil Service Commission's "Division Organization Manual" in the following way:

> The request for a new examination usually originates in the Certification Division when it has a call or when it anticipates calls from appointing officers in the Government agencies for eligibles which cannot be properly met from current registers. . . . The requests for announcements are forwarded to the Stenographic Unit of the Examining Division, where they are recorded and indexed, and referred to the Assistant Chief of Division for designation of an examiner to handle the announcement. The request is then transmitted to the Examination Control Unit where the files of past announcements in similar fields are reviewed, and those closely related are attached to the request, which is then forwarded to the Medical Unit for determination of the physical requirements. The file is then sent to the examiners assigned to the actual drafting of the entrance requirements as to education and experience.[6]

---

[4] Nothing said here should be construed as a reflection on any political party, or even on the institution of patronage itself. Such considerations, however important they may be, are outside the scope of this work. The writer's only complaint, in the present instance, is that the patronage-dispensing mechanism, from a procedural point of view, did not operate more effectively.

[5] Since the appointments were "back dated," employees were paid from the time they began to work.

[6] United States Civil Service Commission, *Division Organization Manual*, Third Edition (1939-1940), Volume 3, pp. 34-35.

ADMINISTRATIVE PROCEDURE

The preparation of the announcement is a task demanding skill and exactness since it is necessary "to make the specifications, such as age and education or experience, sufficiently strict so that too many who are entirely unfit will not apply and at the same time not so strict as to eliminate those who could do the work." [7]

The examiner who drafted the announcement forwards it, on a prepared form, setting forth the general provisions applicable to all announcements, to the Stenographic Unit, where it is reviewed for form and general conformity with established procedure, and typed in draft form. This draft is then returned to the examiner for his approval, and referred to the Examination Control Unit, where a brief is made of changes from former announcements for the information of officials reviewing the proposed draft. Upon its return to the Assistant Chief of the Examining Division, a conference is called of the Committee on Announcements. The new announcement is compared with similar previous announcements; questions of language, grade, salary, and qualification are reviewed, and attention given to matters affecting policy. It may be necessary to bring these changes to the attention of the department concerned for comments and suggestions. Any changes occurring as a result of this study by the Committee are incorporated in the draft of the announcement by the Stenographic Unit, after which the announcement goes to the Chief of the Examining Division. Finally, unless it is for an examination which is already standardized, the announcement is reviewed by the Executive Director and Chief Examiner [8] and by the Commissioners.[9]

Approved announcements, except for positions to be filled through the district managers, are forwarded to the Information and Recruiting Division, which arranges for their production by the Government Printing Office and distributes them throughout the country.

Incoming applications are received by the Application Division, which sorts them, and checks them for age, citizenship, etc. If the examination has educational or experience requirements the papers are then sent to the Examining Division to be checked on qualifications in the case of "assembled" (written) examinations, or for rating if the examination is "unassembled." The applications of those who have passed are later returned to the Application Division for more detailed scrutiny, at which time applicants are given an opportunity to correct or complete their applications if necessary.

Meanwhile, papers for written examinations are being prepared by the Examining Division, going through a routine similar to that of the announcements. It is of course necessary to preserve secrecy so that questions will not be improperly divulged. Arrangements are made with local boards to hold the examinations. The papers are

---

[7] *Ibid.*, p. 36.
[8] This is the title of a single official.
[9] *Op. cit.*, p. 37.

ADMINISTRATIVE EXECUTION—PERSONNEL

then returned to the Examining Division where they are graded by examiners who specialize in the technical field involved. In "unassembled" examinations, the applications, together with the supporting papers, theses, etc., are graded in much the same way.[10]

After the examination ratings have been determined, the ineligible papers and all reports of rating (both eligible and ineligible) are sent to the Application Record Section where the index cards for the applications are drawn from the files and sent, together with the papers, to the Examination Record Section. Here the ratings are noted on the cards and the ineligible papers sent to "dead files" in the Correspondence Division. The reports of rating are returned to the Application Record Section where they are kept until the register is established, when all reports of rating are mailed to the competitors at one time.

The Application Record Section forwards eligible papers to the Certification Division, which prepares record cards containing names and addresses, ratings, acceptable salaries, and other pertinent information. These cards constitute the register, which is turned over to the appropriate certification-unit (such as clerical, professional, etc.) which supplies eligibles to departments are requests are received.

There is a considerable sequence leading up to the request for eligibles by a department. Before a position can be filled it must be established. To do this, or to change the classification [11] of an existing position, the personnel office of the department concerned must prepare a classification sheet allocating the position as to service and salary grade and send it to the Personnel Classification Division of the Commission for approval. This division generally allocates simpler positions which conform in all respects to existing standards (clerks, stenographers, etc.) as requested without special inquiry,[12] but classifications of an unusual character or involving "complex or high-grade" positions are assigned to investigators.

The investigator first studies the information given on the classification sheet and familiarizes himself with the organization and functions of the particular unit, section, or bureau in order to get the appropriate background and the organizational relationship of the position to the other positions in the unit. He then contacts the classification officer of the department concerned, after which the employee's supervisors and the employee himself are questioned. When the employee is interviewed (preferably at his own desk), exhibits of his work are observed, and he is given an opportunity to submit any facts which he considers important in the allocation of the position. If the position is a vacancy (frequently the case), information is secured from the heads and supervisors of the organization in which the position is located. In many cases a study of material in the Commission's own files,

---
[10] See *Division Organization Manual*, Volume 3, p. 43.
[11] In terms of the Classification Act of March 4, 1923, as amended July 3, 1930.
[12] *Division Organization Manual*, Volume 1, p. 51.

ADMINISTRATIVE PROCEDURE

particularly the record of similar or allied positions, must be made for the sake of comparative analysis.[13]

The investigator's report is either approved by the Assistant Chief of the Division or returned for further investigation. The report is then submitted to the Chief of the Division and, in the case of positions paying $5600 or more, to the Chief Examiner and the Commissioners. The department is then notified that the position has been approved.

Once a position has been established an appointing officer [14] may initiate a request for eligibles. The preliminary operations within departments are sometimes complicated, involving review of the required qualifications by a number of bureau and department officials. Sometimes there is also an excess of paper work, such as the transcribing of the request from a bureau form to a department form and then to a Civil Service Commission form.

The Commission's Certification Division has as its operating objective "twenty-four hours service" on requests for eligibles. It is not always possible to meet this standard, because a variety of technical factors affecting "availability" must first be considered and because in many cases the need for special qualifications over and above those set up for the regular as a whole makes "selective certification" necessary. Eligibles are certified in groups of three,[15] their entire files (applications, examination papers, reference letters, theses, etc.,) being sent to the department, which routes them to the appointing officer. This official may either select on the basis of the papers before him, or he may (as is more usual) correspond with and/or interview the applicants before making his choice. Appointment is offered directly by the appointing officer, on behalf of his agency, and acceptance obtained before recommendation is made to the personnel division. As a rule, the certificate of medical examination by a recognized Federal medical officer must be approved by the Commission before appointment.[16] Formal appointment is usually made by the director of personnel of the department or agency concerned, on the basis of the Civil Service certificate, the appointing officer's recommendation, and

---

[13] *Ibid.*, p. 52.

[14] This term is generally used, as here, to mean the official who actually selects the appointee, not necessarily the one who legally appoints.

[15] If more than three are certified, only the first three may be considered. However, if one of these declines appointment or fails to answer the letter addressed to him the fourth name may be considered, and so on.

[16] If appointment is made before the medical certificate has been accepted by the Commission and it is then rejected, the appointment is voided. To eliminate this contingency, appointments are seldom made before its approval, except in emergencies.

the notice of approval of the medical examination. Notification is then sent to the appointee, who reports for duty.

The number of steps in the classification and appointment procedures under Civil Service varies with the requirements of each case. The length of the sequence depends, more or less, on the number of offices which take part. While some speeding up can be, and in several departments is being, accomplished by reducing the operations which occur before requests are made to the Commission, any fundamental simplification will probably require some re-distribution of personnel functions. The volume of Federal personnel work is necessarily enormous, requiring a large and complex organization with highly specialized subdivision of work. Consequently, the administrative sequences within the Commission tend to be fairly long. Although purely routine actions are handled with reasonable expedition, any case outside the normal (involving, for instance, slightly unusual qualifications, eligibility questions, etc.,) requires special routing and is consequently delayed.

It is generally recognized that the Civil Service Commission is woefully undermanned, and that a certain acceleration of the work could be realized by merely enlarging its units. It is quite probable, however, that the volume of personnel work in the Federal Government has grown beyond the amount which can advantageously be handled in full detail by a centralized body, no matter how well managed. There seems to be an optimum size for organizations in each line of activity, beyond which they become progressively less efficient, for reasons directly attributable to their size. It may be that the Civil Service Commission has reached that point, though it is not yet definite that this is so. However, the possibility of shortening the procedures of classification and recruiting by decentralizing to the larger departments and agencies certain activities now concentrated in the Commission is at least worth investigating.

POSSIBLE CHANGES IN CIVIL SERVICE OPERATION

In recent years there has been a consistent movement toward supplementing the Civil Service Commission by the creation of elaborate personnel offices in the several departments. Much care has been taken to staff these units with highly qualified experts in the various branches of personnel management, and hardly a Federal agency now exists which does not have competent classifiers, examiners and investigators, employee relations technicians, and statisticians. It is therefore much safer to entrust to departments greater responsibility

ADMINISTRATIVE PROCEDURE

for operating the merit system, particularly as it relates to specialized line activities, than it would have been six or eight years ago. It is desirable to do so, not only in order to utilize fully the abilities of the departmental personnel experts, but also to provide procedural simplification by carrying out detailed operations in units small enough to have short administrative sequences and reasonable work loads. Four of the six suggestions made here derive from this idea.[17]

As means of expediting and improving Civil Service procedure the following proposals are made:

1. *Decentralize preparation of specialized examinations.* While examinations for positions common to several or all departments (such as clerk, stenographer, laborer, messenger, mechanic, accountant, statistician, etc., and general technical occupations) can best be prepared by the Commission as at present, those for special positions peculiar to a department because of its functions (such as cotton technologist, forester, aeronautical inspector, etc.,) could be as well planned by department personnel officials in accordance with general policies and standards laid down by the Commission. A division of work of this sort, the details of which could be regulated by

---

[17] Decentralizing Civil Service operations is open, like many other proposals, to various objections, the validity of which would depend on how it is carried out. One official to whom the writer submitted the idea stated the following reasons against it:

"1. That to give the many agencies final control over examinations would result in favoritism, political manipulations, and a rapid breaking down of standards. . . . Instead of having one agency with one set of standards, you would have 50 agencies with 50 sets, with resulting chaos.

"2. Civil service examining is a profession. It requires training and experience. It should not be handed over to a widely scattered group without a background in this profession."

The answer to these objections can only be that special care would have to be taken to prevent them from materializing. In relinquishing the actual conduct of operations, the Commission should keep the function of control. It should set standards for compiling and grading of examinations, and it should enforce them by systematic inspection and frequent spot checks. It should review the operating procedures of department personnel offices to make sure there are adequate safeguards of impartiality, and it should order the removal of officials found guilty of irregularities. It should also provide the necessary training in examination technique.

It goes without saying that the Civil Service Commission should have power to demand any departmental records pertaining to personnel matters, and that it should have ample power to enforce its decisions. It should, with respect to those functions to be decentralized from it to the departments, have an authority comparable to that of the General Accounting Office in financial matters.

It would seem logical that the method of decentralized operation combined with centralized control would be no more fraught with danger in the handling of personnel actions than in the handling of money. Nor is such decentralization, so far as it is proposed, entirely a new experiment. The TVA, the State Department, and the armed forces have always operated independently with respect to personnel matters, yet no one would argue that a career service, with at least as much regard for merit as in the other departments, does not exist in these agencies.

working agreements, would assure line agencies of specifications suited to their needs, since departmental staff officials have a familiarity with operating requirements which an outside agency usually does not possess. It would also eliminate much of the delay caused by negotiation back and forth between the departments and the Commission over details. It would permit departments to deviate somewhat from the Commission's tendency to express qualifications in terms of narrowly channelized sequences of experience, which is necessary in a central agency to avoid an unmanageable volume of applications.

To prevent filing by persons who are not reasonably sure they can qualify it might be better to

2. *Charge a fee for Civil Service Applications.* Reasonable fees, ranging from $2.00 to $5.00, would limit the volume of applications. The proceeds could be made available to finance Civil Service work. Those who are not really interested in government employment or who are not sure they can meet the qualifications would be more or less automatically excluded. A parallel expedient, stricter grading of examinations for professional positions, has already had beneficial effects.

The Civil Service Commission should continue to handle the mechanical phases of printing papers and conducting examinations, as it alone has the facilities for doing so. But it would be desirable to

3. *Decentralize the grading of specialized examinations.* The present delay between the holding of an examination and the grading of papers often holds up the making of urgent appointments to specialized posts. The departments could do much of this work, particularly when they had prepared the examinations. Since the examiners in departments would presumably have a good knowledge of the subject-matter of the examinations, it would be possible to get away from the purely mechanical type of examination which has heretofore been usual in assembled tests. Of course there would need to be adequate safeguards to insure impartiality. Each rating would have to be made by someone who could certify that he was not acquainted with the applicant, except as the result of official interviews which are part of the examination. Registers compiled by departments could then be reviewed by the Commission, without too much loss of time. They would be administered by the Commission's Certification Division in the same way as other registers.

4. *Abolish veterans' preference and the apportionment.* Relative standing should be determined solely by merit. The apportionment of Washington positions by states favors those who have the good

fortune to come from the right state against others who may be more qualified. It is a relic from days of exaggerated sectionalism, when communication as we know it today did not exist. Veterans' preference tends to clutter up registers with applicants who are not sufficiently qualified, and causes repeated certification when veterans who do not seem suited for the jobs in question are rejected. The actual result of veterans' preference has been to build up a prejudice *against veterans* in the minds of many appointing officers.

5. *Decentralize classification.* Nearly every department and independent agency now has classifiers who have been thoroughly trained in the techniques of job analysis and correct allocation. Why not give them authority commensurate with their skill and experience? If the Civil Service Commission maintained control by issuing a standard manual of instructions, and by making periodic classification audits of each agency, changing erroneous allocations, this should prove an adequate sanction against deviating from established policy. It would still be possible for a department to refer to the Commission any classification about which it felt doubtful.

6. *Authorize departments to approve changes in status.* When the qualifications for a position have been established, the department personnel officials should be allowed to determine whether an employee proposed for transfer or promotion is eligible. Control could be maintained by submitting personnel actions to the Commission for post-approval, failing which the employee would revert to his original status.[18]

The foregoing considerations were specific applications of the idea urged throughout this book, that operation in any field should be decentralized so far as possible, without sacrificing adherence to basic programs, policies, and standards. Centralized staff operation, in personnel, procurement, building management, or any other field is only justified so long as it results in greater economy and efficiency which is not outweighed by increased procedural complexities. As an organization grows, it reaches a point at which the value of a central staff agency is negatived by the complexity of its administrative structure and sequences, and at which the subordinate units have grown sufficiently to support complete staff mechanisms of their own. This point varies with respect to different staff activities; for instance, it is extremely doubtful whether more than a limited centralization

---

[18] The Civil Service Commission has recently authorized departments to approve changes in status in the first three grades of the clerical service, in exactly the manner proposed here. *Departmental Circular No. 257*, April 26, 1941.

ADMINISTRATIVE EXECUTION—PERSONNEL

of purchasing for a Federal department (let alone the entire Government) is profitable. Beyond the optimum size for efficient operation, staff agencies should progressively divest themselves of detail, bending their efforts toward definition of objectives, planning of model organizations and standard operating procedures, and exercise of broad-gauge control. The Civil Service Commission, like the Procurement Division, can serve best by concentrating on the improvement of policy and technique, and by promoting the legislative and administrative changes needed to delegate as much as possible of the detailed work to the departments.

Chapter IX

ADMINISTRATIVE CONTROL— THE CONCEPT OF CONTROL

CONTROL is the third major phase of administration. Following closely upon planning and execution, it seeks to make sure that performance is proceeding according to plan and remaining consistent with policy. It may be general or particular, applying either to overall accomplishments or to operating details. On each level of administration we find control operations: tasks consisting of supervision and review of work assignments, and authorization and approval of specific acts.

Control exists at various points in our political and business machinery. It is only necessary to mention in passing the external controls exercised upon administration: by legislatures and courts in the Government and by stockholders and creditors in business. We are concerned here only with internal administrative control: that brought to bear by the responsible head of an organization and by his subordinates for the purpose of checking tentative accomplishments and evaluating final results.

> Control is the examination of results. To control is to make sure that all operations at all times are carried out in accordance with the plan adopted—with the orders given and with the principles laid down. Control compares, discusses and criticizes; it tends to stimulate planning, to simplify and strengthen organization, to increase the efficiency of command and to facilitate co-ordination.[1]

That this rosy picture of control is seldom duplicated by the actual processes and mechanisms found in administrative establishments is not due to inherent unsoundness in the idea of control but to mistakes in choosing and applying control devices. Some administrators make a fetish of detailed control, strewing clearances and reports promiscuously about them without being aware that they are multiplying the work of their subordinates and slowing down production. The best systems of control are carefully planned, simple

---

[1] Henry Fayol, "Administrative Theory in the State," Gulick and Urwick, *Papers on the Science of Administration*, p. 103.

ADMINISTRATIVE CONTROL CONCEPTS

in their operation, and interfere as little as possible with the normal flow of business. Within reasonable limits, the best control is the least control.

It is important that overcontrol be avoided. The need for a proper balance between freedom and control is discussed by George H. Shepard as follows:

> We realize that in industry a subordinate must have discretion to deal with the unstandardized conditions with which he comes in contact. The same thing holds true in all management. To tie a subordinate down any closer than that by strict detailed orders destroys his ability to get results. At the same time wide discretion of subordinates impairs the effectiveness of the higher control. As an undertaking increases in magnitude the importance of the higher control increases as some higher power of the magnitude. Finally this impairment definitely limits the size of the undertaking with which success is possible.[2]

This brings us to a concept which is very important for the administrative analyst—the *span of control*. This is the limit within which any one administrator can exercise direct supervision, without delegating executive power to subordinates or intermediaries. The span of control has been the subject of much historical and mathematical research. Studies have been made of the hierarchical and functional structures of ancient and modern armies and churches,[3] and progressions have been plotted to show the number of direct and group relationships which can exist between a supervisor and any number of subordinates. It has been concluded in some quarters that an executive should never give direct access to more than six subordinates in the bottom layers of an organization or three at the top.[4]

The "three-to-six" estimate of the span of control is useful for abstract investigations and also for tentatively planning organization structures in situations where operating conditions cannot be predicted. Its applicability to practical situations, however, is obscured by *ceteris* which refuse to stay *paribus*. The workable span of control depends on the kind of operations supervised and the environment in which they are carried on, the form of organization, the types of papers handled, the executive decisions required, the legal limitations on administrative discretion, the qualifications of subordinates, and

---

[2] George H. Shepard, "The Problem of a Planned Economic Order," *Bulletin of the Taylor Society and the Society of Industrial Engineers*, November, 1934, pp. 22-28.

[3] Mooney and Reiley, *The Principles of Organization*, 1939, Chapters 6-7, 12-17 particularly.

[4] V. A. Graicunas, "The Span of Control," in Gulick and Urwick, *Papers*, etc., pp. 184ff.

ADMINISTRATIVE PROCEDURE

even the political background. Within the limits of the objective situation the span may still be varied by changing the methods of control. The span of control is determined by the volume of work required in controlling rather than by the number of people whom the controller directs. The area which an executive can cover effectively without intermediaries can be fairly well estimated by a survey of the work flowing across his desk, such as that suggested in Chapter IV. Unessential items should be marked for delegation; the rest should be classified by function and by unit of organization. By counting up the time spent on each function and in each organizational relation, over a long enough period to constitute a good sample, there can be shaped a span of control commensurate with the time required to handle each subject-matter and with the number of minutes in the working day.

The simplest control device is incomplete delegation of function, in which the superior officer retains specified executive powers in the operating fields of his subordinates. This has the advantage of bringing administrative sequences under official scrutiny before decisive steps are taken; it has the disadvantage of holding up operations in cases where inspection of papers is unnecessary. Under a fairly tight concentration of authority, such as prevails in some of the older Federal agencies, incomplete delegation brings under "clearance" not only major decisions within the fields of subordinate units but even minor ones when contact with the outside is involved. Thus, it is common to reserve the signature of interdivisional mail to division chiefs, and interbureau and outgoing letters are often signed only by bureau chiefs and their immediate assistants. This creates a heavy drain on the time and energy of high officials and lessens their spans of control. It induces unnecessary administrative moves in interdivisional sequences and gives rise to operating steps which, although in accord with the theoretical concept of contact up and down the lines of authority, violate the practical criteria of efficient routing.[5]

A variety of incomplete delegation is the divergent delegation of specialized processes in a line function which goes with staff functionalization.[6] Divergent delegation to staff units is normal for "professionalized" functions such as accounting, personnel, purchasing, etc. It is also found frequently in mechanical operations such as stenography and filing. Centralized offices performing or supervising

---

[5] See Chapter IV, "Evaluating an Administrative Sequence."
[6] See Chapter V, "Enter Staff Organization".

ADMINISTRATIVE CONTROL CONCEPTS

"business" functions provide technical control in the fields with which line administrators have least time to be concerned in detail. These areas may be as vital to success as the more strictly line phases of work. It is important that a proper balance be kept between staff processes and line objectives; basic administrative sequences should never be delayed for the sake of "perfect" filing, accounting, or copy work. There is always a danger that operating staff units will run away with things, so that particular processes become ends in themselves and basic purposes are obscured.[7]

It is unnecessary to emphasize that incomplete and divergent delegation are complementary phases of concentration of authority and staff organization, and are subject to the same procedural tendencies. The change in nomenclature results from looking at the same phenomena from another angle; from viewing, for instance, the withdrawal of accounting operations from a line unit not as a means of keeping the books more efficiently but as a way of checking the propriety and prudence of expenditures made by the line officials. We may think of the same situation in one way or the other depending on whether our main concern at the moment is getting things done or seeing that what is done is the right thing.

There are other control devices which, if well utilized, can yield as effective administrative information as the clearances that go with incomplete delegation. The most important of these are reports, conferences, and periodic inspection.[8] Any of these can be shaped to meet a variety of needs, and none need cause a block in the flow of regular activity. It is often thought that reports and conferences tend to waste time needed for "direct" action. This is true only if they are superimposed on detailed review and piecemeal supervision. However, if a single report is substituted for a hundred case-by-case clearances, or if a weekly production conference will do instead of routing most of an executive's business across the desk of his chief, then there is a net saving of time and money.

DIMINISHING RETURNS OF CONTROL OPERATIONS

Each task in an administrative sequence should contribute positively to the desired end. Each operating step should have a definite

---

[7] The relations between ends and means, likewise line and staff offices, may become particularly strained over the legal phases of a program. While the legal advisor must have a definite interest in over-all policy, he must restrain his instinct for legal perfectionism at times. He must also resist the temptation to eclipse a line executive's regular superiors.

[8] See also the remarks on the "general staff", Chapter XI.

ADMINISTRATIVE PROCEDURE

purpose, and each control step should prevent loss or waste of money and effort in proportion to its cost. While the value of a control step may be measured only if results can be observed both with and without it, it is a good general rule that each one added is worth less than the last. This is logical because each control operation leaves less need for the next one. To illustrate, let us suppose that a merchant is losing $1000 a month through errors in checking the credit of customers. He introduces an extra operation which catches half of these errors, saving $500. If the monthly cost of this operation is $200 the merchant's net gain is $300. Since there are still $500 worth of errors, he may introduce another control step, of similar cost and effectiveness. It catches half the errors—$250—and costs $200, so the merchant's second net gain is only $50. Other things being equal, the two control operations are justified, but if a third one is introduced it will catch only $125 worth of errors—$75 less than it costs. In the language of economists, the second control step is the marginal one and the third is submarginal.[9]

It must also be remembered that control steps are just as much subject to error as operating steps. This is particularly true when a large volume of business reduces "control" to the mere initialing of a stream of papers. Nor is there any guarantee that detaching and transferring portions of functions (divergent delegation) will produce better performance, unless there are specific points at which the special skills of staff officials can be brought into play. The possibility of error through misunderstanding may actually be increased. The vagueness of responsibility and the confusion which are banes of administrative sequences overloaded with control steps create a need for more rigid review at the end. For excessive control breeds more control. It is thus imperative that administrative controls be as simple as possible, and that those which delay operating sequences be cut to the bone.

It is always necessary to think objectively about questions of control, so that checks and reviews may be made sufficient and no more than sufficient to attain the end desired. In other words, we must be sure of our objective. Too frequently executives set up control devices without any idea why they are doing so. The real motive may frequently be fear—fear that subordinates will compromise them, fear of "sticking their necks out," fear of being "called on the carpet." That is why really good administrators are always men of consider-

---

[9] This idea was introduced in the writer's "A Note on Executive Planning," *Society for the Advancement of Management Journal*, July, 1937, p. 113.

ADMINISTRATIVE CONTROL CONCEPTS

able personal courage. The human mouse has to set up a maze wherein he can hide. He hates responsibility, he is afraid to delegate, he trusts neither his own judgment nor that of another, and he always evades answering important questions. It is this type of personality that is responsible for most of the needless red tape in administrative organizations.

Control, like any other phase of administration, should be planned. The objective should be made clear and the best means to attain it rationally determined. The planning of control should start with analysis of the functions and sequences which are to be controlled. The total objectives and those of each component task in relation to the whole should be drawn from authoritative sources. From the data obtained through the three types of administrative analysis the following factors which relate particularly to the problem of control can be determined:

1. *Operating Standard*—What characteristics must the finished product have to achieve the objective? What is the "tolerance," i. e., the permissible degree and frequency of variation from the standard?

2. *Normal Deviation*—In how many cases arising under the function or sequence, in proportion to the total load, are there deviations from the standard greater than the tolerance allows? Are they more frequent than the tolerance will admit? What are the consequences of these deviations?

3. *Control Observation*—What ways of observing operations under way and finished products will detect deviations? What kind of person is best qualified to observe, and where in the organization should he be located to best assure corrective action?

The best kind of control for any set of operations is the simplest and most decentralized which will apply the operating standard within the limits of tolerance. For instance, to get back to purchasing procedure, the operating standard in buying through competitive bidding is the acceptance of the lowest bid (with due consideration of discounts, freight rates, etc.) which meets the specifications. The tolerance varies with circumstances; in Federal purchasing it is theoretically zero but actually is determined by the probable magnitude of deviations and the cost of 100 per cent control in the particular case.[10] Whatever the particular activity, standard, and normal devi-

---

[10] The Comptroller General has ruled that purchases from bidders other than the lowest are not proper charges against public funds and that contracting officers are

ation involved, it is always better to obtain compliance by placing fully qualified people in divisional and field executive jobs, and by training them to produce what is required, rather than by relying on second-rate performance plus centralized correction. Control should begin with the job itself; the man who does it should know what standards he will be judged by, and should be trained to apply them to his work as he goes along. In many types of work the most effective control is obtained by encouraging voluntary adherence to a standard.

CONTROL OF COMPLEX ACTIVITIES—DANGER OF DUPLICATE ADMINISTRATION

In administering large and complex undertakings, particularly in new fields of endeavor, more elaborate controls are needed, both because of the ramifications of each problem (and hence the more serious consequences of mistakes) and because the subject-matter may be so technical that controls must be highly specialized. This is particularly true of such public activities as housing, flood control, power development, reclamation, and resettlement; in business, it applies chiefly to the launching of new products and new marketing schemes.[11] In these fields the operating standards include engineering, economic, legal, social, psychological, and frequently political factors, and their application requires the participation of experts in each of these fields. In setting up control operations, provision must be made for adequate review of plans, proposals, and technical determinations by the proper professional people. From a procedural point of view it is important that these specialized control operations be synchronized and so far as possible consolidated. It is also important that the controlling officials remember that they are not primarily the executors of the work they are reviewing. Control should always be specific and so far as practical, appear in terms of definite standards. If a project plan coming up for review meets the standards, it should as a general rule be passed, even though it may not be framed in exactly the same way as the controlling officer himself would have done it.

It is very easy for an action agency, particularly a new one not yet

---

personally liable for mistakes. In practice, however, no officer is ever assessed except when charged with collusion or other irregularity. The rigidity of the original interpretation has been gradually modified to recognize the cost of control steps. A-66668 of October 31, 1935; A-84043 of March 5, 1937, 16 C. G. 815.

[11] The Department of Commerce Bulletin, *Check Sheet—Introduction of New Consumer Products* (1935), says that "there are literally scores of studies which must be made, if a new product is to be successfully placed on the market," and it lists seventeen fields for investigation.

settled down, to suffer from administrative paralysis caused by duplication of activities. This may stem from the existence of multiple units with identical or overlapping jurisdictions or from repetition of work by individual units. It may be a symptom of either too little control or too much or—paradoxically enough—too much *and* too little. There may be too much haphazard control over individual plans and decisions, and too little delegation of power to act independently, and at the same time not enough control in terms of definite standards of accomplishment and of orderly administration.

Control mechanisms should be planned not only to produce a definite result but to do so in the simplest and shortest way. Preferably they should not delay functional operations, but if they must do so, the stoppage should be as brief as possible. Reports and inspections are always preferable to clearances where they will effectuate the operating standards: clearances and reviews should be scheduled and subject to time limits. The various technical phases of a project should be examined at the same time rather than in succession, and if necessary a co-ordinator should synthesize the various professional opinions. Due allowance should always be made for the motion delay of control steps and the flow of work planned accordingly, so that operating officials will not be left twiddling their thumbs.

For unstandardized executive work it may not be possible to work out the same kind of standardized and specific controls which can be set up for recurrent major projects of the same general kind. But even in a job where each day's work is different, a survey is likely to show a greater number of recurrent subjects and situations than would be suspected offhand. The best control to apply to a shifting work load is thorough education in over-all policy, and a common-sense classification of subjects which will help the subordinate to perceive what he should bring to his chief's attention and what he may dispose of on his own account.

Attention should be paid to the practical span of control—the limit on the volume of work an administrator can do. Control operations should be assigned, not in terms of theoretical responsibilities, but to fit the specific situation. For instance, an executive who is away on field trips half the time should not be asked to sign all of a division's outgoing correspondence or to clear requisitions for supplies. Nor should one whose duties include minute supervision of a number of subordinates be expected to perform technical reviews requiring intensive analysis. If the volume of control work which

ADMINISTRATIVE PROCEDURE

an administrator cannot get rid of is still too much for one man, he should have a sufficient number of executive assistants [12] to be extra eyes and ears for him. By collecting the information he needs to make rapid decisions, and by relieving him entirely of many minor affairs, they can help him to dispose of each matter promptly and thoroughly.

Most important, control operations should be kept down to the minimum. Efficient procedure is simple procedure with short administrative sequences. Controls should be consolidated and made as effective as possible after careful study of operating methods, objectives, deviations, and techniques of observation. Control should be **high** in quality and low in quantity.

---

[12] These executive assistants would constitute a "general staff," using the word "staff" here in its narrower sense to mean those who help an administrator in planning, executing, and controlling. A staff assistant of this sort would not usually be a technician in any particular "staff function".

To avoid confusion in the use of the word "staff" care has been taken to provide footnotes whenever it is used in this limited sense. When no notes appear, it always means an administrative function based on process, or something pertaining to such a function.

Chapter X

ADMINISTRATIVE CONTROL—
A PATTERN OF CONTROL

THE previous chapter dealt with control in a general way: with what it is supposed to accomplish, with ways of applying it, and with its procedural implications. Problems were presented in terms of administration in general; it was necessary to be abstract so as to keep from being too particular. This theoretical discussion can best be supplemented by a factual survey of the control mechanism of a real organization, in order to see how the various problems are met when they arise in concrete cases. What is to be described here may seem empirical and not related to theory at all. Techniques are often developed without reference to theory, to meet practical situations. If these techniques work it will usually be found that they are perfectly in accord with theoretical principles.

For illustration there has been chosen the Forest Service, one of the bureaus of the Department of Agriculture discussed in the chapter on planning, both because this organization has systematically studied methods of administration longer than any other Government agency or private concern, and because it has made available a great deal of information about its administrative techniques. It is generally considered to be a well-managed bureau, with a notable absence of "red tape" and bureaucratic confusion.

The Forest Service is generally responsible for developing and effectuating a national policy for conserving, improving, and utilizing the 630,000,000 acres of forest land in the United States. Its activities, which have an economic and social rather than a merely technical orientation, include the direct management of 158 National Forests and 37 "Purchase Units" (future National Forests) aggregating 175,843,405 acres,[1] and co-operative and supervisory service to state organizations administering more than 700 forests in 39 states. This

---

[1] Including land authorized for acquisition as of June 30, 1939. *Annual Report of the Chief of the Forest Service, Fiscal Year 1939.* Washington, 1939, Government Printing Office.

ADMINISTRATIVE PROCEDURE

includes administration of the Federal funds which are allotted, subject to certain restrictions, to states for improving forest practice on private land, and it also includes technical advice and service to private owners of forest land in every state.

The National Forests are managed on the "multiple-use" principle, under which each area furnishes timber, water, forage, wildlife, recreation, and other forest values, all at the same time, each resource being developed according to its relative importance. In addition to strictly forest operations, such as planting, timber sales, fire control (including the construction of firebreaks, lookout towers, telephone lines, and trails), and protection from insects and diseases, there is also development and management of grazing ranges and of camping and recreational facilities, as well as protection of water supplies, and erosion and flood-control work.

The Federal Government, under administration by the Forest Service, offers financial aid to and co-operates with 41 states and Hawaii to bring private and state-owned lands under protection from fire. The Forest Service also co-operates with the states and with private owners in the reforestation of areas in 41 states, Hawaii and Puerto Rico. With the aid of Federal funds administered by the Forest Service, state forestry departments or comparable agencies grow and distribute planting stock at low cost for the establishment of windbreaks, shelterbelts, and farm woodlands. The Forest Service also works with the states in aiding farm woodland owners in managing and caring for their timber, and through meetings, demonstrations, and consultations it promotes silvicultural and management techniques.

The Forest Service is also responsible for the Prairie States Forestry Project, a part of the Department of Agriculture's soil conservation and land-use program. From 1935 to 1939, it planted 10,954 miles of shelterbelt strips in the project area of the six Prairie States. Underlying the direct action programs administered by the Forest Service there is continuous research not only in the technical but also the economic and social aspects of forestry.

The volume and scope of this program make necessary a large and internally specialized organization. The Forest Service has nearly 500 permanent employees in Washington and more than 5,000 in the field, not including CCC and WPA workers. It sometimes employs as many as 20,000 additional temporary workers on construction and fire suppression. The Chief's Office in Washington is

ADMINISTRATIVE CONTROL—A PATTERN

divided into six branches made up of twenty-four divisions. Seven divisions are concerned with various phases of National Forest management, three with state and private forestry, two with land acquisition, five with forest research, three with the Civilian Conservation Corps, and there are four "general service" divisions of Fiscal Control, Personnel Management, Operation, and Information and Education. These divisions (except the research group) are represented, as their activities occur, in the ten regional offices, each headed by a Regional Forester. The regional offices supervise the National Forests (each under the charge of a Supervisor and divided into Ranger Districts) as well as the co-operative work with the states and with private forest land owners. The research divisions function through twelve regional experiment stations and a Forest Products Laboratory.

The management of an organization of such size raises many control problems, both of internal integration and of co-ordination with other Federal agencies and with state governments. While specialized controls can be and are used for particular recurrent operations, the most difficult problem, because it is the most indefinite, is that of general administrative control. By such control is meant observation of the whole performance of functions and sub-functions, and seeing that policy and operating standards are adhered to, even in the handling of non-recurrent (and sometimes unprecedented) problems. In this field all control devices must be used to some extent—incomplete delegation, inspection, reports, and other means.

It is here that the high executive runs into danger of violating the "span of control" principle; creating too large a work load for himself by going into excessive detail, particularly if he insists on case-by-case clearance rather than relying on inspection, reports, and conferences.[2]

Most important to effective control is properly planned delegation. As much as possible should be handled as far down the line as possible, and yet the administrator and each division chief should retain personal supervision over matters which involve over-all or divisional policy or which transcend the competence of subordinates. To obtain sufficient delegation without disintegration there must be a well-

---

[2] It should be remembered that the span of control is determined more by the volume of control work than by the number of people supervised. It is to this extent a problem with which the executive himself may deal. An official rendering close supervision to three subordinates, signing all their mail and reviewing each of their acts in detail, may have more to do than an official giving simply policy supervision to as many as eight or ten. At the same time he may very likely be less informed as to what is going on.

ADMINISTRATIVE PROCEDURE

understood classification of administrative and executive actions. Since these actions normally result in or are expressed by correspondence, working classifications are usually assignments of the signing of different types of letters and documents, allocating each to the proper hierarchical level and functional branch.

THE FOREST SERVICE CLASSIFICATION OF CORRESPONDENCE

Every organization has some system of standing assignments fo the signature of particular types of communication. When such a system is rigid, being a plurality of individual determinations rather than a set of principles, it tends to bring too many insignificant items across the desks of high officials. To avoid congestion in central offices there must be developed a flexible classification which can be applied by officials on each level. The Forest Service has undertaken to provide this by dividing all mail into seven general classes, specifying the qualitative characteristics of each, and leaving it to the good judgment of subordinates to determine in which class each item belongs. These types of correspondence are called departmental, service, divisional, regional forester-director, field divisional, forest, and ranger district. The first three occur in the Washington office, the last four in the field.

Departmental correspondence is described as follows:

> Communications to heads of Executive Departments other than Agriculture, to Committees of Congress, and, when matters of more than routine import are involved, to heads of Independent Agencies of the Federal Government such as the Bureau of the Budget, the Comptroller General, Works Progress Administration, et al. Replies prepared for signature of the Secretary of Agriculture or other officials of this Department in response to communications referred to the Forest Service by the Secretary's Office. Initial communications to any agency or any individual which involve Departmental policy or which, in the judgment of the Chief, Forest Service, are of sufficient importance to warrant signature by the Secretary or Acting Secretary.[3]

Departmental mail is subjected to the highest administrative control: personal review by the Chief of the Service or an Acting Chief, and then by appropriate officials in the Secretary's Office, whose inspection is intended to assure co-ordination with department policy. This class properly includes determinations of the highest quality,[4] having important subject matter, requiring the widest technical and administrative competence, and involving grave consequences in case

---

[3] *Forest Service Manual*, p. GA-14-1, 1.
[4] The word is used here in its technical sense. See Chapter IV, "Analysis of Individual Tasks."

ADMINISTRATIVE CONTROL—A PATTERN

of error in fact or judgment. There is some sifting within this class to weed out letters which have to be signed by the Secretary for purely formal reasons. Since department regulations and governmental custom require that all letters to certain agencies, such as the General Accounting Office, have to be signed by at least an Acting Secretary or, in some cases, by the head of a departmental staff office, routine communications of this sort are farmed out to divisional officials of the Forest Service for initialing.

Service correspondence is of somewhat lesser weight than departmental, since it does not commit any official outside the Forest Service. It includes the following:

> Communications to the Secretary of Agriculture, to the Directors of the major Divisions of his office (Personnel, Finance, Extension, Information, Research, Solicitor)[5]; to Chiefs of other Bureaus of this Department or of other Departments or Independent Federal Agencies when Departmental policy or matters of more than routine import are not involved; to Senators or Representatives in Congress when the communication from the legislator is addressed to the Chief, Forest Service, or an Assistant, or when either an initial communication or a reply involves Service (as distinguished from Regional or other field unit) policy or action. Any and all other correspondence which, in the judgment of an Assistant Chief, Division Chief, Regional Forester or Director, is sufficiently important to warrant signature by the Chief, Forest Service, or Acting Chief.[6]

This class of correspondence receives no departmental clearance, but is subjected to the highest control within the bureau. While departmental correspondence is always addressed to persons outside the Forest Service, service correspondence may be internal; for instance, orders to Regional Foresters which establish bureau policy and instructions to division chiefs. The former may be initiated by a division or by several in collaboration, while the latter are usually prepared by the Chief's immediate office unless they deal with staff functions. Service correspondence is always signed by the Chief or Acting Chief and, when going to a region or laboratory, is addressed to the Regional Forester or Director.

Divisional correspondence, as its name implies, stays within the field of a single division, being defined as follows:

> Communications to Regional Foresters, Directors of Experiment Stations, Forest Products Laboratory, or other field units; other Divisions of the Chief's Office [the entire Washington office], or other agencies or individuals, on matters which do not

---
[5] The last four are now technically separate units rather than branches of the Secretary's Office, as formerly.
[6] *Forest Service Manual*, loc. cit.

ADMINISTRATIVE PROCEDURE

involve policy beyond the Division of origin, and which are not included in the Departmental (1) or Service (2) classifications.[7]

Communications of this type are not subjected to control outside the originating division. Each division in Washington may write directly to the Regional Forester on subjects within its field, and such letters are normally referred immediately to the regional counterpart of the Washington division. A letter from a division in Washington intended for the attention of *another* division in the field would, however, be addressed to the Chief of that division in Washington for forwarding, unless concerning only a routine matter of information. The first three classes of mail are mainly confined to business originating in Washington, including instructions to the field. Occasionally departmental and service letters are written in the field and sent in for signature. There are only two classes of regional correspondence, since the department (as distinguished from the bureaus) has no administrative officials in the field except the two Great Plains Co-ordinators.[8] Letters from the regional offices and experiment stations dealing with subjects of bureau-wide interest in the area, with inter-divisional questions, personnel actions, and the like, are classed as regional forester-director correspondence. This type includes:

> All communications to the Chief's Office; to other Regional Offices or Experiment Stations; to officers of Federal Departments, Bureaus, or Agencies (other than the heads of such units in Washington—see classes 1 and 2); to Senators and Representatives in Congress when a Congressional communication . . . involves only Regional or Station policy or action. Communications materially affecting the standing of an appointed employee; any other correspondence not in the Departmental (1) or Service (2) classifications which the Regional Forester or Director may prescribe by local standard for inclusion in this classification; or which, in the judgment of Assistant Regional Foresters or office chiefs of comparable status, are of such nature as to warrant signature by the Regional Forester or Director, or their designatees as "Acting."[9]

This classification of mail, all of which is signed by the Regional Forester or Director [10] and his immediate assistants, is more inclusive than that of service correspondence in Washington. But since the volume of business in a regional office is much smaller, the greater concentration is not so likely to produce congestion. On a par with

---

[7] *Op. & loc. cit.*
[8] Letters signed by these officials might properly be classed as "field departmental" correspondence. There are also a few field branches of the Departmental Solicitor's Office, but these are mainly concerned with the affairs of particular bureaus.
[9] *Forest Service Manual,* loc. cit.
[10] Of an Experiment Station.

ADMINISTRATIVE CONTROL—A PATTERN

Washington divisional correspondence is the field divisional, consisting of:

> All correspondence with Federal, State, and private agencies dealing with matters within the field of the Division or Office and not covered in the Department (1), Service (2) or Regional Forest-Director (4) classifications foregoing.[11]

Field divisional correspondence does not usually pass through the office of the Regional Forester or Director; each division writes directly to Supervisors of National Forests and outsiders on matters within its field.

The two remaining classes, forest and ranger district, cover all correspondence signed in the offices of National Forest Supervisors and of their subordinates, the District Rangers. These offices contain from 7 to 40 and from 1 to 3 respectively, and do not need formal decentralization, although the Forest Supervisors do, in some fields, delegate the signing of mail.

The Forest Service classification is designed to apply enough control, but not too much, to each communication and to the executive act behind it. The important point is that the decision as to how much control is necessary lies in many cases with the official who is to be controlled. Standard routings have been established for many kinds of recurrent letters, but for non-routine matters the Chief of the Service must decide whether the Secretary of Agriculture should sign; the Division Chiefs are responsible for seeing that the Chief of the Service receives for review each item important enough to warrant his attention, and so on down the line.

This "honor system" of control in execution depends for its success on a number of factors which exist in the Forest Service and may or may not be found elsewhere. There must be thorough and integrated planning. There must be complete confidence between the Chief and his assistants in charge of divisions and regional offices: suspicion and friction would lead inevitably to extended detailed control. There must be uniformity of purpose, custom, and policy, based on traditions, ideals, and on a process of education within the organization. And then there must be a clear understanding of where individual fields of jurisdiction begin and end.

OTHER MEANS OF ADMINISTRATIVE CONTROL IN THE FOREST SERVICE

The fact that the Forest Service has decentralized control over

---
[11] *Ibid.*, p. GA-14-1, 2.

ADMINISTRATIVE PROCEDURE

detailed execution indicates that its other means of co-ordination are well developed. Service-wide understanding of objectives and operating standards is fostered through the Forest Service Manual, which provides a working fund of information on all phases of technique and administration. The manual is not a set of ex-cathedra regulations concocted by an inner circle, but represents the basic experience and objectives of the various operating units. This is assured by the democratic process by which the various sections of the manual are prepared.

> The various functional Divisions of the Chief's Office are initially responsible for all original and amendatory text growing out of their respective fields of effort. Operation [the Division of Operation in the Chief's Office] will receive all text as written or reviewed and approved in the Divisions, edit solely from the standpoints of arrangement and form of presentation, place in line for final approval, and, upon such approval, follow through on the production and distribution phases.
>
> The appropriate Assistant Chiefs and the Chief or Acting Chief will review and approve all text prior to publication.
>
> Features of policy or practice concerning which there may be important question may be referred to field units for preview and comment before inclusion in the Manual.[12]

The Regional Foresters and the Directors of experiment stations are expected to supplement the manual by issuing administrative handbooks which relate the objectives and standards of the service to local problems. These handbooks "should present clearly and concisely the duties and responsibilities of the regional, station or other local organization, and the organization structure itself."[13] They need not be cleared through the Washington office; field officials are trusted to integrate their handbooks with the parent manual and to avoid duplication or conflict. The manual and the administrative handbooks are further supplemented by a series of technical handbooks, developed over a long period, which set forth the "best ways" to do various recurrent jobs. These cover fire-fighting, surveying, appraising and measuring timber, range, wildlife, and water management, and various phases of engineering.

As described in an earlier chapter,[14] planning in the Forest Service extends down through the regional and forest organization to the District Rangers, who are on the "firing line." This produces a high degree of natural co-ordination. The plans coming from various units are consolidated in "project work budgets" which incorporate all

---
[12] *Forest Service Manual*, page GA-C2-1, 1.
[13] *Ibid*, p. GA-C2-2, 1.
[14] Chapter VI, "Planning in the Forest Service."

ADMINISTRATIVE CONTROL—A PATTERN

work "other than that which would normally be performed by the regular year-long executive, technical, clerical, and facilitating personnel." [15] These budgets and the normal recurrent budgets are based on operating studies and job-load analyses carried on at each administrative level. These studies not only provide control information—analysis of past accomplishment and data for planning future activity—but they are also a means of training forest officers. By making everyone conscious of objectives and operating standards the need for detailed control of performance is reduced. The men know how to do their jobs because they have had a hand in planning them and in judging their own work. The objective aimed at (although not yet completely realized) is to have each District Ranger and each member of a Supervisor's staff carry on some administrative study as part of his regular duties. Studies are required to have (a) the preparation of a carefully drawn-up program covering immediate needs; (b) uniformity of method; (c) rigid regularity in making observations; and (d) adequacy of reports.[16]

The Forest Service program of operating studies is valuable not only for judging performance, but as a source of information for budgeting. The comparative needs of operating units are evaluated objectively, which minimizes the tendency to apportion funds according to the debating ability of Supervisors and Rangers. In each regional office there is a special consultant in charge of administrative studies who reviews the operating studies made on the forests, suggests improvements in method, and arranges for the pooling of experience. This officer is also in charge of integrating administrative and research [17] activities.

In line with the Forest Service's policy of decentralized administration, the application of operating standards is entrusted in the first instance to the officials directly performing each kind of work, and then to their immediate superiors. The standards themselves have been gradually developed over a long period and are set forth in detail in the manual, which, with the administrative handbooks, contains detailed instructions regarding each function and subfunction. The service-wide standards are supplemented by regional standards promulgated by the Regional Foresters.

---

[15] *Forest Service Manual*, p. GA-C3-3, 1.
[16] "Administrative Research in the Department of Agriculture," a report prepared by the writer on the basis of personal investigation and transmitted June 23, 1939.
[17] This includes the activities of the Division of Research, whose duties are confined to "pure" research on scientific subjects.

ADMINISTRATIVE PROCEDURE

Adherence to operating standards is further insured through a comprehensive program of inspection. Each Forest Supervisor makes frequent trips to his ranger districts, to instruct on execution of plans and application of approved methods, and to co-ordinate the activities. The regional offices provide "functional inspection;" officials of each division look after the work in their respective fields. To avoid the confusion of multiple authority, regional divisional inspectors make their recommendations through the Regional Forester to the Supervisor, who relays them to the Rangers. The Regional Foresters and their assistants make tours of "general inspection" during which they observe the accomplishment of the program as a whole within each National Forest and in co-operating state and private forests. There is always special attention as to whether the expenditures for the various activities are properly balanced, or whether undue emphasis is being placed in one or two fields. Regional inspection is supplemented by periodic visits of Washington officials. Each of the more important officers in the Chief's Office is expected to spend a good deal of his time in the field. Those in divisions give "functional inspection" to their several activities, while the Chief and his staff make "general integrating inspections" of the whole work of the different regions.

"General integrating inspections" are carefully planned as primary instruments of control to bring to the Chief of the service the information he needs for over-all appraisal of progress and for the translation of experience into policy. Each region is inspected about once every third year, at which time two Washington officials, either Assistant Chiefs of the service or division heads, spend six or seven weeks visiting the regional office, the National Forests, state and private forest lands, and the experiment stations. They consult with Forest Service personnel of all ranks, with representatives of other Government agencies, with state foresters and timber operators, and with representative citizens. Each major line and staff function is scrutinized, the inspectors keeping an eye open for possible improvements. Recommendations resulting from these inspections are seldom made from a purely technical point of view (as would be the case with "functional" inspection) but are based on long-range considerations. For instance, the instructions given to inspecting officials in 1937 called for attention to the following items, from a social as well as technical point of view:

1. Condition of the basic resource—the soil—primarily, and of the living resources dependent on it.

ADMINISTRATIVE CONTROL—A PATTERN

2. Major projects in the work program, including Research, and their organization. Objectives with past accomplishments and plans for the future.

3. The "spiritual" qualities of the administration . . . including (a) leadership shown both inside and outside the Service, (b) relationships with permittees, other users [of National Forest land] and the local public, (c) relationships between the administrative and Research personnel, (d) esprit de corps of the personnel, (e) general social philosophy, as expressed in plans, attitude toward various programs, etc., (f) sense of financial responsibility.[18]

These factors constitute a framework for arranging and interpreting the many facts, observations, and opinions which the inspectors encounter. They are not an outline for the report but a set of fundamental criteria to be kept in mind. This becomes evident upon even a casual review of an inspection report made according to these instructions. The report of the inspection of Region 8 (the Southern region, including the coastal states from North Carolina to Texas, Tennessee, Arkansas, and Oklahoma) covered the following subject-matter: [19]

I. Forest Service relationships in the South.
   a. With the public.
   b. With the State Foresters.
   c. Research and administration. Liaison between the research and administrative field services. Needs for co-ordination of program and policy.
   d. Forest Service Personnel. Morale.

II. The Major Resources.
   a. The forest growth.
      1. The condition of the forest resource and steps being taken to improve it.
      2. Trends in forest operation. Needs for future development of forests, fire protection, etc.
      3. Public demand for regulatory legislation.
      4. Forest Service transactions with the public. Use permits. Timber sales policy.
      5. Distribution of planting stock. Activities of state nurseries.
      6. Fire control.
   b. The recreation resource.
   c. The wildlife resource. Management problems arising from joint Federal-state game control.
   d. The water resource.
   e. The range resource. Problems of range management.
   f. Land acquisition.
      1. Alternate types of land.
      2. Abstracting and fiscal procedure.

---

[18] Forest Service, "Instructions for General Integrating Inspections," 1937.
[19] The outline is necessarily given in highly condensed form.

ADMINISTRATIVE PROCEDURE

III. The Forest Service as a Landlord.
    a. Policy considerations. Need for study of tenancy problems. Cost of houses.
    b. Possibilities of improving economic condition of tenants.

IV. Organization and Sense of Financial Responsibility.
    a. Overhead (regional office). Comparison with other regions. Analysis of volume of work supervised.
    b. National Forest organization and financial control. Advantages in dealing on a state-wide basis. Quality of financial management.
    c. National Forests as demonstration areas.
    d. Ranger district manning. Regional policy on local units.
    e. Possibility of subdividing the region.

V. Miscellaneous.
    a. Buildings. Ranger stations, fences, location of fire dispatchers. Research buildings. Roads.
    b. Paper work. Need to reduce volume of records and reports.
    c. Public relations. Evaluation.
    d. Washington office inspections.
    e. Joint activities with TVA.
    f. CCC program. Fiscal problems and economic effects.
    g. Research. Organization problems. Location of research stations in relation to regional office. Problems needing research.[20]

In order to cover effectively the wide range of Forest Service activity, the Regional Foresters and Supervisors need to (and always do) co-operate fully with the Inspectors, helping them to plan their itineraries to include a cross-section of the Region, and personally conducting them over a large part of the journey. The regional officials deal with the Inspectors with complete frankness, showing them the bad spots as well as the show-places, and pointing out difficulties and failures as well as successes. To make this possible the Inspectors must be equally frank; they are expected to discuss their reactions along the way, and to inform the Regional Forester [21] of the contents and conclusions of their report.

Once the report has been written—preferably before but sometimes after the inspectors have returned to Washington—it is considered at length by the Chief and his assistants in a series of staff conferences. Necessary elaborations are made by the Inspectors, and conclusions reached, on the basis of which the Chief writes a letter to the Regional Forester transmitting the report and giving both general and specific instructions on the subjects covered therein. The Regional Forester usually answers the Chief, commenting on the report, and outlining

---

[20] Forest Service, "Report of General Integrating Inspection in the Southern Region, 1937," by Earl W. Loveridge and J. A. Fitzwater.
[21] Also the Regional Experiment Station Director, so far as research activities are concerned.

ADMINISTRATIVE CONTROL—A PATTERN

the steps being taken to comply with the recommendations. The report and the Chief's letter [22] then become the basis of general policy, which is executed in the Region under the functional supervision of the appropriate divisions in Washington.

GENERAL PRINCIPLES OF CONTROL IN THE FOREST SERVICE

In developing its system of administrative control the Forest Service has kept away from the "line of least resistance"—it has resisted the bureaucratic tendency toward incomplete delegation and centralized clearance of executive decisions. It has endeavored instead to build up a sense of corporate responsibility, and a natural instinct against overstepping fields of authority or violating established policies and plans. That is, it promotes *self*-control, and minimizes *imposed* control. It has worked out a program of inspection and reporting which keeps the central office informed of progress, developments, and difficulties in the field, and a method of democratic participation in planning and observation which eliminates any suspicion of dictatorship from above.

Decentralized execution and control "after the fact" as practiced by the Forest Service require a precisely built organization. There must be no serious overlaps between fields of work, and the possibility of conflicting orders avoided by thoroughgoing voluntary co-operation between the several divisions. This is particularly true because the work of the service consists of closely interlocking functions rather than discrete areas of operation.

Control in the Forest Service flows along the lines of authority, which are functional [23] rather than hierarchical. This type of organization has been described as follows:

> Under the functional type orders are a joint product formulated by the various functional officers within whose spheres of activity such work may be. Each officer carries authority and responsibility for his respective part in the issuance of an order. He needs no further authorization either by direct approval or through tacit consent; his own signature is sufficent for the part he plays. . . .
>
> When the subordinate, by his possession and presentation of the facts, actually determines the decision, why not let him make it, subject only to co-ordinating and precautionary control by the superior executive.
>
> Authority, according to this view, should not arise from delegation but from function. In other words, the man who possesses the facts should be the man

---

[22] They are also historical records of progress.

[23] The functional type of administration indicated here, in which the functions are largely purposes and not processes of administration, should not be confused with "functionalism" as introduced in Chapter V and described in more detail in Chapter XII under the heading, "Functionalism in Administration".

who decides. Conformity to this rule would change the procedure of many companies which require "rubber stamp" decisions by higher executives.[24]

Adherence to this principle assures direct and simple administration. Sequences of all kinds flow directly to and from the officers contributing directly to the work: they consist almost entirely of operating steps with the absolute minimum of control steps. Control is kept within bounds—there are ample means of observation, criticism, and guidance, but there is no reversion to higher officials of tasks which can and should be done by subordinates. The top administrator and his staff,[25] as a result, have their time largely free for developing policies and for broad-gauge co-ordination and planning. Herein lies the secret of the Forests Service's reputation for consistent efficiency and quality of accomplishment.

---

[24] Henry P. Dutton, *The Principles of Organization*, New York, 1931, pp. 157-8.
[25] The word "staff" is used here in its limited sense.

Chapter XI

MANAGEMENT PLANNING

A DISTINCTION urged throughout this book is that between administrative purposes and processes. Both are subjects of planning, execution, and control; we have administration of *program* and administration of *procedure*. The first deals with the *what* of administration—the activity which is being run and all its specialized problems. The second deals with the *how*—the machinery of administration, the working relationships between individuals, and the digestion of major projects into practical tasks and sequences. The two activities have been called direct (program) administration and administrative (procedural) management. Each consists of planning, execution, and control within its proper sphere.

Administration and administrative management are distinct activities, even though their exercise is often intermingled. Their techniques are different, and they deal with different kinds of problems. For instance, program questions in an automobile company would be whether to use heavier gauge steel for fenders, whether to buy tires or make them, how much to charge for the car, and whether to carry a line of convertibles. But questions of procedure are whether to pay commissions through a Detroit bank or through local banks, whether to have letters signed by department heads only or by their subordinates, and whether to have departments in branch plants report to one or several executives in the home office. The two kinds of problem call into play different types of knowledge; the first can be best dealt with by those who know the automobile business as such, while the second demands a knowledge of administrative technique.

The relative importance of training and ability in the particular subject-matter and in administration as such varies according to the size of the enterprise managed. A man in charge of a small factory or a technical division of a government agency is essentially a specialist in his field. He plans, executes, and controls the process of manufacture, research, or regulation, as the case may be. His organization is not large enough to have complex administrative problems: he does not have to worry much about communication, routing of business, or demarcation of fields of authority. But when the plant manager is promoted to the presidency of his company or the division chief is placed at the head of his bureau, the picture changes. The new job is not just an extension of the old one; it contains new elements which require not just knowledge of the line activity but specialized skill in administration. The thoughts of Henri Fayol, the leading French exponent of scientific management, on this subject have been summarized as follows:

> Many of the failures to conduct large combinations successfully may be traced to lack of administrative knowledge in men who have been highly successful in charge of smaller concerns, that is in positions demanding a relatively larger proportion of technical capacity. A man with high administrative qualifications who has never been inside a steel or a biscuit works may succeed. A man with all the knowledge of biscuit making in the world, but who lacks the requisite level of administrative knowledge and capacity will certainly fail.
> Unless and until Fayol's thesis on this point wins universal acceptance, avoidable losses will occur.[1]

A "professional administrator" appointed to head a large concern or agency, but lacking technical knowledge in its specialized field of work, could operate successfully provided he had sound advice from specialists on technical policies. Fayol did not apparently consider the converse proposition, that a technician placed in charge might do equally well if problems of organization and procedure were solved for him by experts in administration. The important point is that in a large organization *both* technical and administrative knowledge must be brought to bear, whether through the person of a single official, or by experts in each field working together.

To be realistic, it must be recognized that the leadership of many, if not most, organizations is in the hands of people who have spent most of their lives in the particular fields in which these concerns operate. This will probably continue to be the case. Nor is this unreasonable, since administration exists only to carry out a program, and the head of an organization must be sure *what* he wants to do, which is not always easy.[2] Program and policy must always be

---

[1] L. Urwick, in *Papers on the Science of Administration*. A case in point is the taking over of the bankrupt St. Regis Hotel in New York, from 1934 to 1935, by Professor Raymond Moley of Columbia University. Professor Moley, who knew very little about the hotel business but a great deal about administration, made a notorious success of it.

[2] On this point, see White, *Public Administration*, p. 309.

MANAGEMENT PLANNING

sound in terms of the technique of the activity involved. They precede administration, determine and evaluate it, and re-shape its purposes. Without policy, administration cannot function. There is no use buying an expensive automobile, putting in gasoline, and starting out unless you know where you want to go. Administrative objectives should, of course, be conceived in terms of the whole field of activity and not just that part of it in which the administrator was formerly occupied. To this extent administrators should be "generalists" rather than specialists.

Fayol's apparent neglect of the need for policy is due perhaps to the fact that in his day business objectives were standardized and simple: to produce as much as possible with the least expenditure for men, materials, and overhead; to buy cheap and sell dear. Today, many axioms of a few years ago have dwindled to uncertainties, and administrators are beset with doubt as to where they should aim and what economic and political conditions to expect. This is particularly true in the Government, which is expected to shape policy not only for itself but for everyone else, and which is handicapped by having no private faucet at the fount of wisdom. The need for policy leadership during a time of economic crisis was well phrased by Leon Brown, a high official of the NRA, who in commenting on the management of that organization, wrote:

> Saving the lack of competent personnel, the lack of policy has been, perhaps, the greatest handicap to administration. So much of the work of the deputies has been so largely in the dark. Yet they have been so eager to be guided. Generally, they have not desired a loose rein; generally they have sought policy. When some morsel of policy has come to them, the avidness of their seizure of it has been almost pathetic. Most of them have been conscious of a vast willingness to strive, but uncertain of the direction in which their efforts should be put forth.
>
> Mind, I said this lack of policy was a handicap. I did not say it was a fault. It may have been unavoidable. Well I know that it is difficult to cut policy out of whole cloth. I know also that there may be periods when it is expedient to have no policy. I do not say that this was a fault of administration, but only that it was a handicap. The object of the observation is only to urge that, insofar as practicable, policy be broadened, detailed, amplified, so as to cover as much of the ground of conjecture as is possible.
>
> It is not extravagant to say that certainty and consistency of administration will result in exact proportion to the definiteness of policy, and that speed of administration will be much enhanced.[3]

The administrator must inevitably be concerned with program and policy, not only on the highest level of ultimate aims, but down

---
[3] Leon Brown, *N. R. A. Administration*, memorandum (unpublished) to the National Industrial Recovery Board, March 5, 1935.

ADMINISTRATIVE PROCEDURE

through each function until it reaches the individual task. He must be enough of a technician to know the possibilities and limitations of a sphere of activity, and to be able to relate it to the other fields of work, to other organizations, and to the public. He must supervise planning, and review proposals from a technical point of view; he must evaluate progress and accomplishment with the authority of specialized knowledge. This is why the Secretary of the Treasury must be a banker or an economist (preferably both), why the Secretary of Agriculture must have had practical experience with farming, and why the Federal Works Administrator must be an engineer. If experts versed exclusively in administration are appointed to these posts, their organizations may run like clockwork, but the basic responsibility for program planning and evaluation will have to be passed on to others.

Even if an administrator is an organization and management specialist as well as a technician, he will never have time for both policy supervision and administrative management. This point was also brought out by Brown, who said:

> Only when the administrative officer is permitted to delegate his *complete responsibility* so that he has *nothing to do*, will he have time really to do all that which is essential to proper execution. This may be a paradox, but it is so. Even when the administrative officer has delegated *all* his responsibility, he will still have a capacity load of observation, consultation, discussion, analysis, study, and planning.[4]

It goes without saying that the modern administrator must have assistants. If the distinction between the administration of technique and the technique of administration is observed, these will fall logically into two classes. First, there will be a "general staff" composed of officials who bear such titles as "Assistant Administrator,"[5] "Assistant to the Administrator," etc. These are said to be "extensions of his personality" and are charged with carrying out his plans and policies in detail. These men will handle most of the routine contact with line division chiefs; they will be avenues of guidance for subordinates and of information for the administrator.[6] But other assistants are needed—those who are experts in administration as such. These will not be concerned with the content of programs but

---

[4] Brown, op. cit. It would be more proper to say that the administrator should delegate the exercise of his authority, as he cannot escape the final responsibility for the work of his organization.

[5] An Assistant Administrator having direct supervision over certain divisions or units would not be included in this category. "Staff" is used in the limited sense here; see Footnote 3 in Chapter II and Footnote 12 in Chapter IX.

[6] For the development of the general staff, see Mooney and Reiley, *The Principles of Organization*, Chapters 17 and 18.

MANAGEMENT PLANNING

only with the means for carrying them out. They will be charged with devising the administrative structure, with planning the distribution, routing, and timing of business, and with working out means of administrative control. Such officials have various titles in different organizations, but here are called *administrative analysts*.[7] Their most significant duty is planning facilities and methods of administration. They might also be called management planners or even administrative managers,[8] since they not only plan administrative machinery but help to keep it running.

THE ORIGINS OF MANAGEMENT PLANNING

Although specialized planning of work methods has existed for a long time in industry, and in mechanized office activities such as underwriting and mail-order merchandising, its application to administration is fairly recent and is still in the experimental stage. In the past, heads of establishments have generally been expected to deal directly with organization and procedure as well as policy and program operations. Some separation of routine administration from policy making was achieved by appointing general managers who kept much detail away from the desks of presidents. But the managers were nearly always burdened with day-to-day tasks: they could rarely make any administrative studies except in their spare time. Research, such as it was, centered in the universities and was directed more toward the solution of limited problems in specialized zones than to administration *per se*. In governmental research the emphasis was on municipal and state affairs. In any case, the helter-skelter of the war period and the comfortable surpluses of the 1920's tended to keep *administrative* economy and efficiency from becoming a vital issue.

The trend toward the creation, in large organizations, of groups of experts divested of line functions and devoting their time to questions of administrative technique came slowly, and derived not from private business so much as from the Federal Government. The start was made in the Bureau of Efficiency, which existed from 1916 to 1932, the duties of which included "the investigation of duplication of work and methods of business in the various branches of the

---

[7] The term has been introduced in earlier chapters, but is first discussed in detail in the following pages.

[8] This term should not of course be construed as meaning that they usurp the functions of operating executives, but rather that they assist these officials in solving administrative problems.

139

ADMINISTRATIVE PROCEDURE

Government service".[9] This bureau suffered from having too broad and vague a field of authority: [10] its activities included duties which have since passed to the Budget Bureau, the General Accounting Office, and to the Civil Service Commission (of which it originally was a division). It had supervision over the efficiency rating system for Federal employees, an activity which belongs in the field of personnel and not of management planning. It also contributed to the formation of the present personnel classification scheme, and did considerable constructive accounting before the General Accounting Office took over that function. But it also did some pioneer work in organization and procedure, one of the most noteworthy projects being the investigation which led to the abolition of the nine sub-Treasuries in 1921. It is interesting to note that many of the Bureau of Efficiency's early suggestions, which went unnoticed at the time, have since been carried into effect. The bureau observed in 1920 that the Executive Branch of the Government was quite irrationally organized, and pointed out, among other things, that the Supervising Architect's Office and the Public Health Service did not belong in the Treasury Department, nor the Bureau of Public Roads in the Department of Agriculture. It outlined a scheme for a functional grouping of government agencies much like that which was initiated seventeen years later. It also proposed an agency to co-ordinate all Federal statistical work, and actually began to issue an informational bulletin quite similar to the *United States Government Manual* now published by the Office of Government Reports. The Bureau of Efficiency itself has, for all practical purposes, been restored to life by the creation of the new Division of Investigation and Administrative Management in the Bureau of the Budget.

There were also groups in various bureaus which worked intensively on administrative problems, such as the Field Supervisor's Office in the Bureau of Prohibition. But the real drive toward specialized management planning took place under the Franklin D. Roosevelt Administration. When in 1933 the Government had to develop a broad social and economic program to meet an unprecedented national emergency and get this program into operation as quickly as possible, there was no time for research on administrative technique. The "New Dealers" had to make the best possible use of existing government practices. When they set up the alphabetical agencies they were

---

[9] U. S. Bureau of Efficiency, *Annual Reports*, 1916-32.
[10] The Bureau of Efficiency was never closely associated with the President, but moved more in the sphere of influence of former Senator Smoot. White, *Public Administration*, p. 67.

MANAGEMENT PLANNING

forced to call upon "experts" from old-line departments. Accustomed neither to haste nor originality, these traditionalists could only cast the new agencies in the image of the old ones.[11] The result was that our moss-grown system of Federal administration came near collapsing under the strain. It was as if the owner of a cross-roads general store had been placed in charge of the A & P and had tried to run that concern by his usual business methods. It is not surprising that many "New Deal" agencies, organized on "Old Deal" principles, wallowed in bogs of red tape. The wonder is that they were not completely paralyzed.

Thus the stage was set for administrative reform. The New Deal brought into the Government many businessmen with a background of scientific management, and a number of students of public administration. The yeast began to ferment. The new administrators resented the "red tape." They began to devise short-cuts, and to rearrange their organizations to work more smoothly. As the pressure of the emergency subsided, there began a period of experimentation, during which administrators paid increasing attention to administrative mechanics. Realization of the complexity of the problem made it more and more apparent that administrative research, and the application of management techniques to administrative work, were a full time job and not just an interesting hobby for heads of establishments.

The first move in the direction of specialized management planning was to set up offices to handle the editing of written instructions. These were offshoots of the immediate offices of the administrators, or in some cases of the chief clerks. Every department and bureau had always followed certain standing rules of procedure in written form, variously called regulations, administrative memoranda, Washington and field instructions, etc.—usually drawn up by staff assistants to department heads, or by chief clerks, and in some cases by personnel heads, budget officers, etc. These rules did not constitute unified codes of procedure but were issued promiscuously in numbered or unnumbered series, often without indexes. In many offices there were several concurrent series, and a single subject might be dealt with in any or all of them. The result was the frequent need for scholarly investigation to find the laws and rules on originally simple matters.

The injection of large numbers of new personnel into the Govern-

---

[11] With several exceptions—among them the Tennessee Valley Authority, the organization of which was planned by outside experts in public administration.

ADMINISTRATIVE PROCEDURE

ment, many of them unfamiliar with administrative law and custom, made it essential to expand and codify written procedure to make it easier to "look things up".[12] A number of bureaus established special units to perform this function. These were called "procedure divisions," or given similar names, and were authorized to write or edit all printed and processed instructional material issued by the agency concerned. The assignment of functions of an early procedure division, that of the Resettlement Administration, read as follows:

I. To assist the Director in the performance of the functions listed in paragraph 3f, I, II, and III.
[the functions referred to are the general functions of all Division Directors as follows:
  I to advise the Administrator with respect to the policies coming within their scope.
  II to recommend standard procedures, forms, and instructions necessary, in Washington or the field, for carrying out the functions within their scope, making such research as is necessary therefor.
  III to observe, for the Administrator, the general application of such of the above as are approved, and to report thereon to the Administrator.]

II. To devise, assist in devising, or review all forms of organization, methods of procedure, forms, and space arrangements.

III. To handle the mechanics of classifying, writing, drawing, editing, recording, and issuing all material required to make the above effective, as charts, orders, instructions, notices, forms, layout plans, and the like, delegating to regional directors such authority as is necessary for expeditious handling.

IV. To draft charts, graphs, maps, pictograms, and like items for the Washington office.[13]

Although the authority given the first procedure divisions sometimes included, as in this case, authority to deal with management problems, their tendency was at first to concentrate on the production of written material, viewing it largely as a literary activity. Many of these divisions had lawyers and former teachers of English on their staffs, who were wont to polish the language without due regard to the organizational implications of the meaning. Some of these writers suffered from "lack of terminal facilities" and procedure manuals burgeoned into nine- and ten-volume encyclopedias. The result was that in some quarters procedure work fell into disrepute, and operating officials began to ignore formalized instructions.

---

[12] A comparable experience occurred in Germany during and immediately after the World War. See Brecht and Glaser, *The Art and Technique of Administration in German Ministries*, p. 14.

[13] Resettlement Administration, *Administration Order 2*, June 11, 1935. The Resettlement Administration has since been succeeded by the Farm Security Administration, and the statement quoted has been revised.

MANAGEMENT PLANNING

But the procedure writers learned by doing. As they acquired practical experience they became increasingly aware of organization problems and the need to simplify both administrative routines and the instructions expressing them. Originally bulky documents were condensed, legalistic phraseology gave place to simple English, and the procedure staffs began to find ways of cutting out unnecessary operations. The procedure divisions have slowly developed into organization engineering units. There has been growing emphasis on the application of management technique, both in the older procedure divisions and in those set up in newer agencies such as the Social Security Board and the Railroad Retirement Board. The change in orientation is illustrated by the statement of functions of a recently reorganized staff, the Management Planning Office of the Civil Aeronautics Administration in the Department of Commerce. This unit functions on the agency level, and parallels the Administrative Management Division in the Office of the Secretary of Commerce.[14]

This statement of functions is sufficient to permit thorough and well-grounded management planning, since it grants not only authority for the planning itself, but for the necessary surveys and investigations. The emphasis in the statement is on organization and management rather than on the writing of manuals, which is as it should be, since a good manual is an expression of sound administrative thought and not primarily a literary masterpiece.

FUNCTIONS OF THE ADMINISTRATIVE ANALYST

It is now generally recognized that management or procedural planning is a distinct and legitimate phase of administration, and that a large organization may properly have a special unit or division for this activity and for the other phases of administrative management.[15] The work of the administrative analysts who carry on management planning must always be related to the specific problems arising in each organization. Therefore only a general outline of what they should do can be given here. To begin with, there are some things which the administrative analyst should *not* do. He should not attempt to formulate programs and policies: the purposes of administration. The shaping of basic public or private policies is the function of the legislature or board of directors, and that of programs for

---

[14] See figure 14-A on page 153.
[15] In many agencies the application of administrative management has not gone beyond the planning stage. In a few others, management execution and control (scheduling and progress reporting) are separated from management planning. The author would rather see them together.

ADMINISTRATIVE PROCEDURE

fulfilling them is the duty of the administrator(s). The determination of essential line operations is part of administrative and not management planning. Here the administrator will seek assistance from line technicians—economists, chemists, or production men as the case may be. The administrative analyst enters the field when the organization and procedure needed for the program are considered. He advises the administrator as to the best functional and hierarchical arrangement of operating officials, and he plans the channels through which they will receive and pass on their work. He does not, however, try to specify the details of technical tasks, nor does he attempt to pass on the quality of execution. His duty is to arrange ways and means for the line executives to initiate, supervise, and control operations in their fields with the minimum amount of interference to direct activity.

The administrative analyst should constantly observe the operation of the administrative machine. He should apply analysis by function, by units of organization, and by administrative sequence to the facts and situations he finds. He should study the relation of administration to operation, and keep the administrator informed on whether the organization is adapting itself to changing objectives, conditions, functions, and techniques. He should have the data prepared for planning necessary changes in structure and procedure, so that rearrangements may be made with the least confusion. As Glover and Maze put it:

> As business and economic pressures are exerted upon an enterprise its objectives, plans, and policies change. As these changes take place the organization structure must be adjusted accordingly. This is a conscious process carried on by the management, and unless every changing demand is met by a corresponding change in the organization structure, balance cannot be maintained for long.
> With the disturbances which lead to waste, duplication of effort, slowing up of work, indifferent or unfriendly human relations and other conditions of a similar nature will quickly develop. The only way in which good balance can be retained is for the responsible executives to maintain such a close watch over each activity of the business that its needs are always known and met without delay. . . . The ability of the executives to know that the change is needed is not sufficient; they must possess the ability to devise new policies, plans, and methods to meet those needs and to bring about their prompt and effective adoption.[16]

The administrative analyst is a contributor to administrative flexibility since he relieves line officials, with their eternal load of direct administration, of the extra burden of preparing organizational changes and new procedures.

---

[16] J. C. Glover and C. L. Maze, *Managerial Control*, pp. 36-37.

MANAGEMENT PLANNING

The organizational responsibility of the analyst who carries on management planning has been outlined by Gladieux, as follows:

The principal responsibility of an administrative planning and research [management planning] unit is to study the effectiveness of the basic plan of organization for the agency and to develop improved plans to facilitate the accomplishment of the objectives for which the agency is responsible. This phase of planning and research activities is concerned with the proper division and functional distribution of the work of the agency; the establishment of a sound structure of authority and control; the provision of appropriate staff facilities and services; the elimination of jurisdictional conflicts; and proper program co-ordination. This part of the planning and research job is concerned with the development and continued maintenance of an organization which will enable the chief administrator to energize and coordinate all subdivisions of the work to the end that the major purposes of the agency may be achieved effectively.

If the agency has a regional or field organization, the administrative [management] planning unit will have many additional management problems to study. Examples of field administration problems are the geographic distribution of offices, the types of functions to be decentralized, and the working relationships between the field and central offices. . . .

This basic analysis, appraisal, and planning of organization structure is a continuing process. No governmental organization remains static, and no administrative structure can be established or reorganized in a final form. There must be provision for constant adjustment to meet changes in technical methods and to care for increases or decreases in operating activities. Without continuous appraisal and planned revision, an organization tends to become inflexible and unable to keep pace with new developments.[17]

The activities which Gladieux ascribes to management planning units are not purely theoretical: they are currently being carried on in a number of Federal agencies. The Co-ordinating and Procedure Division of the Social Security Board, for instance, has been recently making a complete analysis of the internal procedures of the Board's Bureau of Employment Security. There have already been tangible results, notably in the simplification of the handling and recording of mail, and the restriction of administrative visé (clearance) to letters affecting important policies. The number of copies of certain documents was reduced, and several recurrent sequences shortened and simplified. The objective of this study is to help the Bureau simplify and streamline its operations as completely as possible. The management planning unit, to be fully effective, should not have to sit on the sidelines until a line executive specifically requests its services. It should be authorized and required to play a major part in the planning and periodic revision of the organization structure and

---

[17] Bernard L. Gladieux, *Administrative Planning in the Federal Government*, pp. 5-7.

ADMINISTRATIVE PROCEDURE

assignment of functions. It should also supply the analytical and technical data and attend to the mechanical details of reorganization.[18]

It is now customary for a management planning unit to be a clearing-house for all kinds of standardized written procedure such as rules and regulations, instructions, and flow charts. It may frequently have the function of approving printed and duplicated forms. One such unit, the Co-ordinating and Procedure Division in the Social Security Board clears *all* orders for printing and duplicating, even for informational bulletins. But this is unusual. Many management planning units undertake to map out each recurrent administrative sequence so that all may know just what executive actions are contained therein, the order in which they follow, and who is responsible for them. Some are charged with the routing of non-recurrent administrative sequences,[19] and some with timing, scheduling, and controlling the flow of work. In general, they have varying degrees of responsibility for seeing that organization, distribution of functions, and procedures are harmonious, and that the size of the various units is adjusted to their work loads.

THE PROCEDURE MANUAL

The arrangement and distribution of procedural material is managed differently in various organizations. Every company and Government agency has its written procedures in one form or another, but there is no uniformity in the way these are published and circulated. The most common practice is to have several concurrent series of documents, with titles which suggest their relative importance, the authority on which they are based, and the subject matter. The number of such series varies from two to three up to seventeen or twenty. As a rule, documents of this sort are numbered consecutively according to the date of release. Sometimes check lists and indexes are provided.

Concurrent series of documents numbered by date present several problems. It is often hard to decide in which series a rule, instruction, or announcement should be issued, and it is generally difficult to fit new material into a previous release without reissuing the whole

---

[18] Except personnel actions, which are of course handled by the personnel office. The administrative analyst may, in connection with a planned reorganization, prepare a schedule of proposed personnel actions, but it is preferable that he have little or nothing to do with personnel changes other than indicating the *positions* to be established or eliminated. Likewise, the personnel worker should keep out of the administrative analyst's field.

[19] This is more usually a duty of line executives and their assistants, but in many cases could be handled under the administrator's supervision, by a management planning or scheduling unit.

MANAGEMENT PLANNING

document. The result is that various phases of the same subject may be treated in each of several series and under different numbers within each. It is sometimes confusing to decide what is obsolete and what is current, as new releases may modify or partially supersede old ones without completely negating them. To assemble and interpret all the material on a given matter may be a sizable task.

The present trend is toward the establishment of consolidated manuals and digests, arranged by subject matter. These bring together relevant citations of laws, decisions of legal and accounting authorities, rules and policies, assignments of function, and specific instructions. The objective is to enable the user to find all he needs to know about any one subject in one place. The value of such manuals is much more apparent in the Government than in private business, which does not have so many legal and fiscal requirements. However, they are to be found in a number of large corporations.[20]

No "best way" of arranging procedure manuals has been found: most organizations are experimenting. The current tendency is to arrange them by major functions, breaking down by sub-functions and sequences. When sequences cover more than one function, it is usually thought best to treat them completely under the heading of the dominant function, taking care of subordinated functions by cross-references. Since the functions of each organization are different, the manual must in each case be assembled to fit. To show the general method of approach, however, there is presented a typical classification scheme—that adopted by the Farm Security Administration in August, 1939, at which time all the releases formerly issued in numbered series were rearranged under functional headings. This classification is shown in Figure 14.

It will be seen that the Farm Security classification arranges material by both line and staff functions. The first four major heads—Administration, Business Services, Employment, and Fiscal Services—cover staff functions without regard to their relations to line functions or places in sequences involved in carrying out programs. The other five headings—General Program, Resettlement, Farm Tenancy, Rehabilitation, and Cooperatives—arrange the material by program, and incidentally cover a number of staff functions.

---

[20] The International Telephone and Telegraph Company and the Hoffman Beverage Company, among others, have manuals which resemble closely those of Government agencies.

ADMINISTRATIVE PROCEDURE

UNITED STATES DEPARTMENT OF AGRICULTURE
FARM SECURITY ADMINISTRATION
CLASSIFICATION OF PROCEDURE

0 Administration	1 Business Services	2 Employment
00 General		20 General
01 Organization	11 Communications	21 Appointive Employment
02 Routine	12 Files and Records	
03 Official Records	13 Travel	23 Non-Appointive Employment
04 Information Service	14 Transportation (things)	24 Conditions of Employment
05 Investigation	15 Property & Services	25 Safety, Health & Compensation
06 Legal Services		26 Employee Relations
07 Statistics & Reports		
3 Fiscal Services	4 General Program	5 Resettlement
30 General	40 General	50 General
31 Budgeting	41 State RR Corporations	51 Planning & Initiation
32 Encumbrance & Disbursement		52 Land Acquisition
33 Administrative Audit		53 Loans
34 Pay Roll		54 Development
35 Non-Fund Accounting		55 Operation
36 Fund Accounting		56 Collection
37 Audit		
6 Farm Tenancy	7 Rehabilitation	8 Cooperatives
60 General	70 General	80 General
61 Families	71 Initiation	81 Planning & Initiation
62 Farms	73 Standard Methods	82 Land Acquisition
63 Loans	74 Emergency Methods	83 Loans and Grants
64 Development	75 Operation	84 Development
65 Operation		85 Operation
66 Collection	76 Collection	86 Collection
67 Other Services		87 Other Services

Figure 14

The objectives, authorities, and principal routines for carrying out programs (with operations arranged in the order in which they are performed) are arranged under the "program" classification headings. Staff functions, which are involved in accomplishing line operations but not as parts of particular line sequences, are classified under the "staff" headings, even though they may be performed (as with travel) by line officials. When staff functions are closely tied in with line sequences, being performed in a particular way with respect to a particular program, they may be included under the "program" headings. For example, while the collection and deposit of funds due the Government is clearly "fiscal," the collection procedures are integral in the sequences of program operations; policies and routines vary

MANAGEMENT PLANNING

between the several programs. For this reason, the last four "program" headings each have a section on collection. These sections cover the parts of the collection procedures which are specialized and which are performed by the field men of the line divisions. Those aspects of collection which are common to all programs or which are handled by the fiscal officers are covered in the "fiscal services" part of the manual, with cross-references in the "program" sections.

The practice followed by the Farm Security Administration is one answer to a question which confronts everyone who undertakes to set up a procedure manual. Since every executive act represents not a line or staff function alone, shall a subject be classified according to the line function or the staff function to which it belongs? What criterion can be used to decide this problem? A general answer, as revealed by the study of a number of manuals, is one to the effect that the material is classified according to whichever function is dominant in the situation. Insofar as organization reflects function, and a correct balance exists between line and staff units,[21] this criterion may be practically applied by grouping activities for which line units are mainly responsible under line functions, and those which staff units perform or supervise in detail under staff functions. This is what the Farm Security Administration has done. Some staff activities (processes) are necessarily carried on by line officials—for instance correspondence, filing (when not centralized), and traveling—but each of these is subject to standardization by a staff authority.

There is also a "no man's land" of activities in which the line and staff aspects are of seemingly equal consequence. This area will inevitably cause trouble for the classifier of procedure. Only insofar as the boundaries and assignments of functions and subfunctions are refined and clarified, and the zones of competence clearly marked out, will the structure of the manual in this middle ground become clear. The manual is not a detached and purely logical code but is a compilation of the organization's standing administrative determinations. It necessarily reflects the clarity or confusion of the over-all procedural management.

PLACE OF ADMINISTRATIVE ANALYSTS IN AN ORGANIZATION— NATURE OF THEIR AUTHORITY

The administrative analyst has a functional authority in his own

---

[21] See the section in Chapter V under the heading, "Balancing Line and Staff Organization".

ADMINISTRATIVE PROCEDURE

field, but since he operates not *in vacuo* but in close relationship with the administrator who formulates and the line officers who execute policies and programs, his work must be co-ordinated with direct administration. Most of his output relates not to administrative management alone, but to methods, specifications, and schedules for carrying out the plans of the administrator. The *hows* are necessarily intermingled with the *whats*. To this extent it is desirable for the results of procedural surveys to be reviewed by line officials, and for the plans and instructions formulated by administrative analysts to be issued by the administrators or executives responsible for the policies and programs to which they refer. This rule is not derived from considering the basic sources of authority but is purely pragmatic. It is desirable to assure the line executives that the functional authority of management planning is always being exercised co-ordinately with delegated or retained authority for administrative planning. In other words, it would be awkward for subordinates to receive instructions on *what* to do from one official and on *how* to do it from another. So far as the product of management planning relates exclusively to techniques of administrative management (instructions for work-unit installations, scheduling methods, flow charts, etc.), the chief administrative analyst should promulgate it over his own signature, as it represents his field of functional authority.[22]

To be more specific, the administrative analyst will prepare rules and regulations, assignments of functions, and instructions and procedures which are effective throughout the organization and/or which

---

[22] Certain authorities would differ with the writer on this point. Those who use the word "staff" in its limited sense, defining a staff officer as an adjunct to the administrator or an extension of his personality, tend to think that the administrative analyst, as a staff officer, has no authority to make determinations in his own name. Gladieux expresses this point of view in saying that "the administrative planning and research unit may not properly make determinations or issue decisions in its own name or right. It simply acts for the administrator in the study of particular problems, and makes recommendations to him, which, following his approval, become binding upon the entire organization. The administrative [management] planning personnel thus constitutes a staff unit in the true [?] sense of the term." (op. cit., p. 24)

The writer considers the administrative analyst to be a staff officer in the larger sense of the word, being on a par with the personnel officer, the fiscal officer, and the purchasing officer, each of whom may issue determinations and decisions by virtue of the functional authority delegated to him so long as he does not encroach on the fields of jurisdiction assigned to line officers. The routing of management plans through the appropriate administrator is virtually more a matter of self-restraint on the part of the management planner than a limitation of his authority.

Administrative analysts, except when their status is uncertain, usually make most working contacts directly rather than through line superiors. When they have prepared procedures for specific line divisions of equal (not superior) rank, the heads of such divisions usually accept these procedures on the "suggestion" of the chief administrative analyst unless they have extremely valid reasons for objecting.

regulate the activities of all personnel or of more than one division for the signature of the highest administrator. This category will include both administrative (policy) determinations, with respect to which the administrative analyst's function is largely editorial, and management (procedural) instructions, which represent his substantial authority. Material relating to the functions of a single line division will usually be issued over the signature of the division head, and that pertaining to a staff activity will be signed by the proper staff officer. The limited volume of material which concerns administrative management or procedure as such should be signed by the administrative analyst.[23]

The distribution of authority to sign suggested above preserves the flexibility obtained by having each functional office issue documents in its own field. It does not prevent the use of a co-ordinated manual. There is a tendency on the part of Government agencies with procedure manuals to require that all material included therein be approved by the administrator or the "board," as the case may be. This concentration of authority is unnecessary and undesirable, since it takes back responsibilities already delegated. It is much better to have a universal classification of material and, within this classification, to allow each division head to sign instructions within his jurisdiction. There should be reserved to the administrator only those matters crossing divisional lines or otherwise warranting treatment on the highest level.

The signature of procedural documents is of course only the culmination of a process. The shaping of procedures should be a co-operative undertaking in which the analyst pools his administrative knowledge wih the technical skill of the line officer. It is the latter's responsibility to state the objectives and basic operations. The administrative analyst must learn what these are and assist the line officer in the arrangement and specification of tasks. This is to say that in planning organization and procedure the analyst will work in collaboration with the appropriate operating officials. There may be times when agreement is not possible—in such cases the administrative analyst will refer the matter to the superior of the official in question and if necessary to the administrator. He should avoid appearing as a special pleader for his ideas and recommendations, and

---

[23] This may include instructions for preparing and signing correspondence, and for filing if this function does not come under the Business Manager or an official of equivalent rank.

should merely assemble the necessary facts so that the superior may have an objective basis for decision. The conflicting recommendations of the analyst and the line official may then be given, separate from the factual presentation, so that, whatever decision is reached, neither can feel that anything has been "put over".[24]

The adminstrative analyst must be able to deal on a direct and co-operative basis with all line and staff officials with whose activities he is concerned. To assure the impartiality of his position, he should be placed in a position directly subordinate to the responsible administrator or in a division concerning itself with problems of management rather than detailed staff operations. He should not be in the personnel or legal office lest he be influenced too much by the specialized outlooks of practitioners in those fields.[25] While the same tendency toward bias may attend his being placed in the budget office if that branch is bent upon securing monetary savings without regard to their consequences or implications, a more liberal budgetary objective—minimizing expenditure *in relation to results achieved* or more simply getting the most for the money—will not impede or warp objective management planning.

In large and complex organizations management planning units on various levels may be desirable. For instance, in a department composed of a central "Secretary's Office" and a number of bureaus, it is advantageous to have a central management planning office reporting to the Secretary either directly or through the Co-ordinator, Comptroller, or Budget Officer. Such a unit would be responsible for dealing with organization and procedure on the departmental level and would be supplemented by management planning units in each bureau of sufficient size to warrant one. While the bureau units would report to the bureau chiefs, they would receive technical supervision and assistance from the central office. If the volume of detailed personnel, procurement, or accounting business handled through the Secretary's Office is large, it might even be worthwhile to have branches of the departmental management planning office functioning in those fields and reporting to the staff, officers in charge.

The administrative analysts, regardless of where they may be located in an organization, should co-operate to the utmost with each other and with the operating officials for whose activities they

---

[24] See Brecht and Glaser, *op. cit.*, p. 28, on the technique of presenting problems to higher officials for decision as developed in Germany.
[25] Gladieux, *op. cit.*, pp. 18-23. The administrative analysts will of course have technical and informational contact with operating staff officials.

MANAGEMENT PLANNING

plan organization and write procedure. While they must strive to make administrative processes as simple and economical as possible they must avoid the type of perfectionism which interferes with program accomplishment. The emphasis should always be on coordination and facilitation, and above all on co-operation.

CIVIL AERONAUTICS ADMINISTRATION
Washington, D. C.

May 27, 1941

Functions of
MANAGEMENT PLANNING OFFICE
(Office of Executive Officer)

Under the general direction of the Executive Officer, provides over-all management planning and advisory services to the Administration in the advancement of administrative determinations, development of directives and evaluation of performance, and specifically:

1. Advises staff and operating officers with respect to administrative determinations involving (a) planning of work programs, (b) operations under approved work programs and (c) establishment of management controls to evaluate work programs.

2. Conducts surveys or analyses involving major problems of the Administration, including: organizational structure (in whole or in part), functions, staffing requirements, performance, and their interrelationships both with respect to programs and to offices.

3. Develops and assists in development of over-all administrative reports and controls for the evaluation of performance in terms of progress, cost and efficiency.

4. Controls issuance in manual form of published directives to the Administration, including orders, practices, instructions and notices, through preparation or review of such material.

5. Assists operating officers in installations involving major changes in activities or equipment.

Figure 14-A

Chapter XII

MANAGEMENT EXECUTION— WORK DISTRIBUTION

THE administrative analyst's planning work begins with design of plan (the fourth step in Dr. Person's sequence [1]), which is specified as "bringing ways and means into exact quantitative, qualitative, and functional relationships." This provides the means for deciding when each task [2] shall be done, by whom, and where the doers shall be placed in the organization structure. Design of plan must reconcile function, unit of organization, and administrative sequence so that each will contribute to the basic objectives. It must visualize a network of interlocking channels through which passes the administrative traffic; it must weigh the capacity of concentration points and processing units; and it must so weave the pattern that the organization's multiplex ends and means do not conflict.

If an organization's work program is to be shaped in a logical pattern, and not be a patchwork of hit-and-miss assignments, the first step is a precise delimitation of fields of work.[3] Of course, when operations are completely routinized, it is sometimes possible to get along without any defined spheres of administrative jurisdiction, there being only lists of specific duties and authorities. Planning is then confined to procedure making for various recurrent sequences, and the work loads of individuals and units are assortments of disconnected tasks rather than integrated responsibilities. But this state of affairs leads to confusion as soon as the work deviates from the predetermined norm.

In non-routine administration in fields in which the specific problems change unpredictably from day to day, design of plan must proceed from function and project rather than sequence. In other words, it is impossible to plan in terms of standardized sets of acts

---

[1] See the second paragraph in Chapter VI.
[2] Deciding *what* tasks are to be done (at least so far as their content is concerned) is part of the third step, formulation of program.
[3] Particularly in zones where line and staff offices would be most likely to conflict.

MANAGEMENT EXECUTION — WORK DISTRIBUTION

always done the same way and in the same order. Instead, there must be considered the content of the work belonging to each branch of the organization, and the kind of sequences and tasks in which this content is likely to occur. The sphere of work for each division must be defined in terms of subject-matter, and the flow of each sequence allowed to evolve from the natural order and content of its tasks. For instance, if an engineering firm has one unit to design machinery, one to lay out wiring, and another to plan buildings, the specifications for a power plant will necessarily pass through these units in succession.

Standing work-assignments should be made in terms of the content of tasks rather than the tasks themselves. When a new task appears its assignment will in most cases be predetermined. Marking out the areas of operation should be a joint undertaking of administrators and administrative analysts. The broad fields of work will usually be mapped out by the head of the organization, following which the analyst may draw the lines more exactly, making charts and descriptions of functions. While the administrator may hold the administrative analyst to account for the feasibility of his recommendations, he cannot sidestep the primary responsibility for the division of work between major units.[4] He should review the material prepared by the analyst, being sure that he agrees with it, for any faults of organization and basic planning will certainly be laid at his door.

The planning of fields of work and organization units to suit them is by no means a matter entirely of paper work, nor is it done once for all and then forgotten. In a going concern there should be continuous survey and analysis based on first-hand inspection and fact-gathering. The conclusions obtained through co-operative study by administrators and administrative analysts can and should be used for re-defining, re-planning and re-organizing. An agency or company whose organization structure has not been changed within remembrance is likely to be a stagnant one.

WORK DISTRIBUTION WITHIN AND BETWEEN UNITS

Work distribution within a unit of reasonable size is a matter of execution rather than management planning. Tasks are normally assigned according to their character, difficulty, and relation to other tasks, with the objective of giving each individual a balanced work load. The methods of approach outlined in Chapter III, "Analysis

---

[4] Bureaus within a department, divisions within a bureau, etc.

by Units of Organization," will be useful in working toward this end, as will the criteria suggested for evaluating administrative sequences.[5]

There should be constant search for the measurable elements in various tasks, and work units should be applied as widely as practical. When the basic units are different for various operations taking place in the same office, it is well to reduce them to a common denominator such as the work-hour. Systems of work units applicable to common operations such as transcribing, typing, filing, auditing vouchers, etc., can be found in the manuals of Government agencies and corporations, as well as in text-books; it is unnecessary to go into them here. Units for recurrent specialized operations may often be developed by observation. Even for highly variable tasks, which require the exercise of authority or creative power, units can sometimes be derived when work records are kept and analyzed periodically.[6] So far as possible, work loads within a unit should be equalized according to objective bases.

The distribution of work between units cannot be considered apart from the question of organization, since the functions and volume of work of an office determine its organizational character as much as its personnel and lines of authority. What is said here must necessarily overlap the discussion of organization contained in an earlier chapter, even though it proceeds from a different point of view.

In distributing work between units a balance must be struck between two not fully compatible objectives. It is desirable to seek the most direct channels of administration: the accomplishment of each sequence with the fewest moves. At the same time the skill and experience of specialists should be used as effectively as possible. If an undertaking has many divergent technical phases a compromise must be reached between the two extremes, so that the product will be sufficiently sound and yet the procedure not too complicated.

An organization's specialists should be so placed that its various types of recurrent projects can be kept within major divisions as far

---

[5] These criteria, described in detail on page 46, are as follows:
  1. Each task should contribute positively to the basic purpose.
  2. Similar tasks should be combined.
  3. Administrative moves should be as few and short as possible.
  4. Each task should be well-balanced.
See also the preceding section, "Analysis of Individual Tasks."

[6] E. W. Loveridge, *Job-Load Analysis and Planning of Executive Work in National Forest Administration*, Washington, U. S. Forest Service, 1932. Also Public Administration Service pamphlet, *The Work Unit in Federal Administration*, Chicago, 1937.

MANAGEMENT EXECUTION — WORK DISTRIBUTION

as possible, and so that interdivisional contacts will be mostly on policy rather than detail. This is desirable even at the cost of having apparent duplications of function. The Farm Security Administration, for instance, has sections for co-operatives in both its Resettlement and Rural Rehabilitation Divisions. From a superficial point of view these sections should be consolidated, yet to do so would complicate operating procedures enormously. When one or more functions appear in several diverse programs, it may be best to split up these functions.

Consolidation of staff operations such as purchasing, personnel, and accounting, if carried too far, increases the volume of detailed interdivisional contact. If a large number of administrative processes are centralized this factor definitely hampers administration. This is often recognized by administrators who allow theoretically centralized staff operations to be carried on in a decentralized way. Such an arrangement, with over-all staff agencies serving mainly as advisers and co-ordinators, is often better than centralizing detailed staff operation.

FUNCTIONALISM IN ADMINISTRATION

Some of Frederick W. Taylor's followers have argued that the work of an administrative organization should be completely "functionalized." [7] According to this theory, all the work coming within any one staff function or process should be done within (or in any case directly supervised by) a single administrative unit, regardless of the line functions or purposes involved. A functionalized administrative structure would have large staff divisions doing detailed work, and small line divisions whose direct operations would be largely confined to distinctive activities existing only in their special fields. Of course, both "processes" and "distinctive activities" are subject to varying interpretations. It is conceivable, however, that under advanced functionalism a line division might be divested of all power to operate directly, each process involved in its work having been drawn off to a staff division. The line division would then become solely a co-ordinator of staff divisons. The result would be a topsy-turvy situation.

The process of "functionalizing" is worth explaining, because it is frequently advocated as a panacea for bureaucratic diseases. To be specific, we may compare the basic operating procedure of "Agency A" as it exists and as it might be under "functionalist" management.

---

[7] William H. Leffingwell, *A Textbook of Office Management*, Chapter VI.

ADMINISTRATIVE PROCEDURE

"Agency A" is not a functionalized organization, in fact it has been taking steps in the other direction such as transferring operative planning in engineering matters out of a central planning division into the line units.

"Agency A" is run by an Administrator, to whom report the General Administrative Officer, the General Counsel, and the Comptroller. Those staff functions which are centralized are administered by the Management Division through its Personnel, Finance, Legal, Materials, Land Acquisition, and Information Sections. As has been indicated with respect to supply work and personnel actions, the Management Division acts promptly at the request of operating units, not undertaking to judge their wants, but merely filling orders as quickly and accurately as possible. It is definitely a service organ, and in the event that it fails to act, the operating branches have authority to proceed on their own initiative.[8]

The line functions of "Agency A" are distributed between three major divisions, each of which administers a certain kind of project. The work is so divided that each branch operates with a maximum of freedom and very little detailed liaison with other offices. Each carries its distinctive activities through from beginning to end, performing tasks embracing a number of physical, technical, and administrative processes. Each line division has its administrators, its research workers and planners, its engineers and draftsmen, its clerks and stenographers and its laborers. These are assigned to the different projects, the manager in charge of each being responsible for integrating all processes needed to attain his purpose. In other words, he is told to get a certain job done and then, subject to general policies, is left alone to get it done. Control is generalized, not particularized.

Under extreme functionalism, the picture would be entirely different. Each process would be concentrated in a staff division, and line divisions would be reduced to skeleton crews of co-ordinating administrators. There would be a research and planning division performing not only broad program planning but also detailed operative planning, a general engineering division, a clerical devision, and a labor division, in addition to the customary staff units. The planners, engineers, clerks and laborers (including foremen) would be responsible to the heads of their respective staff divisions, through which all formal orders would have to be cleared.

Under functionalist organization a manager of a project embody-

---

[8] The possibility of this happening has always been a sufficient sanction to assure prompt action by the Management Division, so that it never has happened.

ing several centralized staff functions could only give definite orders (as distinguished from informal directions) to those working on it through the proper divisional channels. The staff divisions would not merely pass the manager's orders along but, having a *functional authority* for their parts of the work, would change them to meet their standards. And these standards would be those of excellence in *process* and might be either irrelevant or detrimental to the best accomplishment of the administrative *purpose*.

It is a good thing that "Agency A" has been kept out of the hands of the "functionalists." The picture just given of "functionalism" may seem like an administrative nightmare, but it is only the intentional exaggeration of a tendency which actually exists in many organizations. While a limited centralization of some staff activities, such as purchasing, personnel, accounting, and miscellaneous office services, is a good thing since it frees line officials of duties not related to their special fields, carrying it too far can and does result in confusion.[9]

Functionalism is a type of organization developed in manufacturing, and carried over into administration without a full appreciation of the essential differences between hand-work and brain-work. The factory worker may concentrate on process to the exclusion of purpose: he may turn out machine parts made to precision requirements without any idea of their uses. The administrative worker, even on the lowest level, must have a good idea of the purpose of what he is doing. It is, for instance, hard to file papers properly without knowing what they are about, nor can clerical work be done very effectively in a vacuum. While a typist *can* make an acceptable job of a letter which is Greek to her, she can do better with familiar subject-matter. In direct administrative work the technique of purpose (knowledge of the activity administered) is usually more basic than that of process (administrative and other facilitating methods). While processes should be made as efficient as possible, the way to do it is to have adminstrative analysts assist and guide the line officials, rather than taking integral parts of their work away from them.

Functionalism is particularly bad in administration because it multiplies the number of moves through which each sequence passes. This does not matter in manufacturing, where the production

---

[9] On the bad effects of too much functionalism in Federal agencies, see Harry Arthur Hopf, "Administrative Coordination," *Advanced Management*, April, 1940, pp. 50 ff.

ADMINISTRATIVE PROCEDURE

line assures proper timing, but if the work consists of making decisions and giving technical treatment to a series of variable cases, motion delay cannot be avoided. Because so many administrative acts involve the assertion of the human will, dividing the work among too many offices obscures responsibility and causes intense jurisdictional conflicts. It is impossible to conduct an undertaking effectively if those engaged in its direct phases are directed by several different chiefs, each with his own policies and methods, who must be wheedled and cajoled before integrated performance can be had.

Administrators planning to centralize staff phases of their activities would do well to think twice, considering the effects on executive responsibility and channels of contact. This is not to argue that all staff units are baneful—in proper fields they may be valuable in saving the time of line officials. In general, the activities most advantageously centralized in staff units are those least related to the specific subject matter of administration and having standard techniques applicable to any field of activity. Under this head can be included purchasing of common items (but not of specialized apparatus or machinery), personnel work (except the recruitment and final appraisal of specialists), office services, duplicating, photography (except when a knowledge of the subject-matter is required), building management, transportation, and like activities. Direction in these fields by staff officers will not usually impede the line officers' freedom to act. Those activities not susceptible to centralization include technical research and planning (except management planning which requires specialists in administration rather than in subject-matter), engineering, most clerical work (particularly when clerks are potential executives), and management of labor forces. This is not a hard-and-fast dichotomy, but it is generally applicable.

A justification of "functionalism" is that it minimizes waste of time caused by slack periods, particularly in organizations having an irregular flow of business. It is possible to have fewer employees if they can be shifted about wherever they are needed. This objective might perhaps be attained by the following alternative devices:

(1) Giving each unit enough personnel to handle the normal volume of work. Taking care of peak loads with a reserve force or "pool" of clerks, statisticians, research workers, executives, etc., who would be assigned to particular jobs by the management planning or personnel office. Such a "pool" would serve as a valuable training ground for new employees or those being groomed for advancement.

(2) Establishing a personnel exchange service, through which

employees would be loaned from one unit to another for brief periods. Each unit would, of course, have a prior claim on its own employees.[10] The head of each unit having a variable work load would indicate, by means of a weekly "unit production chart," [11] how many employee hours in each class and grade he might wish to give or receive during the ensuing week. It would have to be understood that willingness to lend employees would not jeopardize their security of tenure. The personnel exchange service could be operated most conveniently in conjunction with the aforementioned reserve force.

The arrangements just described would not sacrifice the integrity of line units, nor cause the additional administrative moves produced by functionalism. Properly managed with simple procedures, they might reduce the waste of working time.

THE "ADMINISTRATIVE BOTTLENECK"

A simple maxim can be applied to the functional distribution of work: as a general rule, tasks should be distributed by line function rather than staff function. The exceptions have been noted. A similar principle with respect to the distribution of work between administrative levels might be stated thus: tasks should be assigned to the lowest levels consistent with proper performance. Refusal to recognize these practical rules inevitably creates "administrative bottlenecks."

An "administrative bottleneck" is like a highway bottleneck. It is a place where streams of traffic converge from many directions, going through a single passage. Highway bottlenecks exist at the entrances to important bridges and tunnels, across or through which traffic must pass to and from tributary areas. Administrative bottlenecks are found in the offices of executives who undertake too much or try to clear too many papers going to or coming from their subordinates. On the highways, when there is more traffic than can pass through the bottleneck, cars pile up in a traffic jam. In an office, when a key official has more work than he can dispose of promptly and there is no way to "short circuit" his office, there will be an administrative traffic jam. If the congestion affected only the official in question it would not be too serious, but it frequently ties up the work of a whole division or even a bureau. There are two ways of dealing with administrative bottlenecks. One is to widen them, that

---
[10] Loaning of employees is of course a common practice, but is seldom done on a systematic basis.
[11] See Chapter XIV, "Reporting Current Unit Work Loads."

ADMINISTRATIVE PROCEDURE

is to divide up the work among a sufficient number of officials; the other is to re-route business around them.

Bottlenecks are usually caused by undue concentration of executive authority and by excesses of functionalism. An example due in part to both factors was the bottleneck which existed several years ago in the Finance Division of "Agency B." This organization unwittingly involved itself in "red tape" by setting up an over-elaborate fiscal control system, which undertook to examine minutely the operating plans of the line divisions. The latter were each charged with certain projects involving social and economic planning, construction, and financial management. The line divisions had plenty of economists, sociologists, land experts, engineers, and cost accountants, and were headed by well-paid and presumably capable executives. No one ever accused them of turning out inadequately considered plans. Yet, under the guise of "budgetary control," the finished plans were minutely analyzed by the Finance Division, which dissected cost estimates, revamped project budgets, and checked every last detail for conformity with administrative policy.[12] The control operations were themselves highly functionalized, resulting in a welter of administrative motion within the Finance Division. The number of projects ran into the hundreds, so that the "control" officers were swamped, especially as they were not very familiar with the line activities they were trying to control. It took months to clear plans through the Division, the resulting delay in getting projects under construction being so great that "Agency B" became an object of considerable political abuse.

Cost planning and project budgeting are integral parts of detailed program planning. They should be assigned to those having direct responsibility for the work, with fiscal experts providing policy supervision. To give detailed control duties to a superimposed staff division, as in "Agency B," shows an apparent failure to consider the following essential points:

(1) The necessity or non-necessity of control functions; their duplication of line controls.

(2) The time required for the performance of control functions.

(3) The load of these functions on the officials performing them.

"Agency B" also suffered from other bottlenecks. The one in its Personnel Division, particularly in connection with political clear-

---

[12] "Budgetary control," as advocated by progressive authorities, concentrates on major aspects of program rather than on infinitesimal detail, and presupposes the technical competence of line officials.

MANAGEMENT EXECUTION — WORK DISTRIBUTION

ance, has already been cited in Chapter VIII. Another bottleneck with widespread effects lay in the centralized channels through which the entire correspondence of the agency was routed. Incoming letters were opened by a central mail office, where a clerk prepared record slips in quintuplicate. One slip was filed in the central office and the letters were forwarded with the remaining slips to the divisional mail office where another clerk detached a slip and sent the letters on to the sections where they were to be answered. Here a third mail clerk detached still another slip for his collection, and then presented each letter to its recipient. The time required for this procedure was never systematically measured, but officials of the agency have estimated it as from four to six hours.

Outgoing mail in "Agency B" was subjected to a corresponding process of involution. Letters were usually signed or initialed by section chiefs, checked by the sectional mail clerks (who transferred the proper slips from the "pending" to the "answered" files), and then were submitted to division chiefs for review, no matter how trivial their contents. After passing through the divisional mail office, where the slips pertaining to the incoming letters were transferred as in the section, mail went on to the central office where the process was again repeated. This office contained a visé unit, which read each letter through, checking the form, spelling, grammar, punctuation, and contents. The volume of mail was too much for the unfortunate visé clerks, who regularly worked until nine or ten in the evening and still had a full day's work piled up. The inconvenience produced by the correspondence bottleneck finally moved the Administrator of "Agency B" to take action. The visé unit was abolished, as were the divisional mail stations, clearance by division chiefs was restricted to matters meriting their serious attention, and the movement of correspondence was speeded up immeasurably. The extra control functions were never missed, because they were quite unnecessary.

The bottlenecks in "Agency B" were due to the attempt to control line activities in detail through staff units. The review of plans and correspondence by those who may be called amateurs so far as the controlled activities were concerned, did not improve the product. Since the clerks in the mail office did not, for the most part, know what the letters were about, the best they could do was to catch split infinitives. Control, insofar as it is exercised through clearance of papers, should be in the hands of superior line officers and their assistants who have a working knowledge of the subject matter. Placing it elsewhere is a misassignment of function.

ADMINISTRATIVE PROCEDURE

The place of work distribution in the planning process has been indicated, as have its general objectives and methods. The "functionalist" tendency and its results have also been noted. To sum up, there are a few simple maxims which administrators or administrative analysts should consider. These are as follows:

1. *The basic division of administrative work should be according to the organization's major purposes (line functions).* Certain processes (staff functions) common to several line functions may be carried on in staff divisions, if this will improve quality of performance and make line work easier. But the staff divisions must not be allowed to obstruct the work of line divisions, nor should their technical controls go out of bounds.

2. *Responsibility and authority for performance should not be separated.* When an executive is responsible for action, he must have power to act, without awaiting approval by a non-responsible control agency.

3. *Work assignments should allow as short administrative sequences as possible.* Yet differentiation of fields should proceed from function and project rather than from specific sequence.

4. *Qualitative and quantitative capacity should be considered.* Each official, each unit, and each division should be given functions, sub-functions, and tasks within known abilities and skills. No individual should regularly be given a greater volume of work than he can dispatch promptly and without overworking.

These principles, as applied to administration in general, are necessarily somewhat abstract. Yet they will become concrete when applied to specific organizations and programs of activity.

Chapter XIII

MANAGEMENT EXECUTION—TIMING AND SCHEDULING

DESIGN of plan, which includes management planning, consists of setting up three series of relationships: quantitative, qualitative, and functional. These relationships apply in work distribution, which divides the work into functions, sub-functions, and assignments; they also apply in organization, which is the arrangement of personnel in divisions and units and the establishment of working contacts and channels of supervision. A particularly important quantitative relationship is that of *time;* it is necessary to plan when things will be done and how long they will take.

After management planning, there follows execution, in which the paper organization comes to life and projects start on the sequences laid out for them. The planner must follow through to see that his plans work properly; he must be able to spot needs for adjustment. He must keep the administrator assured that work is proceeding in an orderly way or, if not, that steps are being taken to correct the situation.

When plans fail to work as they should, the reason is likely to be in some way related to time. Usually not enough time has been allowed for an operation. Sometimes it is the other way around; something happens before it is expected. The administrative analyst has to pay particular attention to time, both during the planning process and afterwards. He must find ways to tell how long a job will take and then, while it is going on, find out whether his original time estimate was correct. Unless the time factor can be thoroughly mastered, management planning can never be fully effective.

It is seldom easy to measure the time required for administrative processes; it is hard to lay hands on facts which can be exactly measured. The primary methods of administrative analysis, by function, units of organization, and administrative sequence, are qualitative and logical rather than arithmetical. Yet it is necessary to have precise knowledge, since the output of organizations is judged in

ADMINISTRATIVE PROCEDURE

terms of the amount of work done, and their resources have quantitative (budgetary) limitations. The administrator must plan to get a certain number of definite things done, and both he and those who direct him (legislators or stockholders) want to know how much they will get for their money. It is thus important for the administrative analyst to develop as fully as he can the techniques of exact observation and measurement which will fit the organization's work, so that he can tell the administrator how much each unit can produce on a given budget.

Quantitative planning specifies the amount of materials and labor required to produce a desired result. In the administrative field it is concerned mainly with personnel requirements: the need for executive and professional effort. The time required for an operation times the rate of pay equals the wage cost; without time wage cost cannot be determined. The total time for an administrative sequence is the sum of the individual job-times plus the aggregate motion delay. The total cost is the sum of the wage cost plus charges for materials, space, and utilities. Time and cost are inescapably interrelated; without time accounting there cannot be cost accounting.

The interrelationships of administrative functions make proper time planning even more essential, particularly in complex operations. Construction of buildings must be timed with land acquisition, personnel work, and procurement; planting of trees requires timing of ground preparation, transportation, and supplying tools and fertilizer. If physical operations must be timed, so must the administrative steps required to direct them. The parts of each multiple job must be timed in relation to the other work of each participant. This puts squarely up to the administrative analyst the problem of finding out how long each task (or at least each recurrent task) will take, and what the sum of the job-times and the time in transit will be for each sequence.

TIME ANALYSIS OF INDIVIDUAL AND UNIT TASKS—WORK UNITS

Timing of work, whether manual operations, clerical work, or administration, requires a work unit.[1] In simple tasks the unit is derived easily because of the tangible character of the output and the lack of variation in the work. For instance, the bricklayer's work is measured by the hundred, the roofer's by the square, and the weaver's

---

[1] Work units for budgetary purposes are generally units of completed work within a homogeneous sub-function (miles of sidewalk built, etc.). For scheduling, work units may be established for steps within the sub-function.

MANAGEMENT EXECUTION — SCHEDULING

by the yard. These may be reduced to a common denominator by determining an average or standard time for accomplishing each unit and converting to man-hours. This process is an essential part of estimating and is done, albeit sometimes crudely, by every contractor who bids on a construction job. It is done more exactly by manufacturers in setting their production costs. In either case administration is usually charged in a lump sum to overhead or allocated pro rata to the physical operations. But in large administrative organizations, particularly in Government agencies where construction and production, if any, must be co-ordinated with social and economic programs, there is so much supervisory, executive, and research activity that it must be measured in order to find true costs and time requirements. This need has led to intensive research and to gradual development of executive work load measurement and scheduling techniques in a number of organizations.

Work units for standardized manual and clerical tasks can usually be developed without great difficulty. These tasks may also be evaluated by direct time study. When the size and difficulty of items vary but their general character remains the same, average time values may be obtained by inspecting work records, file copies of documents, and the like, or by keeping count of production. Although particular jobs may vary in bulk and complexity, if the variation is measured a run of a certain number may be assigned a standard time value. When work loads vary not only in the size of items but in their character, particularly when special assignments, planning, inspection, etc., are involved, it is necessary to estimate on the basis of experience and occasionally to resort to outright guessing when a brand-new job comes up. Accurate work records are helpful in reducing uncertainty; some organizations, notably the Forest Service, urge the keeping of diaries. But however hard it may seem to evaluate the volume of work, at least tentative estimates should be made and then corrected as circumstances warrant. An executive who takes periodic stock of the jobs on hand and thinks about the time required to do them is less likely to make promises he cannot keep than one who does his work on a hand-to-mouth basis.

Before trying to set a time estimate for any job, it is necessary to get an all-round picture of it. The data secured in analysis by function, by unit of organization, and by sequence should be adequate for this purpose. The factors suggested for consideration under these heads in earlier chapters are very much like a set of questions outlined

ADMINISTRATIVE PROCEDURE

by Loveridge [2] for specific use in work load analysis. The comparison is as follows:

Analysis by Function	Analysis by Units of Organization	Analysis by Administrative Sequence	Loveridge's Questions
Purpose	Purpose	Contribution of tasks to administrative end	Why?
Necessity	Relationships		What and who?
Method	Method	Possibility of combining similar tasks	How?
Assignment	Work load		
Coordination	Personnel	Administrative motion	Where?
Work load	Conditions of work		When?
Accomplishment		Balance of qualitative factors	

The analyst must be sure that he knows what the jobs are about, even though he can never learn to do all of them himself. He may, in many cases, pool his efforts with the personnel worker who looks for similar information for classification and rate-setting. By keeping his eyes and ears open for relevant information, and enlisting the co-operation of the persons whose work is studied, he may arrive at quantitative estimates of tasks almost as useful for practical purposes as those compiled by more "scientific" methods of time study. Inability to apply a stop-watch to a job is not a deterrent to scheduling, provided sufficient leeway for variations is allowed.

Work load analysis produces two sets of data: load estimates for individuals (necessary for proper work distribution) and approximate times required for performing each task. These facts may be compounded into group work load estimates and times for accomplishing entire projects or parts thereof. The latter must include suitable allowances for motion delay.

TIMING AND SCHEDULING LARGE SCALE ADMINISTRATIVE OPERATIONS

The foregoing indication of the process of timing administrative work may well lead the reader to remark: "Your instructions for evaluating tasks are too vague. Apparently they cannot be made specific except for specific tasks. A trained administrative analyst might make good time estimates, but could he get others to do so?

---
[2] E. W. Loveridge, *Job-Load Analysis*, etc., pp. 17 ff.

MANAGEMENT EXECUTION—SCHEDULING

How could your system be made to work in a large organization?"

These questions can be answered by a concrete example. The Rural Electrification Administration, which since July 1, 1939 has been an agency in the Department of Agriculture, maintains precise schedules for a large portion of its administrative operations. The operating steps in development of rural electric co-operatives and the making of loans for lines and equipment call for a fairly standardized series of administrative actions which fall into a logical sequence. Several years ago officials of the agency realized that by streamlining the sequence, and by adjusting the man-hours required for each step, they could eliminate the piling up of backlogs of current work in the several technical divisions. By doing this, they could carry out their program more rapidly and with reduced administrative costs. Accurate forecasting of work load, not only on the basis of individual projects but for the program as a whole, would permit timely adjustment of personnel strength to actual needs, and would provide data for a measured and calculated budget. It would also make possible accurate prediction of advance needs for poles, wire, insulators, transformers, and other supplies.

The first step undertaken by the management engineer appointed to set up the schedules was a study of the existing steps—the "tentative program of action." [3] This included the technical and administrative steps from the allotment of funds for a project to the approval of the construction contract, and a further sequence of operations leading up to energization—turning on the current. All unnecessary tasks were weeded out, and the remaining essential steps rearranged in a new standard order.

Having refined the standard program of action, the engineer proceeded to the next step, design of plan, emphasizing the time factor (including labor requirements) in each operation. He reviewed work records which showed the past production of various units.[4] Conferences were held with division heads and technicians, at which their functions were critically analyzed, and tentative time estimates determined. These were the result of discussion and compromise, and in

---

[3] This "tentative program" is the product of the third step in planning, formulation of program. See first section of Chapter VI.

[4] Methods engineers generally do not like to use work records for standard setting, as the records may indicate a production below what is actually feasible. However, the operations in this case did not lend themselves to more direct methods of time study. The work records covered a period when REA was carrying the heaviest load it has yet to carry in any one year, and the performance indicated by their analysis proved to be high, satisfactory, and dependable.

ADMINISTRATIVE PROCEDURE

STANDARD OPERATIONS AND TIME PERIODS

WORK DAYS PER YEAR—256   WORK DAYS PER MONTH—21
WORK DAYS PER WEEK—5

TIME POSITION IN WORK DAYS FOR OPERATIONS

After ALT	Ahead of CCA	Symbols General	Const.	Name
		REX		Received for Examination
0	65	ALT		Allotted for All Purposes
0	65	ALR		Allot. Released—All Purposes
0	65		ALR	Allot. Released—Construction
0	65		SSE	Superintendent Selected
0	65	LSE		Lawyer Selected
5	60		ESE	Engineer Selected
5	60	LCS		Loan Contract Sent
10	55	PSA		Power Source Acceptable
12	53	LCE		Loan Contract Executed
20	45	MRE		Mortgage Recorded
25	40		P & S	Plans and Specifications Received
30	35		BRE	Bids Released
40	25		BOP	Bids Opened
50	15		BAP	Bids Approved
65	0		CCA	Construction Contract Approved
175	—		WTC	Weighted Construction
			PER	Poles Erected
			WST	Wire Strung
			SIN	Services Installed
			ENR	Energized

Courtesy of Rural Electrification Administration

Figure 15

each case represented standards accepted by the line officials. The professional workers put up some resistance at first. But when they were shown that their work could be measured by using their regular work records, and that allowances could be made for variations in complexity and difficulty, they came into agreement and times were set for their various activities.

After the job times had been determined, a standard list was made showing them in order, and showing the time after allotment when each should be completed. It was not necessary to schedule *all* the jobs. There were certain tasks the accomplishment of which indicated automatically that specified others had been done. These key actions were designated as "control points" and entered in a standard

MANAGEMENT EXECUTION—SCHEDULING

schedule of operations, each being set a definite number of days after the making of the allotment. The time-table, for steps from allotment to approval of the construction contract,[5] which appears in Figure 15, was made standard for all rural electrification projects. A "production control unit" began applying it to each project, setting definite dates for the performance of each "control" step in the sequence of administrative actions.

It was agreed that job times would be changed if operating experience should show them to be incorrect. The estimates turned out, however, to be surprisingly accurate and only a few minor changes were made. The average time requirement for the handling of all documents, beginning with the allotment and culminating in the construction contract, was 36 weeks during the fiscal year 1936. In fiscal 1937 this was reduced to 22 weeks, in 1938 to 16 weeks, in 1939 to 13 weeks, and in 1940 to 12 weeks.[6] This accomplishment was due primarily to a combination of (a) standard time, (b) adjustment of personnel strength to work load, and (c) maintenance of an even flow of work.

The scheduling method used in the Rural Electrification Administration was developed for activities which could be arranged in a standardized administrative sequence. The tasks performed by each unit have a constant form (although the content is variable) and the decisions are made with reference to recurrent problems. A different method of scheduling is in order when individual and unit work loads consist of an assortment of tasks, particularly when the moment each will come up cannot be exactly predicted. In this case there must be determined not only the time required for each task but also the frequency with which it occurs.

The work loads of District Rangers and Forest Supervisors in the Forest Service are highly diversified and require more complex analysis than they would if they always consisted of the same things. For each National Forest, job lists are made up showing the various tasks which occur, the time required for each, and the number of times each is expected to arise. These lists are first made for a whole year's work, and are then broken down into monthly work budgets, with jobs distributed to the most suitable months. Adjustments are then made by consolidating travel time (planning a number of jobs on

---

[5] REA has other schedules for construction and for steps after construction, but these are not covered here.

[6] Scheduling in REA is on a 5-day week basis, Saturday being used for "catching up."

one trip), transferring work from one month to another so as to balance the load, and distributing non-recurrent jobs so far as possible to the months having the lightest loads of recurrent work. The resulting schedules express the work loads for the various units. In case there is an overload (more work to be done than man-hours available), two schedules are compiled, one for work that should be done and one for work that will be done. A bad discrepancy would serve as a basis for requesting additional funds.

On the basis of monthly work load estimates, work plans are prepared for each unit, grouping field jobs into trips and assigning these, as well as office jobs, to the persons who will do them. Consideration is given to special factors such as fatigue, incidence of unexpected jobs as well as miscellaneous minor tasks which crop up on every field trip, and necessary "time for reflection." Although outside work is planned for definite days, there is enough flexibility to allow for weather and other unpredictable factors. The work plan as a whole is a close approximation of the possible accomplishment of each unit, and the Forest Service has found that these plans are usually adhered to without significant deficiencies.

The Forest Service's method of scheduling was made to fit that agency's organization and type of work. The service has many more or less independent units doing assortments of tasks which, while integrated toward a few basic objectives, are for the most part technically separate and arrangeable in various orders. The Forest Ranger's work, and to some extent the Supervisor's, consists of a number of housekeeping duties; some things have to be done at fixed times, and others (like putting out fires) whenever they come up, but the rest may be shifted around. This flexibility is only possible in administrative work when the operating units can function with considerable independence. In a large central office, where the functions of divisions and sections are closely interrelated, *and* the work load is variable or unpredictable, scheduling must follow still another pattern.

Activities which follow a set form, such as project development in the Rural Electrification Administration, or which are foreseen some time ahead, may of course be scheduled some time in advance. But much of the work of modern organizations is kaleidoscopic. In business and government alike large and involved projects which require the collaboration of many specialists turn up from day to day. These undertakings cannot be scheduled far in advance. Yet if they are allowed to float aimlessly from division to division, or are started

MANAGEMENT EXECUTION—SCHEDULING

without schedules, they tend to get lost—which is what often happens.

For interdivisional activities undertaken on short notice, schedules, if any, must be prepared *ad hoc*. This duty can well be undertaken by the administrative analyst. It should be emphasized that *he* does not usurp the function of the administrator, who decides *what* is to be done. The administrative analyst steps in where the administrator's function ends: he must determine *how* it is to be done. Subject to the operating requirements of each project, he should determine the administrative sequence and routing. The processes which he can use for scheduling non-recurrent work are discussed in the next chapter rather than here, since they are closely related to the subject of procedural control.

THE FACTOR OF BACKLOG

A common error in scheduling, whether for routine or non-recurrent work, is computing the time required for doing a long job as the sum of the individual task times when the tasks are done in different units. To do so is to ignore motion delay, which is always present in administrative organizations, and which is largely responsible for their slowness of operation. The administrative analyst must make allowance for the time required for each move, providing he cannot shorten it. The first and last elements of motion delay, time in transit and time required to process the work, may be arrived at without too much trouble. But the time between the delivery of a paper and the moment when the recipient starts to do something about it is the most elusive. This interval is determined by the "backlog" of the official in question or of the unit to which he belongs.[7]

Physically, an official's backlog is represented by the pile of papers lying on his desk waiting for action. For planning purposes it is more convenient to express backlog in terms of hours of work to be done. Each employee in an administrative circuit must have some backlog to keep him busy; the backlog is the slack which allows for variations in the flow of work. In scheduling, it is necessary to account for the backlog at each point of handling, and to assume that all matters of equal or superior priority on hand must be disposed of before an incoming paper can be given attention. This matter deserves special thought when it is proposed to merge operations or to transfer them to officials having many other duties. It is quite

---

[7] I am indebted to Mr. Oliver G. Brain, Director of the Procedure Division, Farm Security Administration, for introducing me to the problems connected with backlog.

ADMINISTRATIVE PROCEDURE

possible to rearrange work so as to lessen actual job time and yet to delay final accomplishment because of increased backlogs.[8]

The factor of backlog is of course recognized even where it is given no systematic attention: it is common practice to label some papers "rush," attaching colored slips to show their preferred status. The danger is always that the number of rush papers will cause the distinction to lose meaning. One is reminded of the American diplomat visiting Russia who was given, as a mark of courtesy, a permit to buy railroad tickets without waiting in line. When he arrived at the station to take his first trip, he was ushered to the rear of one of two lines almost equally long. When he protested, the station master explained: "But you see, Comrade, this is the line for those who have permits to buy tickets without waiting in line!" In order to assure proper discrimination as to priority it may in some cases be desirable to establish various levels of urgency. The German ministries have two categories: urgent matters (*Eilsachen*) and immediate matters (*Sofortsachen*). Whatever schemes for expediting particular papers are used, they should be restricted to cases of extreme importance.

An official's current backlog can be computed as the sum of the job times for the tasks he has on hand, if these have been estimated or scheduled. His average backlog may be discovered by a series of observations. The employee arranges all his pending papers in a single pile. The paper at the bottom is designated as the "control" paper, and all new incoming papers are placed underneath it in the order of receipt. The time is noted, and then noted again when the "control" paper is reached, at which point the paper then at the bottom of the pile becomes a new "control" paper. An averaged series of intervals between control papers provides an estimate of the employee's backlog. The same result may be obtained by maintaining and analyzing a work diary, in case it is not feasible to arrange the papers in the way suggested. Due allowance must of course be made for special factors, such as variability in the kind of work and the presence of one or more types of material requiring preferred handling.

Backlog has several causes. One is overload, in which case the employee's backlog grows steadily until part of his work is transferred to someone else. Another is interruption, due to extraneous work, absence, etc. The third and most common cause of backlog is the arrival of work in batches, so that the volume of accumulated busi-

---

[8] See the author's "A Note on Executive Planning," *cit. supr.*

ness fluctuates. In many offices backlog varies regularly with the time of day, month, or year. In the Government, for instance, purchasing offices always have a year-end peak due to the consumption of appropriation balances, and budget offices have annual cycles with heavy loads in certain months.

To gain the best utilization of energy and the highest speed in administration, it is necessary to straighten out the flow of work, compensating for unavoidable peaks by assigning temporary employees and moving non-rush tasks to slack periods. Many organizations have already taken steps in this direction; for instance, telephone and electric companies usually stagger their billings, and many large companies pay employees in different departments on separate days. Some offices have scheduled times to order supplies, and others have experimented with starting projects involving considerable administrative work at regular intervals.

The problem of timing and scheduling so as to achieve maximum speed of accomplishment combined with an even flow of work can only be discussed in specific detail when a program has been framed and "control points" established. The objective is to time and route each administrative sequence so that it will not clash with other sequences.

It is, of course, possible for administrative offices to operate without any attempt at scheduling, or even at qualitatively precise planning. Most have gotten along for years without them. But by the same token most such offices, if they have any appreciable volume of work, are slow in functioning. To achieve speedier administration, definite time standards have to be applied. Many executives and technical people always bristle with resentment at anything remotely implying "putting a stop-watch on them." Yet perhaps in the long run such umbrage may seem as unreasonable as irritation at being told when to stop and go by a traffic signal.

Chapter XIV

MANAGEMENT CONTROL

ALTHOUGH control is treated theoretically as the last phase of administration, in one sense it is the first phase. The cycle of planning, execution, and control is continuous; once it gets started there is no greater break between control and (re)planning than between either other pair. Control is the examination of results, not because of abstract curiosity, but for the purpose of testing and re-shaping programs and methods. It depends upon information, but mere information is not control. A driver may see that his car is leaving the road, but he is not controlling the car until the perception leads to appropriate muscular responses and he steers it back on the pavement. Administrators and technicians on each level need the data provided by control observations as a basis for keeping performance up to operating standards or within permissible ranges of deviation or "tolerances."

Control is needed in both direct administration and administrative management. Administrative control is directed at results and processes of direct action; it aims to assure that the product of the activity is as desired in every respect. It is concerned with *what* is being administered—with seeing that the organization is fulfilling its purpose, and that the purpose itself is rightly defined. This kind of control has been discussed in earlier sections, particularly in Chapter X.

But another type of control is needed: that designed to assure the proper functioning of the administrative machinery. The administrative analyst assists the administrator in specifying functions, tasks, and sequences, and works out the details of distribution, timing, and scheduling. To effectuate this planning and execution there must be suitable control. Procedure work is continuous: there must be constant redesigning of structure and method based on observation of accomplishment and on criticism by line officials, customers, and "disinterested" observers. Each operating plan should include means

MANAGEMENT CONTROL

for reporting results to the management planner, so that he can diagnose and correct faults and be prepared to recommend realignments of functions and sequences before the need becomes acute. If there is scheduling, there must be reports to show whether work is proceeding on schedule and where delay is being encountered. These reports must carry enough information, yet they must be simple and easy to prepare, read, and interpret.

The scheduling of administrative sequences which pass through a number of divisions is most effective when there are current reports showing the status of each project and directing attention to delays and snags as soon as they occur. In the Rural Electrification Administration such reports are made weekly by the Production Control Unit in the Management Division, which schedules projects according to the standard time table.[1] As soon as an allotment for a project is made, the Control Unit makes out cards showing the date on which each subsequent action up to the approval of the construction contract is due. These are filed by the Control Unit in a visible record cabinet. Each office performing operations in the sequence makes a report as of the close of work every Friday showing the projects it has processed and the date of each action. This information is posted on the schedule cards. If an action is overdue, a hollow "warning" flag is attached to the space where it should be recorded, showing that the project in question must be rushed to bring it back on schedule. For recording lengthy delays there are red flags showing the number of days overdue. After posting, the cards are stacked in panels and photographed. The result is a series of charts showing each current project, the dates on which administrative actions have been taken, and the warning flags signalling late and overdue projects.

The progress charts are sent to the Administrator and the division heads on the Wednesday following the receipt of data. Every other Thursday,[2] these officials assemble in a "production meeting" at which an explanation of each delay is requested of the official technically responsible for it and steps toward bringing the work back to schedule are agreed upon. The production meeting is not intended to be a device for harrying the delinquent but rather a means for getting at the causes of administrative troubles. Emphasis is laid on planning the necessary action to bring projects back on schedule. If a project is held up because of factors which the organization can

---

[1] The development of this time table was discussed in the previous chapter in the section entitled "Timing and Scheduling Large Scale Administrative Operations."
[2] Originally every Thursday.

ADMINISTRATIVE PROCEDURE

neither control nor correct, such as litigation, it is removed from the schedule and restored only when the obstacle has been overcome. In other cases the schedule may be revised as circumstances warrant. The general psychological effect of the reports and production meetings, however, is to spur divisional officials to get work done on time, thus avoiding membership in the "alibi club."

REPORTING PROGRESS OF INDIVIDUAL WORK ASSIGNMENTS

When scheduling is applied to individual work loads, performance should be reported in terms of the schedule. The simplest method is to issue working instructions with estimated job-times and deadlines. These may be completed as reports by checking the jobs done and entering the time spent on major assignments (but not individual tasks). The Forest Service sets up its work plans this way, covering each man's work load as a whole, and uses the resulting reports for evaluating and re-distributing tasks. An example of the resulting computation is shown in the following case cited by Loveridge:

Case 1—A very competent, experienced, and hard-working junior forester in charge of a district with 2 sawmills, 2 lookout stations, an average of 9 fires annually, 3,100 cattle and 34,000 sheep under permit, a summer-home colony and other land-use activities, as well as a driveway problem and miscellaneous duties.

ACTIVITY	Days in Peak Season Past actual	Job needs as determined by analysis
Non-field	13	24
Field:		
Timber management	34	36
Range management	59	73
Roads, trails, structures	10	12
All fire activities	22	21
Land uses	9	11
Number of days worked	147	177
Number of work days available	129	129
Sundays and holidays worked	18	0

The past actual in this case does not show the complete picture of overtime devoted to keeping things going well in the field, or night work done to keep abreast of the office job. The analysis definitely shows the need for relief from the over-load, if the work is to be well done by a competent man without danger of breaking down.[3]

---

[3] Loveridge, op. cit., p. 54 ff. It should be pointed out that the work plan of

MANAGEMENT CONTROL

The device of preparing a consolidated work plan and completing it as a report is best applicable to loads consisting of large numbers of small tasks, the character but not the exact incidence of which is known in advance. It is also useful for determining whether an employee has too little, just enough, or too much to do.

When an employee's work consists of a few sizable non-recurrent jobs, it may be desirable to keep track of each separately. Methods for doing this have been developed by the Office Service Department of the Tennessee Valley Authority, both for its own use and for that of operating divisions.[4] The TVA systems presuppose exact task specification and, whenever possible, comparison and weighting of the various elements within jobs. The record in each case is a visible index card, the bottom lines showing the title or type of assignment, the date assigned, a symbol designating the employee, and (when scheduled) the date due. On the right-hand side is a percentage scale for reporting progress, running from 0 to 100, with a celluloid strip which may be pulled out to cover it to any point. For scheduled work two strips are used, one of orange to show percentage of work completed and of blue to indicate time elapsed.

Progress is reported at regular intervals. When work is carried on in a central office the supervisor confers with each employee, determining by inspection how much of each job has been done. In the types of field work for which progress records are maintained, it has been possible to assign values to most of the constituent sub-tasks, so that the employee can mail in weekly coupons showing the units of work which he has done. Periodic reports are obtained by placing a cardboard mask containing standardized headings over the job cards, and then photographing them. These reports tell administrative officials the exact status of each project, and also show which employees are free to take on additional assignments.

REPORTING CURRENT UNIT WORK LOADS

The scheduling of recurrent sequences, and that of mixed work loads of more or less independently operating individuals and units, was discussed in the previous chapter. But the scheduling process as applied to a heavy load of unstandardized and multi-functional business carried on within a geographically centralized (or otherwise

---

the forester in question did not necessarily require him to do all that should be done if his time were unlimited; a distinction is always made between the desirable and the possible.

[4] Tennessee Valley Authority, *Office Methods Bulletins*.

highly integrated) administrative structure was left to be covered here. The reason for doing so is that this type of scheduling depends peculiarly on control information—much more than any other kind.

For scheduling non-routine centralized operations, the administrative analyst must have full information in advance regarding the progress of current business and the volume of work on hand in each unit. It is useful to think of him, in this connection, as being like a master switchman in a freight yard. He breaks up incoming trains and makes up new ones, shifting cars from one track to another so as to arrange them in the desired order with as few moves as possible. Like the switchman, the analyst must know whether the tracks he wants to use are free and, if not, how many cars must be cleared first.

The switchman is not interested in the contents of cars, except as this determines the way they are to be arranged. Similarly, the administrative analyst is not interested in technology except as it relates to the proper functional and hierarchical arrangements of tasks, and to the time required for performing them.[5] He will not inquire too deeply into the detailed working methods of the divisions and sections which take part in a sequence, but he must know enough about their operations to size up the situation intelligently. He must also have a usable fund of information regarding similar tasks done before, and he must be able to outline new tasks clearly and concisely, so that those who do them can estimate their time requirements.

In order to bring the administrative analyst the control information needed for scheduling, in condensed form, there has been devised a "Unit Production Chart," which is illustrated in Figure 16. This chart has necessarily been drawn up in general terms, and any office using it as a model will have to make its own adaptation. The official who is responsible for current scheduling should receive such a chart, properly filled out, from each office in his jurisdiction at stated intervals. The chart will indicate the capacity of each unit in terms of man-hours in each occupational classification, and the volume of work which the unit has on hand or expects to receive during the forthcoming production period. Charts for professional and technical units should usually cover the work loads of individuals, whereas those for clerical offices will treat each group of workers in identical

---

[5] This is not meant to imply that he should not have plenty of curiosity, or that he should avoid going further than he needs into a subject which really interests him. He should, however, be a "generalist" except in the specific field of administration. See John M. Gaus, "Should Administrators Be Generalists or Specialists," in *Lectures on Administrative Management*, U. S. Department of Agriculture Graduate School, 1940.

MANAGEMENT CONTROL

positions as a whole. In either case, the unit head is expected to size up the progress of business in his office at regular intervals, which is desirable for its own sake.

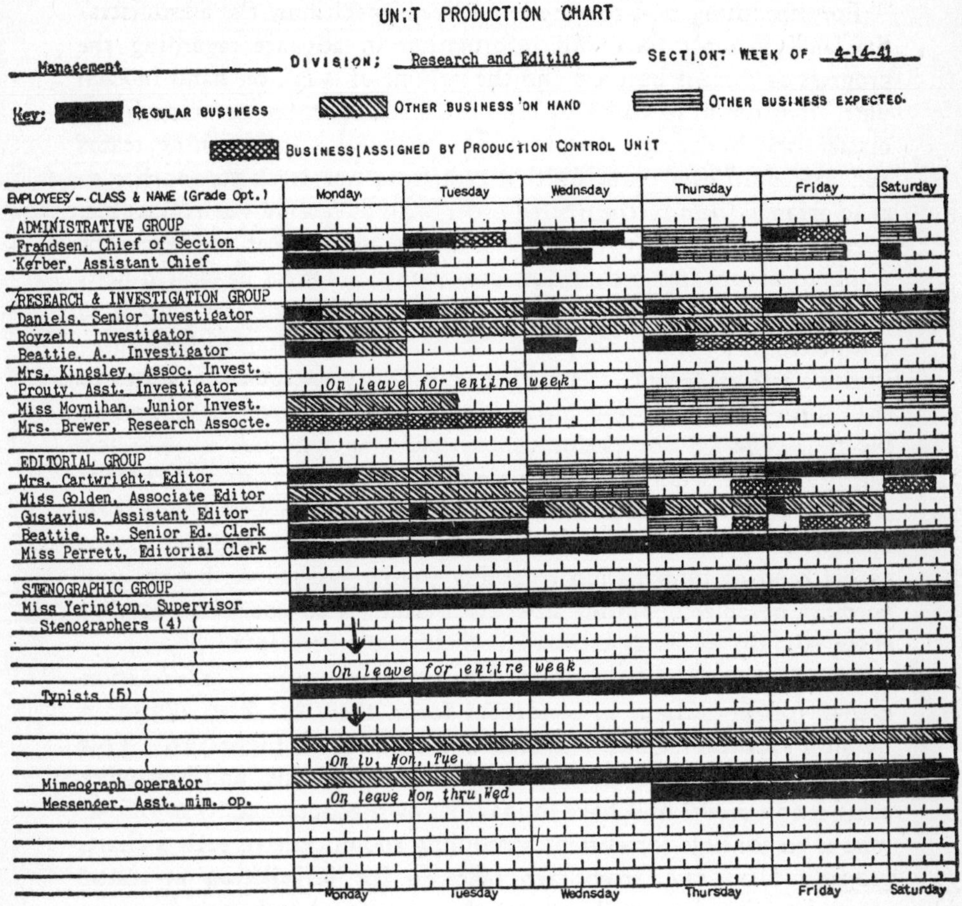

Exchanges Suggested:

1. Could detail Mrs. Kingsley for entire week. She has just returned from leave and has no assignments yet.

2. Daniels wants calculating machine with operator for same Thursday until Tuesday of following week.

3. Messenger on detail here wanted through Wednesday.

Signed: *Henry P. Frandsen*

Remarks: This chart has been made up as it might be in practise. The use of italics indicates entries which would probably be made in longhand.

Figure 16

ADMINISTRATIVE PROCEDURE

To make the chart as simple as possible, all detailed data are eliminated, quantities of time and work being expressed graphically by means of bar lines. With the use of color schemes various classes of work (recurrent and special, ordinary and rush jobs, etc.) can be differentiated. If records of individual task assignments are kept, the chart will summarize the current job cards. Each administrative sequence and major task should be assigned a number, to be used both in the unit's card file and in the central scheduling office. These numbers should be entered on the chart, so that each part of the work can be identified. It is of course unnecessary to provide numbers for small routine jobs. These should be lumped together, along with an allowance for unpredictable work, visitors, correspondence, etc., under a standard symbol.

The unit head should send his production chart to the administrative analyst sufficiently in advance of the ensuing production period. If possible, he should also send a tentative chart for the following period, listing work which can be anticipated that far ahead. The analyst will then know that he can assign work to each unit equal to the vacant work-hours shown on that unit's charts, and that further assignments will require extra personnel, overtime, or postponement of work already scheduled. He should, so far as possible, try to avoid scheduling up to the limit, so as to allow leeway for errors in time estimates, incidence of unexpected work, and "breathing spells."

If the administrative analyst undertakes to schedule non-recurrent projects, he must have the active co-operation of the officials who will perform or supervise the work, so that his efforts will not be arbitrary or meaningless. His plans, particularly the time estimates, must be confirmed by each operating unit concerned, so that they will be plans of the whole organization. Preliminary schedules should be prepared as far in advance as possible, and circulated to participating offices. They will carry statements of the objectives and methods of proposed projects, an outline of the sequence of tasks, and tentative job times and dates for completion. Unit heads will confirm or amend the first time estimates, and suggest any changes they feel should be made in the specifications for the work, and return the papers to the analyst as a basis for definite scheduling.

After reviewing the returned preliminary schedules and securing agreement on any differences, the analyst will make up a definite schedule. After this has been properly approved (unless the analyst is authorized to promulgate schedules himself) he will circulate it to

MANAGEMENT CONTROL

those who are to participate, and also distribute job tickets which are to be returned to him as the individual tasks are completed. A lengthy task may have intermediate tickets indicating, for instance, 25%, 50%, and 75% of completion. After the sequence starts, he will post the data from incoming tickets on the schedule, thus obtaining a running record of its progress.[6]

It is desirable to arrange the schedule so that estimated and actual job times and dates for completion run in parallel columns. This device will permit attention to be easily focussed on work which is behind schedule, and will facilitate assembling agenda for production meetings. Unit heads should be asked to report mistakes in time estimates at these meetings so that current schedules can be revised, and the experience used in future scheduling. The completed schedules will serve to record the relative success of the scheduling, and will afford data for analyzing deficiencies and improving technique. They will also provide material for supporting budget estimates, for reapportioning personnel, and for dealing with organizational problems. Combined with the unit production charts they should present the necessary facts for administrative cost accounting.

Reference is made again at this point to the pool of reserve personnel and the exchange service suggested in Chapter XII as means of increasing flexibility without the disadvantages of functionalism. The value of these services can be enhanced by integrating them with the scheduling process. In this way the capacity of the various units can be kept most nearly commensurate with current work loads, the resources of the organization being consistently applied at the points where they are most needed.

LIMITATIONS OF MANAGEMENT CONTROL

If management control is practiced too minutely, it will defeat its own purpose. It is not advisable to schedule intra-divisional business from a central office, or minor undertakings consisting of small tasks which do not require sustained attention. These should be grouped under the heading of "routine" and allowed for by unit heads when making up their production charts, but they do not merit the special attention of the administrative analyst unless the volume of routine in a particular unit is large enough to warrant study on its own account. Scheduling of standardized recurrent sequences will be semi-

---

[6] It is hardly necessary to state that the analyst can delegate most of the *clerical* work in connection with scheduling.

ADMINISTRATIVE PROCEDURE

automatic, consisting of applying the prearranged routing and job estimates to the current time situation. It is sufficient in this case to fit in the standard sequence with the non-standard and routine work, and to notify the appropriate units that a project of type so-and-so will arrive at such and such a time. For both recurrent and special sequences proper allowances must of course be made for motion delay and backlog.

The administrative analyst should, as a rule, confine scheduling and procedural control to the larger administrative undertakings requiring considerable effort by a number of offices, such as the preparation of development plans, the making of surveys, budget work, consummation of important "deals," and the carrying out of construction and similar programs. He will also, as a rule, arrange or at least be kept informed of important conferences, committee work, and liaison with outside organizations.

The analyst should not try to regulate the assignment of work within units, or within larger subdivisions which are closely integrated: this is the duty of line officials and heads of operating staff agencies. He should, however, keep informed of what is going on in each part of the organization, and should initiate or participate in the elimination of duplications of activity and unessential operations which sidetrack important programs. He must at all times be diplomatic in his relations with unit heads, avoiding "laying down the law" to them. Improvements in working methods should always be initiated as co-operative undertakings in which the operating official receives his due share of the credit. If pressure is necessary, it should be applied through the person of the administrator and seldom if ever directly by the analyst, even though he might have a "functional" right to do so. It is up to the analyst to see that as few questions as possible reach this stage, since successful management planning and control depend on thorough co-operation and a feeling of mutual achievement.

Chapter XV

POSSIBILITIES OF A RATIONAL TECHNIQUE OF ADMINISTRATION

SCIENTIFIC MANAGEMENT as applied to directly productive operations means the standardization of data of human behavior, and the study and correlation of facts so as to facilitate, co-ordinate, and simplify work. It means figuring out how to get the most output for the least input. It is scientific (strictly speaking) only insofar as it sticks to experiential facts and treats them objectively. Where exact factual knowledge is not to be had, management pursues its goal by using inferential logic, which is intellectual dead reckoning. The fact that it is no longer strictly scientific does not nullify its value—it is still better than purely subjective or rule-of-thumb administration.

The administrative analyst or management planner aims at the same objective in managing administration as the scientific manager does in managing industry. But he can not use the same methods: his work is never as clear-cut. It is much harder to measure the output of people's brains than that of their hands, and while a man can be told how to lift pig iron in a few minutes, and how to run a punch press in a few weeks, it is supposed to take four years to show him how to think. Executive tasks are troublesome to size up and specify, and a sequence of administrative and technical operations must always be laid out with some leeway for the unpredictable. The administrative analyst has to deal with relationships between individuals and groups, a subject we know far less about than we do about the relations between chemicals, physical forces, etc. Still, he tries to be as scientific as he can be. By observation and analysis he converts such ideas as functions, units of organization, concentration, and devolution from purely conceptual devices into tools for classifying phenomena. He develops constantly new techniques of measuring and comparing.

No science has ever grown up overnight. Advanced disciplines like physics, chemistry, and astronomy are all products of long develop-

ADMINISTRATIVE PROCEDURE

ment. They began when men started to think about the things they saw happening around them; there followed various stages in which ways of gathering and arranging data were slowly improved and bodies of rational thought were built on pragmatic bases. Management in administration, or administrative technique, is not yet a science. It is perhaps about where chemistry and biology were about two hundred years ago; it has divergent schools of opinion and a limited body of accepted thought.

Some say that the social sciences can never become exact sciences; that they must always rest on abstract and subjective ideas (sovereignty, self-interest, etc.) even though they assimilate scientific methods. Possibly administrative knowledge is in this category. Be that as it may, administration is an every-day necessity: we cannot wait for perfection. We have to apply such administrative technique as now exists, in full awareness of its faults. Because science is a word to be used rigorously, it is perhaps too soon to talk about a science of administration in the present tense. There are today, however, both a considerable body of knowledge and a growing technique of observation and analysis, which are being applied to practical administrative problems, and which give promise of becoming increasingly scientific as they go along.

THE ENVIRONMENT OF ADMINISTRATION

The student of administration, like the student of nature, begins by studying phenomena. These include the individual administrative and executive acts, their functional relation as parts of collective undertakings, their character, and bulk, and their arrangement in sequences. They include also the people who perform these acts, their abilities and potentialities, and the way they are theoretically and actually arranged physically and organizationally.

While the tools of administrative analysis relate essentially to the phenomena themselves, it is wrong to conceive of administration as taking place in a vacuum. The work of human organizations, like that of aggregations of ants and bees, takes place in a complex milieu. The administrator, be he man or insect, cannot confine himself to the limited problem of technique and organization needed to do a particular job. He must also safeguard the survival of his group by anticipating sentiments and reactions of its members, as well as the probable behavior of outside men and animals. So far as human activity is concerned, environmental conditions affecting administrative technique might for convenience be classified in four major groups: the physical, the political, the legal, and the socio-psychological. The first is concerned with objective conditions, which may be natural or man-caused. The last three represent different phases of human behavior.[1]

The various sets of environmental conditions exercise determining influence on both the programs and techniques of administration. For instance, a flood (physical) occasions public demand (political) for government action to prevent future inundations. A flood control measure is passed and found constitutional (legal). Later the agency administering the law encounters local resistance because of fear that established habits of living may be dislocated (socio-psychological). Any workable administrative plan must take account of all four factors; at each stage decisions must be made whether to bend policies to fit the environment, or to try to change the latter—whether to abandon an unpopular activity or try to sell it to the public, whether to plan in terms of the legal status quo or to seek desired legislation. Much of administration consists in responding to environmental stimuli in one way or another.

THE PHYSICAL ENVIRONMENT

The physical environment affects administration principally through its part in determining the subject or problems requiring action and the techniques to be employed. Most administrative activities are concerned with organizing the attack on a physical problem: natural, such as the need for food, shelter, and clothing, and protection against disease, pests, floods, etc.; or man-made, such as war, slums, unemployment, crime, etc.[2] The possible techniques are logical

---

[1] It might seem simpler to divide the environment of administration into two spheres, the physical and the human. But human behavior in a complex society is highly compartmentalized and its study even more so. Thus a man's attitude toward a proposal at any moment may be determined by whether he is thinking politically, legally, or in terms of the proposal's relation to himself and his way of living. His "authorities" might be, for instance, his party leader, the courts, and his church. The criteria of politics, law, and social tradition are different, and the arguments in these fields appeal to different sentiments. (See Graham Wallas, *Human Nature in Politics*, especially Chapters 4 and 5.)

In one sense the political and socio-psychological environment might seem to be identical. But social traditions and instincts run deeper than political programs politically approved may turn out to be socially unacceptable. Thus it might be voted to socialize all land, but doing so would cause wide disturbance of people's peace of mind. Even Henry George recognized the practical need for allowing people to keep nominal "title" to the property they occupied, and charging them "taxes" instead of "rent."

[2] Man-made conditions such as these have a socio-psychological basis, but the problems they pose are in large measure physical.

consequences of the problems themselves. The choice between alternate objectives and methods is determined by political [3] conditions and the will to deal with the problem at all is itself a political phenomenon. But on the whole, the kind of activity to be administered, if there is a desire for activity, is determined by the physical problem as it touches the welfare of those in whose interest the program is undertaken.

Since policy formation—determining what is to be done—is in large part a process of politically recognizing a situation which exists, the physical problem dictates to a large extent the scheme of functions. For instance, if the situation calls for building a dam, there must be assembled a corps of surveyors, engineers, cement workers, stonemasons, truck drivers, mechanics, electricians, and a second line of supervisors, purchasing and personnel men, accountants, doctors and nurses, etc. An administrative mechanism must be developed to encompass and co-ordinate all these. Thus the physical environment, as seen by those who plan, sets up the necessities of administration which, in turn, determine the method.

But the physical environment also affects administration in a more direct way. For instance, the specific techniques employed in building dams (and hence the purposes of administration in this field) are somewhat uniform. But the way an organization constructing dams will *administer* them depends on their distance apart, the presence or absence of a geographic and social region, and the relative availability of central sources of supply and personnel. The Tennessee Valley Authority was able to establish a fully integrated organization to manage the construction of a number of dams (not to forget its other activities), whereas the Public Works Administration, which has public power projects in widely separated localities, has had to rely largely on semi-autonomous local authorities. The physical problem of communication is important in determining administrative structure and procedure; this is patently so in military operations, and only slightly less so in civil activities.

In general, geographic concentration of activity, uniformity of operating conditions, and convenient channels of information permit a centralized and functionalized organization with elaborate staff offices participating widely in detailed operations,[4] whereas their

---

[3] The term "political" is used in a broad sense, to denote a dominance of ideas, even in technical fields, rather than the mere preponderance of a political party.

[4] This is not to gainsay what has previously been said in favor of decentralization. The conditions cited here make centralization technically possible; they do not necessarily make it desirable.

A RATIONAL TECHNIQUE OF ADMINISTRATION

opposites call for decentralization and independence of field units except in relation to major policies. The attempt to impose detailed central control on activity carried on in dispersed places under variable conditions has repeatedly resulted in failure and will always do so.

The foregoing only serves to hint at the way in which the physical environment of administration may influence it. More specific illustrations are at hand in any organization; they will be found both in the way programs are laid out and in the methods of supervision.

THE POLITICAL ENVIRONMENT

Like the physical environment, the political context of administration affects organization and procedure both through the determination of programs and in more direct ways. It is outside our present scope to describe the process by which popular reaction to a physical or social situation is translated into legislative authority and then into administrative programs. Nor need we go into the ways in which basic business policies are formulated by those in final control.

It is important to note, however, that another political process, sometimes in accord with and sometimes contradictory to that going on in the public arena, takes place *within* organizations. Program planning, other than the most routine sort, is essentially a political activity. An agency which makes provision for the sifting upwards of policies and plans, from the operating officials to the top administrator, will be "shot through with politics," although not necessarily a kind of politics objectionable in civil servants. Consciousness of the total aim of a public organization is political consciousness, and its expressions are political even though they may not be considered "politics" in the usual sense. No one would argue that the civil servant should go blindly about his narrow task without a feeling of relationship to the whole job of his bureau and of his department, or that he should suppress such a feeling if he has it. The most effective organizations are those which, instead of suppressing, develop and co-ordinate policy-forming opinion among their employees.

The shibboleth that "the civil servant should be divorced from politics" is meaningless: it expresses an impossibility.[5] Likewise the

---

[5] There have of course been attempts to "sterilize" civil servants by forbidding them to "influence" legislation, even on technical points within their special fields.

distinction between "policy forming" and "non-policy forming" jobs. Each member of an administrative organization has some responsibility for program and policy within his field. The responsibility of subordinates is intermediate, that of the administrator more final, though not completely so. The distinctive thing about the position of a "politically responsible" department head is not that he forms policy but that he interprets it to the legislators and the public. An administrator in a democracy is normally faced with two sets of "political" pressures. One comes from "outside" sources: politicians of varied ilk, special interest representatives, the press, etc., and the other comes from his own employees. Both, subject to certain limitations, are legitimate.[6]

Politicians are not only concerned with *what* is to be administered. They take sporadic but intense interests in *how*. Congressmen, news columnists, reformers, and general busybodies all like to ride administrative hobbies, regardless of how much or little they know about the technical or organizational problems at hand. When an administrative problem comes to issue in the political arena, it is seldom decided on the technical merits of the case. The popular haranguers refuse to let the argument stay within fields in which they do not know the language. If the real question is too involved for the politicians to understand, then another question must be raised and the battle fought over that. The most patent examples of this phenomenon are the Congressional struggle over the President's Reorganization Bill of 1937, and the recurrent dispute as to whether the United States Employment Service should be in the Social Security Board or

---

But anything which tends to close avenues of information to legislators is certain to give way in the face of practical necessity.

A distinction between the kinds of politics which are proper and improper for civil servants could conveniently be drawn by excluding any activity which tends to benefit a particular group at the expense of other groups or the public or which promotes any candidacy for elective office. There is nothing in the Hatch Act which inhibits legitimate policy-influencing by civil servants.

[6] These remarks have been directed at the situation of the public administrator, to whom the urgings of external and internal protagonists of policy are equally audible. The private administrator may wish to cater to public sentiment, but he does not have external reactions thrust upon him. Rather, he needs to take some pains to learn how people feel about his business. His immediate constituency, the stockholders, are normally inarticulate, and the board of directors which is their "legislature" is usually subservient to the management and therefore seldom active, except as an advisory group. The pressures which arise within a private concern, on the other hand, are not so frequently directed at the furthering of programs or policies springing from the professional zeal or disinterested opinions of employees. Unless the management has been unusually skillful in its "missionary work," the latter are more inclined to adopt a "we and they" attitude and to concern themselves mainly with their personal or craft interests.

A RATIONAL TECHNIQUE OF ADMINISTRATION

the Department of Labor.

The administrator cannot always follow objective and reasonable considerations of economy and efficiency. He has to consider the political consequences of events which in themselves may be relatively harmless. For instance, the elaborate precautions taken by most public agencies to prevent any sort of petty graft are not based on the assumption that public employees are less honest than others, or on any estimate of the cost of preventing each marginal dollar of loss. They exist more because of the political repercussions of irregularities than because of the damage caused by the irregularities themselves.

It is thus necessary for the administrator to listen not only to the administrative analyst, who is concerned mainly with getting work done as efficiently as possible, but also to political advisors who "keep an ear to the ground" and who study the reactions and behavior of people with whom the organization deals. The advice of the latter may lead to departures from what seems to be good management, and sometimes to the adoption of purposely cumbersome procedures. For instance, it is often necessary to protect field men engaged in distributing relief or loan money from the importunities of would-be clients. In order to remove from the man "out front" the onus of unpopular decisions, it is usually the custom in such situations to have him refer all applications to a superior office for review and formal action. The latter normally follows the recommendations of the field agent, who can always get out of an embarrassing situation by indicating the action desired and then pleading that he had nothing to do with the decision.

A basic rule of good management is that each function and activity should be precisely defined and allocated, and that responsibility and authority should run parallel. This policy may usually be adhered to, so far as internal administration is concerned. Yet when seekers after special privilege become too insistent, it may be necessary to find ways of "giving them the run-around." This very convenient weapon of bureaucratic defense can unfortunately be abused to cover up error and indolence. But it can never be entirely dispensed with, as it is sometimes the only shield an organization has against flank attacks.

Administration is never divorced from politics; rather it is the implementation of politics—the development in detail and execution of plans roughed out by legislatures. A consistent and deep-seated rift between politicians and administrators is always a sign of a breakdown of democratic control. Yet the administrator is expected to distinguish between legitimate and illegitimate politics. He is asked to respond sympathetically to "proper" requests of statesmen and spokesmen (representatives of the public), while he is expected to refuse "improper" demands of politicians and lobbyists (representatives of special privilege). This is not a very clear distinction. The authors of "proper" and "improper" proposals are often identical; the divergent names applied to them may merely illustrate a difference in attitude, being used reciprocally by two sets of partisans.

The line between "legitimate" and "illegitimate" political pressure depends on the prevailing political ethos of the community. A department head serving under Pendergast in Kansas City could hardly be asked to judge an issue in the same way as his colleague working for LaGuardia in New York. It is useless to moralize about the "subservience to politicians" of individual administrators save in terms of the communal morality which finds political expression. Those socially-minded public servants who have tried from time to time to work effectively in a corrupt political environment have usually ended either by compromising or by going into politics.

Administration, as a whole, tends to reflect public morality, or rather that phase of it which succeeds in expressing itself effectively in politics. The introduction of rational management technique, depending as it does upon criticism of methods, discussion of objectives, and free interchange of information, is only possible when the political objectives are such that they can be analyzed without fear of embarrassment, and when the details of operation contain nothing which has to be hidden.

THE LEGAL ENVIRONMENT

The legal environment of administration consists of the constitutional background and the various laws which authorize, facilitate, channelize, and limit administrative activity, as applied by the courts and by quasi-judicial authorities. A distinction can be drawn between the *functions of legislation*—the establishment of objectives and broad programs, and the appropriation of funds; and the *function of administrative planning*—precise definition of purpose, delineation of projected activity, and arrangement of ways and means for action. This idea implies that legislation should eschew detail, confining itself to stating what results are desired and leaving it to administrators to decide how to get those results.

A RATIONAL TECHNIQUE OF ADMINISTRATION

As a matter of practice, enabling legislation, as we find it in the United States, goes into detail more often than not, and sets forth more or less specific ways and means which administrators are compelled to utilize. If the details are consonant with the realities of the situation, all is well and good. But if they do not work out to advantage, or if circumstances change, administration may be hamstrung. It is of course obvious why administrators try to influence legislation, and why any wholesale ban on "legislative" activities of civil servants is next to impossible to enforce.

It is frequently remarked that our legal structure, on both national and local levels, is far too complicated. Our common-law system of case-by-case construction inevitably leads to further complexity. Each enactment becomes overlaid with a superstructure of interpretation which the administrator must follow. Insofar as the law and its encrustations are complicated, administrative procedure must also be. Yet there could be great simplification without any legal revolution if legislators would keep two things in mind: (1) the administrative processes necessary for executing laws, and (2) the constructive interpretation of laws. If each Congressman or Senator who has fathered a bill and piloted it successfully to enactment would keep an eye on his brainchild, inquiring every now and then as to the possibilities of simplification, the tasks of administrators would be measurably lightened.

There are many laws which, while inspired by laudable purposes, have complicated Federal administration more than is perhaps necessary to achieve the ends sought. One such is the law requiring counting and weighing of mail sent out under frank by Government agencies. Another is the Davis-Bacon law which aims to assure that workers employed on construction contracts for the Government shall be paid "prevailing" wages. There can be no quarrel with this objective. But the way it is accomplished, by a special determination of rates for each craft made by the Secretary of Labor before advertisement for bids, such determinations each applying only to a single contract, adds an average of one month to the time required for consummating a contract.

In other cases, basic legislation is simple enough, but over-construction has made it complicated. Section 3709 of the Revised Statutes, which governs all Federal purchasing except in amounts and categories mentioned in specific exemptions, states:

ADMINISTRATIVE PROCEDURE

All purchases and contracts for supplies and services, in any of the Departments of the Government, except for personal services, shall be made by advertising a sufficient time previously for proposals respecting the same, when the public exigencies do not require the immediate delivery of the articles, or performance of the service. When immediate delivery or performance is required by the public exigency, the articles or service required may be procured by open purchase or contract, at the places and in the manner in which such articles are usually bought and sold, or such services engaged, between individuals.

This is not a complicated statute. Its objective is to secure goods and services at the lowest cost, and it states the method in broad terms. But the Government purchasing agent has to reckon with a number of restrictive interpretations laid down by the Comptroller General. The term "public exigency" has been construed very narrowly, to mean only emergencies such as fires, floods, epidemics, etc. It is not considered to cover operating emergencies, such as unforeseen needs for material, even though the financial loss to the Government through idleness of men and machinery may exceed the possible savings which could be secured through competitive bidding. The type of emergency caused by delay in appropriating funds is not even recognized to the extent of allowing preference for bids which offer immediate delivery, despite the often urgent need of starting operations on short notice.

The Comptroller General has further interpreted Section 3709 as requiring bid solicitations to call for prices "both ways," that is for delivery at point of origin as well as destination. The purpose of this requirement is to assure that the Government will gain whatever advantage may be obtained from its preferential "land grant" freight rates. The use of freight rates in bid transactions involves a series of extra operations and is only worthwhile when there is a land-grant railroad in the picture [7] and when the shipment

---

[7] There are land-grant railroads east of the Mississippi River only in Illinois, Michigan, Wisconsin, Florida, Alabama, and Mississippi.

Since the paragraph touching on "land grant" freight rates was written, the situation has been potentially changed by the passage of the Wheeler-Lea Transportation Bill (Transportation Act of 1940). §321 of this law provides that civilian departments of the Government shall pay full commercial rates if and when the railroads in question shall file releases of certain claims with the Secretary of the Interior. Probably most railroads will do so, although certain western roads may feel their claims are worth more than the increased rates on Government business, particularly as military and naval transportation will still be paid for at "land grant" rates. It is also possible that the railroads may offer the Government a percentage deduction, applicable not only in "land-grant" territory, but elsewhere too. Thus, at the time of writing (10-27-40) the Government freight rate situation is "wide open."

is heavy enough so that the differential in rates will be greater than the rather considerable administrative cost. It would be easy to analyze experience and work out criteria as to when freight rates should be used. The Comptroller, however, has modified his original ruling that rates must be used in *all* cases only to the extent of dispensing with them when shipments weigh less than 200 pounds. Actually 5000 pounds would be nearer the mark, except for certain particular articles, even in "land grant" states; this has been proved by statistical analysis. But most Federal departments, although aware of the needlessness of looking up rates and making computations, have felt it necessary to go on doing so. The sudden discontinuance of freight rate service by the Treasury Procurement Division in March, 1940, however, made it impossible for many departments and agencies to continue compliance with the Comptroller's ruling. Since then, bids for all except very large shipments have been received on a "delivered price only" basis.

It would be possible to cite many other instances of legal requirements which complicate public administration, but the foregoing are sufficient. They are merely instances of what happens when a secondary position is thrust upon the administrator, who thinks of laws as instruments for producing certain results, and who feels that they should be so executed and interpreted as best to serve the desired ends; while at the same time, the upper hand is given to the legalist, who believes with Gilbert's Lord Chancellor that:

> The law is the true embodiment
> Of everything that's excellent.
> It has no kind of fault or flaw,
> And I, my Lords, embody the law.

LEGISLATION AND CONGRESSIONAL CONTROL

A primary reason why Congress tends to enact laws which prescribe so many of the details of administration, why it resists attempts to circumscribe the power of the Comptroller General as a "congressional officer," is its desire not to lose control over the executive branch and not to write "blank checks." Few people disagree with the concept of the executive's responsibility to Congress, or maintain that administration is a precinct in which the legislator should never intrude. What civil servants object to is the ineptitude of certain legislative controls, and the tendency to ossify procedures which should be flexible.

The tendency for legislative control to result unintentionally in hamstringing administration is perhaps more pronounced under our constitutional framework than it is under the British "parliamentary executive" system. Since we are very anxious these days to make our form of government work as well as possible, it is important to counteract this tendency by devising a control mechanism which will not only check upon the executive establishment but also facilitate the "streamlining" of administration. There should be means of transmitting information, and making constructive criticism, in both directions. A step in this direction would be the creation in Congress of a permanent Joint Committee on Administrative Management, which would take over the functions of the recent Select Committee on Government Reorganization, and would consider all problems of organization and procedure, and of the business management of Government offices. This committee would have to co-operate with other committees whose jurisdictions might be concerned, such as the House Committee on Expenditures in the Executive Departments, the two committees on Civil Service, the Joint Committee on Printing, and so forth. Its business would be to discover the *simplest administrative procedures* for carrying out the programs and maintaining the standards enacted by Congress. It would review pending laws with a view to making them as simple to administer as possible.

The Committee on Administrative Management should have a permanent staff of experts to investigate the proposals submitted to it and to advise regarding their feasibility. The staff should look for ways of simplifying Federal administrative practices, and should prepare necessary legislation to this end. While the activities of the Committee's staff would necessarily overlap those of the Division of Investigation and Administrative Management in the Budget Bureau, it is important for Congress to have its own staff of administrative technicians. However objective the Budget Bureau may be, Congressmen always regard it as a creature of the administration. Its recommendations would obtain a more cordial hearing if they were ratified by an independent body responsible to Congress. There is also the possibility that the Budget Bureau, although now highly developed as a center for administrative co-ordination and improvement, might become weakened in succeeding administrations.

The suggested Joint Committee on Administrative Management is not a *sine qua non* for improving administrative technique; much is already being accomplished without it. But rationalization and simplifying of administration can progress only so far without cor-

A RATIONAL TECHNIQUE OF ADMINISTRATION

responding changes in its legal environment. It is important to develop some means of studying the administrative phases of new laws before enactment, and of gradually revising the present legal structure to permit more efficient operation.

THE SOCIO-PSYCHOLOGICAL ENVIRONMENT—"HUMAN NATURE"

In the first chapter the point was made that administrative procedure is, among other things, a pattern of human behavior and, therefore, hard to change. Men may readily trade in their automobiles and sometimes even their wives, but they cling to their habits. They hate to be reorganized. While an administrator may become convinced that a rearrangement of functions and persons is essential, he may have a long struggle to convince his operating chiefs. Of course he may simply order people about in spite of objections, but if he is wise he will not do this, because he will want subordinates to work with him and for him, and not merely under him.

Resistance to change is a deep-seated instinct, arising from centuries of uncomfortable experience with changes. It is largely a common-sense instinct, since it inhibits men from rearranging their lives without prospective gains sufficient to offset the costs of adjustment. In administrative organizations resistance to change is bound up with a variety of motives such as fear of losing one's job, dislike of moving into strange situations, and the desire to entrench and enhance one's position. These are perfectly normal sentiments. Yet sometimes, in the mass-psychology situations which often exist in offices, particularly those conscious of inadequacy or superfluity, they lead to a peculiar group sensitivity to outside stimuli and cause irrational responses. There are units which, at the approach of an investigator or personnel classifier, fall into panic. Wild rumors of wholesale dismissals get started, and the work becomes totally disorganized, often for no real reason.

The instinctive reactions of individuals and groups sometimes hamper the administrative analyst in securing work load data, and occasionally prevent him from finding out even what offices do. If working methods seem susceptible of improvement, the implication that operating officials are to be blamed for not having already improved them is hard to suppress. If an administrative analyst, through mischance, places an operating unit on the defensive, it will make superhuman efforts to prove the necessity of each of its tasks and to dig up every conceivable reason why each should be done exactly as at present. Because prestige is thought to be related to the number of subordinates, unit chiefs do not like to give out work load information if they think it will lead to reduction of their forces. For the same reason they resist simplification, hoping that recognition of the difficult work they do will lead to reward. From an objective point of view, jobs can be best protected and individuals most easily advanced in accordance with their merit if organization is flexible and working methods efficient. But people do not always act rationally when their personal interests are concerned.

The administrative analyst trying to apply rational technique to administration must show by his actions the falsity of the widespread prejudice against scientific management, which exists among administrative as well as industrial workers. There is a stereotype of the "efficiency man" which pictures him as a Simon Legree whose peculiar delight is abolishing as many jobs as he can and making one man do the work of three. This image, which has figured prominently in the mythology of organized labor, originally had some justification in the fact that some industrial concerns, and occasionally the Government, perverted some of the devices of scientific management to anti-social ends. Organizations which did this were not practicing scientific management: they were acting counter to its basic philosophy.[8]

During its years of experience, scientific management has developed a code of ethics, an important tenet of which is that the benefits of efficiency should be shared by all concerned—the entrepreneur, the worker, and the public. It is true that many of those who control industry still think in terms of scarcity. Scientific managers, on the other hand, believe that the best cure for economic troubles is to produce *more*, particularly more of the things which are most needed, and to increase demand by lowering prices. In fields where capitalism, in its economic sense, has been supplanted by the "special-interest socialism" of monopolies, technological unemployment will exist. Where capitalist dynamics are really effective, or where special-interest price fixing is superseded by public-interest price fixing, it can be kept under control. Labor's real quarrel is not with the scientific manager, but with the reactionary entrepreneur who prevents him from being fully effective.

---

[8] Anyone who has any doubts as to the social consciousness of Frederick W. Taylor should read his little book, *The Principles of Scientific Management*. Taylor was very emphatic on the point that his methods were not intended as tools for exploitation.

A RATIONAL TECHNIQUE OF ADMINISTRATION

So far as the Government is concerned, scientific management presents little or no danger to employees. The amount of desirable work a public agency can do is almost limitless; the volume of activity is bounded only by its budget. Whenever improved operation or administration releases employees, the money saved can always be used to set up new positions where their work will be more productive. Wholesale reductions in the Government service occur for only two reasons: abandonment of an activity and curtailment of funds. Cases of net reductions traceable to increases in efficiency are practically non-existent. In any case, a Federal or state agency which can show that it spends its funds with the least waste is far more secure than one open to attack on charges of inefficiency.

It is of course necessary that the connection between the abolition of a job and the discharge of its incumbent be severed, even at the cost of maintaining a few workers in comparative idleness until suitable transfers can be arranged.[9] Workers displaced could be used to staff the "reserve pool" suggested in Chapter XII, or they could be given courses of training for new positions. When reductions are unavoidable, the line of least resistance—dismissing those whose particular jobs are terminated—should be avoided. Instead, "separation registers" should be set up on an organization-wide basis, according to the most objective information available. These things are necessary if workers are to be induced to think and act, not as members of a particular unit, section, or division, but as active participants in the larger undertaking of the whole organization.

To sum up, consideration of the socio-psychological environment of administration means recognizing the human factor in every administrative problem, and studying the way in which people respond to situations as individuals and groups. It has been discussed here in terms of the relations between management and the employees; but much of what has been said can be applied, in slightly different terms, to relations with the public. The main point is that an administrative organism is not a machine composed of inert elements, to be tinkered with at will, but a collection of individuals, each of whom reacts in his own personal way to the situations with which he is confronted.

---

[9] It is sometimes literally more economical to pay employees to do nothing than to maintain useless functions which may interfere with the progress of essential work.

ADMINISTRATIVE PROCEDURE

MAKING MANAGEMENT DEMOCRATIC

All of the foregoing leads up to a final point. Administrative management, or the application of rational technique to administration, must be thoroughly democratic. It must not be a mystery propounded in esoteric terms by a caste of intellectual priests, but it must be a common way of doing things accepted by everybody. The administrative analyst must not be an exalted and remote "staff officer," but should approach each office he studies with an attitude of wanting to learn as much as possible, not only from executives and supervisors but also from the operators and clerks who perform the direct labor. He can never have immediate personal knowledge of all the functions and activities his work covers, but he should develop his capacity for listening and understanding. He must speak the common language so that he can quickly get at what he wants to find out, and so that he can sell operating people ideas in terms of their own experience.

The administrative analyst must always remember to work *with* people. He must accept the fact that few of his results, at least few that are worthwhile, will be peculiarly or exclusively his own. While he may sketch out the first draft of a plan of organization or a procedure, the final result will usually be a synthesis of ideas gathered from operating officials, plus those of his own which stand up under criticism. He should not of course attempt the impossible task of securing complete agreement from everybody—he should be quick to recognize and discount obstructionism. But, as a rule, the wider the participation in shaping a plan, the easier it will be to put it into effect.

A lesson learned during our few decades of experience with giant corporations and ten-thousand-employee Government agencies, is that democratic management is better management. Since authority to execute must be delegated and re-delegated to many levels, it is necessary to delegate also the desire for efficient accomplishment which in a small plant may be translated into specific task instructions by a single manager. This can only be done by giving operating officials and workers, all the way down the line, their share in influencing the functioning and growth of the organization. It is important to cultivate the feeling of proprietorship, so that employees will of their own accord think about better ways of doing their jobs as individuals and groups, and so that they will welcome changes which improve production.

A RATIONAL TECHNIQUE OF ADMINISTRATION

Some of the planning systems described in earlier chapters to illustrate procedural problems are significant as experiments in democratic management. The "project work budget" and "job load analysis" used by the Forest Service are examples of program and management planning on the first level of administration: the Ranger District. The county planning program of the Department of Agriculture enlists the active collaboration not only of bureau field men, but also of farmers—the "customers." Both are illustrative of the new trend in management, which calls for "two-way planning"—from the bottom up as well as from the top down. The same tendency can be seen in private enterprise; the "multiple management" scheme of the McCormick Tea Company of Baltimore is typical. The first step in Allan Mogenson's "work simplification" program, which is currently creating an impression in business circles, is the education of *all* of a plant's employees in the objectives and philosophy of scientific management. The specific steps undertaken in reorganizing operations are for the most part worked out by those who do the jobs. There is never any "system" planned on paper and installed from outside.

Scientific management as applied to industry, and rational technique as applied to administration, are products not only of specialized knowledge but of the diffusion of that knowledge among those whom it affects. Just as modern medicine is possible only because the public accepts its objectives and methods, management in administration is only feasible if administrative officials understand and approve of the philosophy and logic behind it. The administrative analyst must be a leader and co-ordinator and not a manipulator. He must resist any temptation to exploit the exclusiveness of his knowledge, and must seek always to spread understanding of administrative principles and techniques. Only as the natural laws and human equations which govern administrative organization and procedure are assimilated by all who take part, is sustained progress possible.

BIBLIOGRAPHY

GOVERNMENT DOCUMENTS (U. S. Government unless otherwise indicated)

BUREAU OF EFFICIENCY

Annual Reports of the Chief of the Bureau of Efficiency, Washington, 1916-32, Government Printing Office.

DEPARTMENT OF AGRICULTURE

Planning for a Permanent Agriculture, Miscellaneous Publication No. 351, Washington, 1939, Government Printing Office, 71 pages.

Farm Security Administration Instruction Manual (administrative manual circulated to employees, loose leaf, mimeographed or processed), Washington, revised currently.

Forest Service Annual Report of the Chief of the Forest Service, fiscal year 1939, Washington, 1939, Government Printing Office, 48 pages.

Forest Service Manual (administrative manual circulated to employees, loose leaf, processed), Washington, revised currently.

Instructions for General Integrating Inspections, 1937, Document from files, confidential. (citation approved)

Job-Load Analysis and Planning of Executive Work in National Forest Administration, by E. W. Loveridge, Washington, 1932, Government Printing Office.

Report of General Integrating Inspection in the Southern Region, 1937, by Earl W. Loveridge and J. A. Fitzwater, Document from files, confidential. (citation approved)

CIVIL SERVICE COMMISSION

Division Organization Manual, third edition (administrative manual circulated to employees, bound, mimeographed), Washington, 1939-40.

DEPARTMENT OF COMMERCE

Bureau of Foreign and Domestic Commerce Check Sheet—Introduction of New Consumer Products (Chart with explanatory notes, processed), Washington, 1935.

TENNESSEE VALLEY AUTHORITY

Office Manuals (administrative manual circulated to employees, loose leaf, mimeographed), Knoxville, Tennessee, revised currently.

Office Method Bulletins (Nos. 24, 25, 37, 43, 46, 60, and 78 deal with work units, timing, scheduling, etc.), Knoxville, Tennessee, issued from time to time.

BRITISH MINISTRY OF RECONSTRUCTION

Report of the Machinery of Government Committee, by Lord Haldane of Cloan (Richard Burton Haldane) and others. London, H. M. Stationery Office, 1918, reprinted 1938, 80 pages.

ARTICLES, BULLETINS, LECTURES, ETC.

Gaus, John W., "Should Administrators be Generalists or Specialists?" in *Lectures on Administrative Management*, Washington, U. S. Department of Agriculture Graduate School, 1940.

BIBLIOGRAPHY

Gladieux, Bernard L., "Administrative Planning in the Federal Government," paper presented before the Governmental Research Association at Princeton, New Jersey, September, 1939. This paper, in condensed form, appeared under the title, "Management Planning in the Federal Government," in *Advanced Management*, July-September, 1940.

Glaser, Comstock, "A Note on Executive Planning," *Society for the Advancement of Management Journal*, July, 1937, pp. 111ff.

Glaser, Comstock, "Managing Committee Work in a Large Organization," *Public Administration Review*, Spring 1941, pp. 249-256.

Hopf, Harry Arthur, "Administrative Co-ordination," *Advanced Management*, July-September, 1940, pp. 50ff.

Lilienthal, David E., "Decentralization of Federal Administrative Functions, an Experiment" (about the T.V.A.), *Advanced Management*, January-March, 1940, pp. 3-8.

Person, Harlow S., "On the Technique of Planning," *Bulletin of the Taylor Society and the Society of Industrial Engineers*, November, 1934, pp. 14ff.

Public Administration Service, *The Work Unit in Federal Administration*; papers presented at a meeting of the Society for the Advancement of Management. Chicago, Public Administration Service, 1937.

Shepard, George H., "The Problem of a Planned Economic Order," *Bulletin of the Taylor Society and the Society of Industrial Engineers*, November, 1934, pp. 22-28.

BOOKS

Brecht, Arnold, and Glaser, Comstock, *The Art and Technique of Administration in German Ministries*, Cambridge, Harvard University Press, 1940, 191 pages.

Dennison, Henry, *Organization Engineering*, New York, McGraw-Hill, 1931, 204 pages.

Dewey, Melvil, *Decimal Classification and Relative Index*, 13th edition, Lake Placid Club, N. Y. Forest Press, 1932, 400 pages. Also "extracts on office economy and business methods," from earlier edition of above, Forest Press, 1924, 56 pages.

Dutton, Henry P., *The Principles of Organization*, New York, McGraw-Hill, 1931, 315 pages.

Fayol, Henry, *Industrial and General Administration*, translated from the French for the International Management Institute by J. A. Coubrough, London, Sir I. Pitman & Sons, Ltd., 1930, 84 pages.

Finer, Herman, *The Theory and Practise of Modern Government* (one-volume edition, revised by William B. Guthrie), New York, Dial Press, 1932, 918 pages.

Glover, John G., and Maze, Coleman L., *Managerial Control*, New York, Ronald, 1937, 574 pages.

Gulick, Luther W., and Urwick, L., *Papers on the Science of Administration*, New York, Institute of Public Administration, Columbia University, 1937, 195 pages.

Leffingwell, William H., *A Textbook of Office Management*, New York, McGraw-Hill, 1932, 409 pages.

ADMINISTRATIVE PROCEDURE

Macmahon, Arthur W., and Millett, John D., *Federal Administrators, a biographical approach to the problem of departmental management*, New York, Columbia University Press, 1939, 524 pages.

McCormick, Charles P., *Multiple Management*, New York, Harpers, 1938, 175 pages.

Meriam, Lewis B., and Schmeckebier, Laurence, *Reorganization of the Federal Government, what it involves*, Washington, Brookings Institution, 1939, 213 pages.

Mooney, James D., and Reiley, Alan L., *The Principles of Organization* (first published in 1931 as *Onward Industry*), New York, Harpers, 1939, 223 pages.

Niles, Mary Cushing Howard, *Middle Management, the job of the junior administrator*, New York, Harpers, 1941, 270 pages.

Stevenson, Marietta, *Public Welfare Administration* (written for American Public Welfare Association), New York, Macmillan, 1938, 352 pages.

Taylor, Frederick W., *The Principles of Scientific Management*, New York, Harpers, 1915, 144 pages.

Taylor, Frederick W., *Shop Management*, New York, Harpers, 1911, 207 pages.

Wallas, Graham, *Human Nature in Politics* (third edition), New York, Knopf, 1920, 313 pages.

White, Leonard D., *Introduction to the Study of Public Administration*, revised edition (cited in notes as *Public Administration*), New York, Macmillan, 1939, 611 pages.

INDEX

Accounting, 22, 50, 61, 84, 86
Administration, definition of, 9
  direct, 11, 15, 135, 144, 176
  duplicate, 118
  phases of, 9, 55, 135
Administrator, functions of, 38, 68-71, 112, 134, 135-138, 144, 186
"Agency A," 27-28, 85-86, 101-103, 157-159
"Agency B," 28-29, 85-87, 101-103, 162-163
Agricultural Economics, Bureau of, 74
Agriculture, Department of, administrative (program) planning, 72-76, 201
  committees, 66, 72
  management planning, 76
  uniform project system, 21
  (see also names of bureaus and offices, designated "Agr.")
Analysis, by administrative sequences, 37-48, 49, 144, 167-168
  by function, 17-25, 49, 64-65, 144, 167-168
  by units of organization, 26-36, 49, 129, 144, 155-156, 167-168
  tasks, 45-46, 156, 166-168
Analyst, administrative, 16, 26, 30, 38, 46-47, 113, 139, 143-146, 149-155, 159, 165-166, 168, 176, 180-186, 197-198, 200-201
Authority, administrative, 26, 88-89, 124, 133-134, 149-150, 164
  (see also centralization, delegation)

Backlog, 173-175
Biological Survey, Bureau of, 77
"Bottlenecks," administrative, 161-163
Brain, Oliver G., cited, 173
Brecht, Arnold, cited, 23n, 142n
British Machinery of Government Committee, 62
Brown, Leon, cited, 137, 138
Budget, Bureau of the, 140, 196

Centralization—decentralization, 50-53, 55-61, 64, 80-81, 87, 89-95, 97-98, 107-111, 114-115, 129, 133, 151, 157, 162, 188-189
Channels of contact, 29, 31, 34, 38-41, 46-47, 49, 52-53, 85-88, 114, 124-127, 158-159, 161
Civil Aeronautics Administration, 143, 153
Civil servants and "politics," 51n, 189-190
Civil Service Commission, U. S., 16n, 103-111, 140
Classification, budgetary, 21-22, 81
  files, 23

functions, 18, 21-24, 36, 112, 147-148
  personnel, 45
"Clearance," administrative,
  (see correspondence, also channels of contact)
Cleveland Commission, 21
Committees, 62-67, 72, 196
Communication, 12, 32-36, 38, 40, 46-47, 124-127, 187-188
Comptroller General, 108n, 117n, 194-195
Concepts, 14, 47-48, 185-186
Conferences, 115, 132
Congress, relations with administrative agencies, 190-193, 195-197
Control, administrative, 9, 15, 41, 51-52, 57-58, 61, 91, 112-134, 158, 162-163, 176
  devices, 114, 117-118, 123, 127-130, 133
  diminishing returns, 115-116
  management, 176-184
  need for planned, 112, 113, 116-120
  production, 177-183
  span of, 113-114, 119-120, 123, 162
Coordination, 9, 24, 38, 68, 128, 130, 133-134, 158
Correspondence, 47, 50, 53, 114, 119, 124-127, 150-151
County Extension Agents, 74
Cross-analysis chart, 43-44, 59, 90
Custom, effect on administration, 12, 14-15, 44

Data, techniques for gathering, 30, 44-46
  (see also measurement and under planning)
Delegation, in general, 10-11, 31, 34, 112, 115, 123-124, 138
  divergent, 63, 114-116
  incomplete, 114
Democracy in administration, 72-75, 128, 189-190, 200-201
Dewey, Melvil, cited, 23n
Dutton, H. P., cited, 100n, 134
Duty, 31, 38

Efficiency, Bureau of, 139-140
Elimination of unnecessary tasks and functions, 24, 45-46, 169, 199
Employee relations, 99, 197-199
Environment of administration, 186-199
Examinations, civil service, 104-105, 108-109

Farm Security Administration, 78-81, 142, 147-149, 157
Fayol, Henry, cited, 54, 112, 136
Field operations, 29, 87, 91-92, 121-123, 126-133, 145

205

INDEX

Files—filing, 23, 61
Financial limitations, 81-82, 199
Finer, Herman, cited, 51n
Fish and Wildlife Service, 77
Flow charts, 42-44, 59, 90
Flow of business, 13, 88, 113, 173
  (see also channels of contact)
Forest Service, administrative control, 121-134
  classification of correspondence, 124-127
  inspection, 130-133
  planning, 81-82, 128-129, 171-172, 178
  program, 121-122
  work load measurement, 167-168, 171-172, 178-179, 201
Formalism in administration, 46-47, 133-134
Functions, analysis, (see under analysis),
  assignment, 20, 24, 35, 38, 64-65, 70, 139, 142, 146, 153, 155, 157-161, 163
  "auxiliary," 19n, 63n
  classification, 18, 21-24, 36, 112
  definition, 18
  line, 19-20, 38, 54-57, 71, 84, 147-149, 157-158
  line and staff, distinguished, 19, 38, 54-55, 64-65, 143-144, 147
  line and staff, relationship, 20, 29-30, 38, 49, 53-55, 61-65, 94-95, 97, 100, 110-111, 115, 148-149, 160
  relation to organization, 29, 49-50, 61-65, 149, 156
  specialization of, 40, 54, 99, 156-157
  staff, 19-20, 28, 38, 54-55, 61-65, 84, 97, 99-100, 114-115, 147-149, 157-161
"Functional foremanship," application to administration, 11, 133, 149-151
"Functionalism," 63-64, 157-162
Functionality of tasks and duties, 38, 46, 68n, 180

Gaus, John J., cited, 180
General Schedule of Supplies, 88, 94-95
German Ministries, classification of work, 22-23
  decentralization, 51, 52
  political neutrality, 51n
Gladieux, Bernard L., cited, 145, 150n
Grant-in-aid procedure, 57-61
Graphic methods, 26-28, 34-35, 42-44
Gulick and Urwick, cited, 10n, 113n, 136

Hopf, Harry Arthur, cited, 159
Human problems in administration, 13-15, 197-199
Inspection, 115, 130-133

Interpretation of laws, 193-195
Leffingwell, William H., cited, 157
Legislation, relation to administration, 71, 187, 192-197
Line (see Functions)
Loveridge, E. W., cited, 132, 156, 178

Management, administrative, 11, 15-16, 28, 37, 48, 63, 129, 135, 139, 143-146, 169-171, 176, 196-197, 201
  collaboration in, 151-152, 182, 184, 189-190, 200-201
  committees, 65n, 67
  difference between industrial and administrative problems, 14, 37, 54, 159, 185
  planning (see under planning)
  planning units (see procedure divisions)
  standardized sequences, 169-170, 177
  unstandardized executive work, 119, 154-155, 160, 167, 171-173, 179-183
Manuals, 77-78, 103-106, 128, 141-143, 146-149, 151
Measurement, techniques of, 32-36, 45, 129, 156, 165-174, 179-183
Mooney and Reiley, cited, 19n, 37n, 113n, 138n
Morale, 51, 116, 127
Motion, administrative, 39-42, 44-47, 52-53, 85-87, 89-91, 102-103, 114, 134, 156, 159, 164, 174

National Committee on Municipal Accounting, 22
National Recovery Administration, 137
New Deal, effect on Federal administration, 140-143

Operating standards, 117-118, 129-130, 169-170
Organization, general problems, 10, 26-31, 49-67, 113, 140, 144-145
  changes in, 26, 49, 144-145, 155, 176, 197
  characteristics of, 10, 53-54, 99
  charts, 26-28, 35, 52, 56
  complex, 10, 32-36, 54, 99, 122-123
  hierarchical (scalar), 10, 53-54, 63, 113
  line and staff, 30, 53-57, 61-65, 84-85, 95-96, 100, 110-111, 114-115, 157-161, 163
  need for clear statement of, 11, 87, 119, 133, 154
  relation to functions, 29, 49-50, 53-55, 122-123, 149, 156
  relation to procedure, 26, 49-50, 52-53, 56-63, 144, 156-161

206

INDEX

Person, Harlow S., cited, 68-69
Personnel, general problems, 31, 99-111, 146, 198
  appointment procedure, 101-106
  civil service procedure, 103-111
  classification, 45, 101, 105-106, 110
  "emergency agencies," problems in, 101-103
  exchange service, 160-161, 182
  offices, functions of, 61, 99-100, 107-108
  reserve force, 160-161, 182, 199
Phenomena, administrative, 17, 186
Physical environment of administration, 187-189
Planning, administrative (program), 16n, 28, 68-83, 162, 171-172, 189, 192
  areas of, 69-70
  data required for, 17-18, 79, 144, 171-172, 180
  management, 15n, 17, 28, 49-50, 69-70, 76-78, 135-153, 154, 165
  officials, location, 72, 76-78, 81-82
  place in administration, 9, 68-72, 83
  steps in, 68-69, 71, 74, 154
Policy, need for definiteness in, 136-138
Political factors affecting administration, 51-52, 80, 102-103, 187, 189-192
Procedure, administrative, 11-13, 49-50, 84, 135, 141, 196
  classification, 147-149, 151
  difference between public and private, 85, 89, 100
  divisions, 16n, 28, 63, 142-143, 145-146, 152
  manuals (see manuals)
  planning, 72-83
  promulgation, 150-151
  relation to organization, 26, 49-50, 62, 156-161
  (see also management)
Processes of administration, 11, 19, 49, 53-55, 63n, 139, 157-161, 164
Procurement Division, Treasury, 87-88, 90, 93-97, 195
Projects, budgetary, 21, 128-129, 162
Purchasing, in general, 41, 54n, 61, 84-98
  bids, 87, 89-93, 95, 117, 193-195
  Federal, consolidation, 93-98
  open-market, 87-89
  term contracts, 87-89, 96
Purposes of administration, 11, 19, 24, 30, 39n, 46, 64, 136-138, 157, 164, 165-166, 187-188

Pyramiding, administrative, 92

Quality, 45, 68n, 124

Reports, operating, 115, 177-183
Research, 21, 129
Routing (see channels of contact)
Rural Electrification Administration, 169-171, 177-178

Scheduling, 83, 165-175, 177-183
Scientific management, application to administration, 13-15, 37, 48, 185-186, 198, 201
Sequences, administrative, 37-48, 52-53, 72-75, 79-80, 85-87, 101-107, 166, 169-171, 175, 177
Shepard, George H., cited, 113n
Social Security Board, 143, 145-146, 190
Socio-psychological factors, 14-15, 187, 197-199
Staff, meaning of term, 19, 53-54, 63n, 120, 138, 150
  (see also functions)
Staff officer, authority of, 19n, 28, 63-64, 95, 97, 99-101, 110-111, 115n, 133-134, 149-151, 157-159, 163, 184
Stevenson, Marietta, cited, 10n, 55n

Task, 20, 38, 45-46, 155-156, 166-168, 179
Taylor, Frederick W., 11, 157, 198
Technical standardization and control, 93, 95-98, 108-111, 117-118
Technique of activity administered, 20, 69, 84-85, 118-119, 135-138, 151, 180, 188
  of administration, 13-16, 37-38, 46-47, 71, 121, 135-136, 138-144, 151, 185-201
Tennessee Valley Authority, 47n, 108n, 141n, 179, 188
Time study, industrial, 37
Timing of administrative work, 39-40, 45, 72, 75, 85, 89-91, 165-175
Traffic, administrative, 36, 39, 161

Unit production chart, 161, 180-182

Wallas, Graham, cited, 187n
White, Leonard D., cited, 63n, 95n, 136n
Work distribution, 20, 38, 46, 154-164, 182, 184
  load, 25, 31-36, 81, 114, 129, 164, 167-168, 178-183
  units, 32, 156, 166-168, 171-172